USING

google™
adwords and
adsense

Michael Miller

800 East 96th Street, Indianapolis, Indiana 46240 USA

Using Google™ AdWords and AdSense

Copyright © 2010 by Pearson Education, Inc.

ISBN-13: 978-0-7897-4395-4

0-789-74395-7

Library of Congress Cataloging-in-Publication Data is on file

Printed in the United States on America

First Printing May 2010

Trademarks

Warning and Disclaimer

Bulk Sales

Que Publishing offers excellent discounts on this book when ordered in quantity for bulk purchases or special sales. For more information, please contact

U.S. Corporate and Government Sales

1-800-382-3419

corpsales@pearsontechgroup.com

For sales outside of the U.S., please contact

International Sales

international@pearsoned.com

Associate Publisher

Associate Publisher
Greg Wiegand

Acquisitions Editor
Rick Kughen

Development Editor
Rick Kughen

Managing Editor
Kristy Hart

Project Editor
Andy Beaster

Copy Editor
Seth Kerney

Indexer
Cheryl Lenser

Proofreader
Sally Yuska

Technical Editor
Steve Baldwin

Publishing Coordinator
Cindy Teeters

Compositors
Jake McFarland
Nonie Ratcliff

Designer
Ann Jones

Reviewers
Vince Averello
Sarah Perez
Ed Tittel

To Sherry, for no particular reason.

Contents at a Glance

Media Table of Contents

To register this product and gain access to the Free Web Edition and the audio and video files, go to **quepublishing.com/using**.

Table of Contents

About the Author

Michael Miller has written more than 100 nonfiction how-to books over the past twenty years, including Que's *Googlepedia: The Ultimate Google Resource*, *YouTube for Business*, *The Absolute Beginner's Guide to Computer Basics*, and *Using Blogger*. His other best-selling online marketing books include *The Complete Idiot's Guide to Search Engine Optimization* (Alpha Books) and *Online Marketing Heroes* (Wiley).

Mr. Miller has established a reputation for clearly explaining technical topics to nontechnical readers, and for offering useful real-world advice about complicated topics. More information can be found at the author's website, located at www. molehillgroup.com.

Acknowledgments

Thanks to the usual suspects at Que, including but not limited to Greg Wiegand, Rick Kughen, Andy Beaster, Seth Kerney, and technical editor Steve Baldwin.

We Want to Hear from You!

As the reader of this book, *you* are our most important critic and commentator. We value your opinion and want to know what we're doing right, what we could do better, what areas you'd like to see us publish in, and any other words of wisdom you're willing to pass our way.

As an associate publisher for Que Publishing, I welcome your comments. You can email or write me directly to let me know what you did or didn't like about this book—as well as what we can do to make our books better.

Please note that I cannot help you with technical problems related to the topic of this book. We do have a User Services group, however, where I will forward specific technical questions related to the book.

When you write, please be sure to include this book's title and author as well as your name, email address, and phone number. I will carefully review your comments and share them with the author and editors who worked on the book.

Email: feedback@quepublishing.com

Mail: Greg Wiegand
           Associate Publisher
           Que Publishing
           800 East 96th Street
           Indianapolis, IN 46240 USA

Reader Services

Visit our website and register this book at www.quepublishing.com/register for convenient access to any updates, downloads, or errata that might be available for this book.

Introduction

Advertising drives the Internet.

That's surely not something most of us imagined 15 years ago when the World Wide Web was still in its infancy, but it's most definitely true today. The big Internet companies, such as Google, make most of their money by selling advertisements; even smaller websites make a fair chunk of change by allowing ads to appear on their pages. And businesses with products to sell and websites to promote have big budgets for online advertising, which turns out to be a very effective way to drum up new customers.

Like I said, advertising drives the Internet.

One of the great things about this Internet advertising craze is that it's not just for the big boys. Thanks to online advertising networks such as Google's AdSense and AdWords, even the smallest website can host profitable online advertisements, and even the smallest advertiser can make his presence known on the web. Anybody and everybody can either host or place ads online, and that's not a bad thing.

That said, how do you join the party?

Well, if you want to make a little money from your website, you can participate in Google's AdSense program, which places relevant ads on your web pages. Or, if you want to advertise your website or product or business, you can sign up for Google's AdWords program, which displays your ads when people search for a similar topic on Google's search site—as well as places your ads on websites that participate in the AdSense program.

In other words, Google is your one-stop-shop for online advertising—whether you're a host site or an advertiser.

It's not quite that easy, of course—especially if you want to be effective in what you do. Optimizing your site to generate the most possible advertising revenues takes a bit of work, and creating an effective text advertisement is as much of an art as it is a science. In other words, you probably need a bit of help in navigating the online advertising waters.

Which is why you're reading this book, I presume. *Using Google AdWords and AdSense* is your handy guide to everything you need to know about Google's online advertising programs. I'll walk you through creating an account, placing ads on your site, and creating ads to run on other sites. I'll help you maximize your revenues and minimize your costs—at least, as much as possible. There's always a bit of work involved on your part, of course.

Who Should Read This Book

Using Google AdWords and AdSense is written for all levels of users; I don't presuppose any existing online advertising experience. That said, you do need to know or have access to someone who knows a little bit about the technical aspects of running a website. That's because using AdSense and AdWords requires some basic HTML coding to place those ads on a website. If you don't know how to do it, you'll have to find someone who does.

How This Book is Organized

Using Google AdWords and AdSense contains everything you need to know to get started as either an ad host or an advertiser. I'll walk you through the basics of pay-per-click (PPC) advertising and show you what you need to do to place ads on your site or create your own ads.

This book contains 22 chapters, organized into three major sections:

- **Part I: Pay-Per-Click Advertising** provides an overview of how PPC advertising works, from both sides of the table.

- **Part II: Using Google AdSense** is your guide to making money from PPC ads. You'll learn about Google's five different AdSense programs, how to earn sales commissions from the Google Affiliate Network, and how to maximize your AdSense revenue.

- **Part III: Using Google AdWords** shows you how to advertise on the Google AdWords network. You'll learn how to create an account, launch a new campaign, and write your first ads. You'll also learn how to choose and bid on the most effective keywords, how to track your ads' performance, how to create a customized landing page, and how to combine PPC advertising with search engine marketing. You'll even learn how to advertise your videos on Google's YouTube site.

Using This Book

This book allows you to customize your own learning experience. The step-by-step instructions in the book give you a solid foundation in using Google AdWords and AdSense, while rich and varied online content, including video tutorials and audio sidebars, provide the following:

- Demonstrations of step-by-step tasks covered in the book
- Additional tips or information on a topic
- Practical advice and suggestions
- Direction for more advanced tasks not covered in the book

Here's a quick look at a few structural features designed to help you get the most out of this book.

Notes: Important tasks are offset to draw attention to them.

 LET ME TRY IT tasks are presented in a step-by-step sequence so you can easily follow along.

 SHOW ME video walks through tasks you've just got to see.

 TELL ME MORE audio delivers practical insights straight from the experts.

Special Features

More than just a book, your USING product integrates step-by-step video tutorials and valuable audio sidebars delivered through the **Free Web Edition** that comes with every USING book. For the price of the book, you get online access anywhere with a web connection—no books to carry, content is updated as the technology changes, and the benefit of video and audio learning.

About the USING Web Edition

The Web Edition of every USING book is powered by **Safari Books Online**, allowing you to access the video tutorials and valuable audio sidebars. Plus, you can search the contents of the book, highlight text and attach a note to that text, print your notes and highlights in a custom summary, and cut and paste directly from Safari Books Online.

To register this product and gain access to the Free Web Edition and the audio and video files, go to **quepublishing.com/using**.

Media and Support

The Using series lives online at quepublishing.com/using. Visit this site to register your book, gain access to the media files, and complete your learning experience. Media files require the free QuickTime Player software available from www.apple.com/quicktime/download/.

And Even More, Online

In addition, I urge you to visit my personal website, located at www.molehillgroup.com. Here you'll find more information on this book and other books I've written—including an errata page for this book, in the inevitable event that an error or two creeps into this text. (Hey, nobody's perfect!)

And if you have any questions or comments, feel free to email me directly at adwords@molehillgroup.com. I can't guarantee that I'll respond to every email, but I will guarantee I'll read them all.

Get Ready to Click!

With all these preliminaries out of the way, it's now time to get started. So get ready to turn the page and learn more about pay-per-click advertising in general, and Google AdSense and AdWords in particular. It's a great way to both make money from your website and promote your site online.

Pay-Per-Click Advertising

1

How Pay-Per-Click Advertising Works

Google AdWords and AdSense are two web-based advertising programs that utilize pay-per-click advertisements. If you run your own website or blog, AdSense lets you host ads that generate income for your site. And if you want to generate more traffic for your site, you can advertise with AdWords on other sites. It's easy to do, and you only pay—or get paid—when someone actually clicks an ad.

But what exactly is pay-per-click advertising? These aren't those big, splashy banner ads that get in your face at the top of a web page; instead, these are small, relatively unobtrusive text ads that can appear anywhere on a web page. And they're directly targeted at a site's visitors; only ads somehow related to site's content appear on that site.

Before you start using AdWords or AdSense, then, you need to understand what PPC advertising is and how it works. Read on to get educated.

A Brief Look at Advertising on the Internet

 TELL ME MORE   Media 1.1—A discussion about online advertising
Access this audio recording through your registered Web Edition at
my.safaribooksonline.com/9780131388666/media.

You don't have to be a fan of *Mad Men* to consider advertising a fun and interesting profession. Advertising is all around us, in newspapers and on television and even trailing behind low-flying airplanes that buzz touristy beaches. It's pretty pictures and catchy slogans and immensely hummable jingles, trying to sell you on the notion that you need, no, you really, *really* need this product or that one.

Merriam-Webster's dictionary defines advertising as the action of calling something to the attention of the public, especially by paid announcements. It's a form of communication intended to persuade consumers to take some sort of action, typically purchasing a product or service. It's all about enticing you to buy something.

For years, firms wanting to promote their brands and products and services have had their pick of what we call traditional media in which to run their advertisements. I'm talking print ads in newspapers and magazines, commercials on radio and television, billboards along major highways, direct mail solicitations, and the like. But with the advent of the Internet, there are now new places to advertise, and new ways to promote.

It didn't take long after the popularization of the World Wide Web for advertising to stick its nose under the virtual tent. Website owners discovered that they had valuable space on their pages that advertisers would gladly pay for; advertisers discovered that lots of people actually used this web thing, and that there was benefit in courting those users via some form of advertising.

With these realizations, online advertising was born. On the web, that first translated into banner advertisements, those short and wide images that soon took over the tops of many web pages. But banner ads were just the tip of the proverbial iceberg; soon advertisers and web hosts were devising all sorts of ways and places to place ads on websites.

Today, online advertising comprises a wide assortment of different types of advertising. We still have banner ads on web pages, of course, but also small text ads that always seem to have something to do with the content of the web page. These text ads also show up in the search results of Google and other search sites, subtly disguised as "sponsored links" or some such.

And there's lots of online advertising beyond what you see on web pages. Advertisers have devised many different ways to drive traffic to their websites, from engineering their way higher in Google's search results to running their own blogs to infiltrating Facebook, Twitter, and other social networks. Savvy marketers know that to maximize their online presence they must master all these different forms of online advertising and promotion; web-based ads are just part of the equation, albeit a very important part.

Understanding Pay-Per-Click Advertising

Of all the different forms of online advertising, the most popular is *pay-per-click* (PPC) advertising. PPC advertising isn't like traditional display advertising; it doesn't take up discrete space on a given web page, nor does it allow for graphics-intensive advertisements. Instead, PPC advertising is all about getting a small text ad onto a specific search results or content page—putting relevant ads in front of interested consumers.

SHOW ME   Media 1.2—A video about how PPC advertising works
Access this video file through your registered Web Edition at
my.safaribooksonline.com/9780131388666/media.

It Starts with One Little (Key) Word...

PPC ads are different from most ads in that they're highly relevant to the pages on which they appear. That is, PPC ad networks don't display any old ad on a web page; instead, they try to serve up the right ads for the right potential customers. To do this, PPC advertising networks utilize *keywords*, those words and phrases that users search for on Google and other search engine sites.

It all starts when a PPC advertiser purchases a particular keyword or phrase from the PPC ad network. More precisely, the advertiser purchases ad space that appears on search results pages and other websites that relate to the keywords in question. Ideally, the keywords purchased are somehow related to or descriptive of the product or service promoted in the ad.

The keywords purchased determine where the ad is displayed. When a user enters a query on a related search site, such as Google, the advertiser's ad is displayed on the first page of the search results, in the "sponsored links" section that appears at the top or side of the page. As you can see in Figure 1.1, ads are designed to look kind of like an organic search result—the better to entice users to click on the ads. The sponsored links are circled in Figure 1.1.

The second place the ad appears is on individual websites that belong to the PPC ad network. The ad is placed on specific pages that have content that relates to the purchased keyword. These ads, also text-only (as you can see in Figure 1.2), can appear anywhere on the given page; the ad placement is up to the owner of the web page.

So, for example, if you have a website that sells printer ink cartridges, you might purchase the keywords "printer," "ink," and "cartridges." When a consumer searches Google for any of these keywords, your ad appears on the search results page. Your ad may also appear when a consumer goes to an affiliated website that features content containing these keywords.

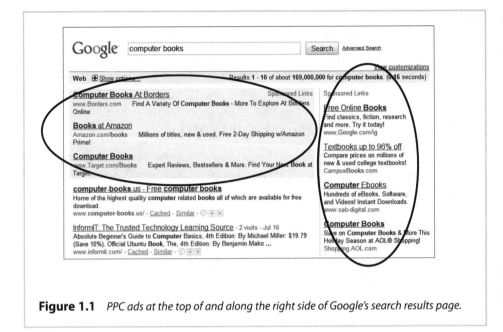

Figure 1.1   *PPC ads at the top of and along the right side of Google's search results page.*

Figure 1.2   *PPC ads on an affiliated website.*

Placing Ads in Context

The neat thing about PPC ads is that they use advanced search technology to serve content-focused ads—that is, an ad that relates to the underlying content of the host web page. An ad that is somehow related to the content of a web page reaches a more targeted audience than a more broadly focused banner ad—and, theoretically, generates more and better traffic.

What this means is that if you're advertising golf clubs, your ad will appear only on those websites that have something to do with golf; it won't appear on sites about women's health, politics, or gourmet cooking. Your ad will also appear in Google's search results when someone searches for golf clubs. It's very targeted placement.

This context sensitivity also benefits the sites that host the ads. If, for example, you host a website about country music, only ads somehow related to country music will appear on your site. You won't see ads for dental supplies or baby shoes or radar detectors; your site's visitors will see ads that are only related to the main content of your site. This makes the ads a little less annoying—and more likely to be clicked.

How does a PPC network serve up these relevant ads? In the case of Google, the company uses the same sophisticated algorithms that it uses to create its search index to determine the content of pages for sites that participate in its advertising program. Google analyzes the keywords that appear on a web page, the word frequency, font size, and overall link structure to figure out, as closely as possible, what a page is all about. Then it finds ads that closely match that page's content, and feeds those ads to the page.

For example, my personal website (www.molehillgroup.com) is all about the books I've written. On the page for my book *The Complete Idiot's Guide to Music Theory*, Google serves up ads titled "Music Theory Made Easy" and "Learning Guitar Scales"; on the page for *Absolute Beginner's Guide to eBay*, there are ads for "Free eBay Beginner Guide" and "eBay Dropshipper Reviews." The right ads for the right content—which benefits both advertisers and host sites.

Paying by the Click

The reason it's called pay-per-click advertising is that an advertiser pays the ad network only when customers click on the link in the ad. (The link typically points to the advertiser's website—or, most commonly, a special landing page on the website.) If no one clicks, the advertiser doesn't pay anyone anything. The more clicks that are registered, the more the advertiser pays.

Pay-per-click advertising is in contrast to traditional *cost-per-thousand-impressions* (CPM) advertising, where rates are based on the number of potential viewers of the ad—whether they click through or not.

Ad rates are calculated on a *cost-per-click* (CPC) basis. That is, the advertiser is charged a specific fee for each click—anywhere from a few pennies to tens of dollars. The actual CPC rate is determined by the popularity of and competition for the keyword purchased, as well as the quality and quantity of traffic going to the site hosting the ad. As you can imagine, popular keywords have a higher CPC, while less popular keywords can be had for less.

This is typically done by having advertisers bid on the most popular keywords. That is, you might say you'll pay up to $5 for a given keyword. If you're the high bidder among several advertisers, your ads will appear more frequently on pages that contain that keyword. If you're not the high bidder, you won't get as much visibility—if your ad appears at all.

A given PPC ad probably won't appear on every search engine results page for the keyword purchased. That's because the number of suitable pages for a given keyword is limited, while advertisers are theoretically unlimited. For this reason, ad networks typically rotate ads from multiple advertisers on their search results and affiliated websites.

While an advertiser pays only when an ad is clicked, there is some benefit gained just by having an ad displayed—even if no one clicks it. That is, some people will view an ad and remember the product or service for later action. The advertiser doesn't pay for this longer-term product/brand awareness, just for the immediate click.

Sharing Ad Revenues

Here's something else interesting about PPC advertising: Revenues from PPC ads are shared between the ad network and the hosting website. That's right—any website where the ad appears gets a cut of the ad revenues paid by the advertiser—which is why sites agree to put PPC ads on their web pages.

If you're an advertiser, this part of the arrangement is transparent; you pay the ad network and they divvy up the funds however they do. If you run a site that hosts PPC ads, however, you get a percentage of all the funds paid by your site's advertisers. The ad network collects the revenues from the advertisers and then passes your share on to you.

Here's the process, in a nutshell:

1. An advertiser creates an advertisement and contracts with a PPC ad network to place that ad on the Internet.

2. The ad network serves the ad in question to a number of appropriate websites (and to search results pages on its own search site, of course).

3. An interested customer sees the ad on an affiliated website and clicks the link in the ad to receive more information.

4. The advertiser pays the ad network, based on the CPC advertising rate.

5. The ad network pays the host website a small percentage of the advertising fee paid.

Remember that no one pays anything until someone actually clicks on the ad. If no one clicks an ad, the advertiser pays nothing—and the site hosting the ad generates no revenue. That's why PPC ads are context-sensitive, the better to entice visitors to click on the ads, thus generating traffic for the advertiser and revenue for the host sites.

Maximizing Ad Placements

If you're an advertiser, it's important that you pick the right keywords for your PPC ads. Pick keywords that no one is interested in, and your ad won't appear anywhere; pick more popular keywords, and your ad appears more often—and ideally generates more traffic back to your site.

The problem then is that the best keywords are also the most popular ones. That is, lots of advertisers will be interested in the same keywords. Because ad networks set their rates by having advertisers bid on keywords, the most popular keywords cost more than less popular ones.

In many ways, competition for keywords among advertisers resembles the activity surrounding an online auction. In fact, because advertisers bid for keywords, the process really is an auction. Those advertisers who bid the highest "win" more and better ad placements. If you don't bid high enough on a popular keyword, your ad simply won't appear as often—if at all.

The temptation then is to bid high on the most popular keywords in an attempt to get more ads displayed and drive more traffic to your website. Be careful what you wish for, however, as this approach can result in very high advertising bills.

Google and other PPC ad networks let you set a daily or monthly budget for your total advertising expenditures. Your ad will run only until your budget is maxed out; at that point, your ad is no longer in circulation.

That said, bid price isn't the only factor in determining how often an ad is displayed—at least not anymore. It used to be that the highest bidder got the most placements, but that didn't always ensure that the most relevant ads got placed. For that reason, the ad networks now utilize a "quality score" factor that attempts to determine the relevance of the ad's landing page—the page that the ad links to. If an ad's landing page consists of low-quality content, that ad gets a low quality score and won't rank highly in the ad network's results. A landing page with high-quality, relevant content will rank higher and thus be displayed more frequently.

To maximize your ad placements, then, you need to consider a number of factors:

- Keywords

- Bid price for those keywords

- Content of the linked-to landing page

- Effectiveness of your ad copy

In other words, you have to bid on keywords that are both popular and relevant, bid the going rate for those keywords, create a high-value landing page for your ad, and write an ad that encourages users to click on it. Fall down on any of these factors and your ad will be less than fully successful.

Auctioning PPC Ads

How much, then, should you bid on the keywords you choose? The answer is simple: As much as you can afford!

As noted, cost per click for most PPC advertising is determined by a bidding process. When you sign up as an advertiser, you pick the keywords you want and tell the ad network the maximum amount you're willing to pay for each ad placement. When it comes time to serve an ad onto a search results page or affiliate website, the ad network runs an automated auction process to determine which ad gets placed. Obviously, the advertiser who is willing to pay the highest price has a better chance of having his ad displayed than does an advertiser with a lower bid.

This automated auction takes place whenever a user searches for a keyword that advertisers have bid on. The ad network takes various factors into account beyond just the bid price, of course; in some instances, the advertiser's location, the date and time of day, as well as the actual content linked to by the advertiser also figure into the equation. And because most search results have slots for several of these "sponsored links," there can be more than one winner for each keyword search. In this situation, the ad from the highest bidder typically shows up first in the list.

This same sort of automated auction occurs when an ad appears on an affiliate website. Whenever a page is visited on that site, the ad network conducts an auction for the ad slots available on that page. As with ads in search engine results, those ads with the highest bids—as well as highest quality content—are most likely to be displayed. When the site has placement for multiple ads, the ad from the highest bidder typically shows up highest on the page.

Ads on affiliate sites typically have lower click-through rates than do ads on search engine results pages. As such, these ads are less highly valued—and typically cost less than the same ads served in Google's search results.

The bidding for PPC ads works much the same way as bidding in an eBay auction. You specify the maximum amount you'll pay and let the ad network's automated bidding software do the dirty work for you. That is, the ad network places a bid for you that is only a little higher than existing bids. If competition forces the bidding higher, the ad network raises your bid accordingly, up to but not exceeding the maximum amount you specified.

The result is that advertisers aren't necessarily charged the full amount of their maximum bids. Because the bid raises are automated and incremental, Google and other ad networks charge the winning bidder just a penny or so more than the next-highest bid. So, if you bid a maximum of $5.00 and the next-highest bid was $4.00, you won't pay the full $5.00; instead, you'll be charged $4.01 for your winning bid.

Putting PPC Ads on Your Site with Google AdSense

If you're interested in generating revenue for your website, you need to sign up as an affiliate with a PPC ad network. The largest such ad network is Google AdSense (www.google.com/adsense), and it places text ads on your web pages; you get paid whenever a visitor clicks on one of these ads.

G *Learn more about using Google AdSense in Part 2 of this book, "Using Google AdSense."*

AdSense places PPC advertisements on traditional web pages, mobile web pages, blogs and blog feeds, and even YouTube videos. When you sign up for AdSense, you agree to provide Google with access to your website's content. In return, Google provides you with a short piece of HTML code to insert in your page's underlying code; this code inserts the PPC ads on a real-time basis.

Whenever someone visits your page, this code reports back to Google. Google then consults its database for information about your page content, and then serves up one or more PPC ads that match that content. It all happens in real time, and the ad appears almost simultaneously with the visitor opening the page.

At the end of each month, Google tallies up how many users have clicked on those ads appearing on your site. It does the internal accounting based on the amount paid by each advertiser and then determines your share of the revenues. This money is then deposited electronically in your bank account, or you can specify that a check be mailed to you.

The amount of work you have to do is minimal, including the sign-up process, of course, which requires you to fill in a few forms and supply your bank account information (so you can get paid). You then have to insert the AdSense code into each page on your site, which is the majority of the work—but a one-time thing. Beyond that, just sit back and let the process work and collect your money at the end of each month.

The process is even easier if you have a blog hosted by Blogger, Google's blogging service. Google will automatically insert the proper AdSense code into your blog pages, so you don't even have to do that.

It's pretty much the same if you have videos on YouTube, which is also owned by Google. You specify that you want to host ads on your YouTube pages, and YouTube does the rest. No coding necessary.

How much money can you expect to generate from being a member of Google's AdSense network? It's impossible to tell. It all depends on how much traffic your website generates, the quality of the content you have on your site, and how popular that content is with advertisers. Some website owners generate hundreds and thousands of dollars a month in ad revenue; others generate just a few dollars. Obviously, the bigger and more popular your site, the more potential there is for higher revenues.

If you're looking to host PPC ads on your site, other competing ad networks include Yahoo! Publisher Network (publisher.yahoo.com) and Microsoft pubCenter (beta.pubcenter.microsoft.com), currently in beta testing.

Buying PPC Ads with Google AdWords

If you want to advertise your website or business, you need to join a PPC ad network. The largest such network today is Google AdWords (www.google.com/adsense).

ⓖ *Learn more about using Google AdWords in Part 3 of this book, "Using Google AdWords."*

Google places ads on its own search results pages throughout its entire network of sites (Gmail, Google Maps, YouTube, and so forth), and on participating affiliate sites. Google claims that its AdWords program reaches more than 80 percent of all Internet users; most advertisers confirm that AdWords generates the overwhelming majority of PPC traffic to their sites.

Advertising with Google AdWords isn't like a traditional advertising buy, as there are no contracts and deadlines and such to deal with. You pay a one-time $5 activation fee and then are charged on either a cost-per-click (CPC) or cost-per-thousand-impressions (CPM) basis. (You can choose either payment method.) You control your costs by specifying how much you're willing to pay (per click or per impression) and by setting a daily spending budget. Google will never exceed the costs you specify.

How much does AdWords cost? It's your choice. If you go with the cost-per-click method, you can choose a maximum CPC price from $0.01 to $100. If you go with the CPM method, there is a minimum cost of $0.25 per 1,000 impressions. Your daily budget can be as low as a penny, up to whatever you're willing to pay.

If you go the CPC route, which is most common, Google uses AdWords Discounter technology to match the price you pay with the price competing advertisers are offering for a given keyword. This is, in effect, Google's automated bidding system. The AdWords Discounter automatically monitors your competition and lowers your CPC to one cent above what they're willing to pay.

When you sign up for AdWords you get down to business quickly. You're prompted to set a budget for your first campaign, create an ad, choose your keywords, and then set your price for those keywords. Your ad then goes live.

At this point, AdWords places your ad on relevant pages, based on your keyword bid amount, until your budget runs out. At that point your ad is withdrawn from circulation until the next budget period begins, or until you increase your budget. This means you can blow your budget in a day, especially if you have a low budget and you've bid on popular and high-priced keywords. That's just the way it works; you have to pay for results, and if you don't have a big budget, you won't get much exposure.

You can opt to continue a given ad indefinitely or to run an ad for a limited period of time only. You can run multiple ads simultaneously, or go with a single ad. You can even create separate ads for different keywords; the more sophisticated your approach, the better your potential results.

At the end of each month, AdWords bills you for the number of clicks on your ads. If no one clicked, you don't pay anything—but then again, you can hardly call that a success. You are only billed, of course, up to the maximum amount of your budget. If the cost of those clicks is under your budget number, you only pay for the actual clicks, not the maximum amount you budgeted.

Over the course of a campaign, you can use AdWords' various tools to monitor the performance of your ads. Monitor your ads carefully, as you can tweak them incessantly; it's not uncommon to change keywords and rewrite ad text over the course of a campaign to maximize your results. The goal, after all, is to generate the maximum amount of traffic to your website (and from there to convert clicks to sales), and AdWords gives you the tools you need to generate the best performance.

The other major PPC networks for advertisers include Yahoo! Sponsored Search (http://advertising.yahoo.com/smallbusiness) and Microsoft adCenter (adcenter.microsoft.com).

II

Using Google AdSense

2

Making Money from Your Website with AdSense

Yes, you *can* make money from your website—and it's easy to do. All you have to do is sign up with Google's AdSense service, which adds relatively unobtrusive text advertising to your website. Whenever a visitor clicks on one of these ads, Google gets paid and passes on a portion of that fee to you, the hosting site.

Any site, large or small, can sign up for Google AdSense and start generating revenues immediately. But how does AdSense work? It's really quite simple, as you'll learn in this chapter.

How to Make Money from Your Website

On the Internet, the way that most big sites pay for themselves is by selling advertising. But web advertising isn't limited to the big boys; any site, no matter how small, can generate significant advertising revenues, using pay-per-click advertising.

As you learned in the previous chapter, pay-per-click advertising involves placing small text ads on the pages of your website. Whenever a visitor clicks through the ad to the advertiser's website, you collect a small fee.

The problem with this scenario, of course, is that you're not in the advertising business; you have no sales force to sell advertising on your site, nor do you have the technology required to place the ads, track click-throughs, and then collect funds due from advertisers. Sure, you might be able to generate a bit of revenue—if only you could get the ads placed and managed.

This is where Google AdSense comes in. The AdSense program places content-targeted ads on your site, sells those ads to appropriate advertisers, monitors visitor click-throughs, tracks how much money is owed you, and then pays you what you've earned. These are typically small text ads, and you have full control over how many ads appear on each page, as well as the size and placement of each ad. You can make the ads as unobtrusive as you like—or make them stand out, the better to catch the attention of your site visitors.

Given that Google does all the heavy lifting, it's hard not to like the AdSense program. Yes, you can—and should—work to maximize the potential for the ads on your site, but you don't have to bother with keeping track of who clicked what and when. Google does its thing in the background, placing the best ads possible on your site and tracking each ad's performance. You get paid just for providing the display space for the ads.

Granted, a typical personal website isn't going to generate millions of click-throughs on its ads; you don't have millions of visitors, after all. But even a few click-throughs a week will generate a bit of spare cash that you didn't have otherwise. All you have to do is sign up for the program, insert a few lines of code into the underlying HTML code of your web pages, and then sit back and let Google do the rest of the work.

Getting to Know the AdSense Family

Google AdSense is actually five programs in one:

- Google AdSense for Content is the primary part of the program, placing targeted ads on your web pages

- Google AdSense for Search lets you add Google search to your website, and thus generate even more traffic and advertising revenue

- Google AdSense for Feeds lets you add AdSense ads to your blog's RSS feed

- Google AdSense for Mobile Content lets you optimize your site for access from smartphones and other mobile devices, and thus serve ads to users with those devices

- Google AdSense for Domains lets you earn revenue from any unused or parked web domains

Next we'll learn more about each of these programs.

 SHOW ME Media 2.1—A video about how each of the AdSense programs works

Access this video file through your registered Web Edition at **my.safaribooksonline.com/9780131388666/media.**

Understanding Google AdSense for Content

The main part of the AdSense program is dubbed Google AdSense for Content. This is the part of the program that puts ads on your web pages, and then generates revenue whenever visitors click on the ad links.

AdSense ads aren't just random advertisements; Google utilizes the same technology it uses to analyze web pages for its search index to determine the content of a page and place a content-appropriate ad on that page. For example, if your web page is about books, it might place ads for book publishing services, as shown in Figure 2.1. If your web page is about teeth, Google might place an ad for dentists, and so on.

Figure 2.1   *A block of book-related contextual ads on the author's bibliography page.*

Google calls this *contextual targeting*, and it really works—more often than not. Google's content parser can only determine which words are used on your page, not how those words are used. So, if you have a page that's critical of the dentistry profession, it will still generate ads for dentists and dental hygienists.

The nice thing about ads that actually relate to your page's content is that they're more appealing to your site's visitors. One can assume that if you have a page about teeth, your visitors are interested in all things teeth-related, and thus are likely to respond positively to ads selling teeth-related merchandise and services. At the very least, the ads Google places should be more relevant to your toothsome visitors than, say, ads for motor oil or Viagra. And the more relevant the ad, the higher the click-through rate will be—which means more profits, for both Google and you.

Even better, AdSense ad selection is automatic; you don't have to do a thing. Google automatically crawls your page to determine its content, and places ads appropriately. Your involvement is to activate the AdSense service, insert the appropriate HTML code (just once), and then sit back and let Google do everything else. You don't even have to notify Google if you change your site's content; AdSense automatically monitors your site for changes, and places new ads accordingly.

⊙ Learn more about implementing Google AdSense for Content in Chapter 3, "Adding AdSense for Content to Your Website."

Understanding Google AdSense for Search

Then there's AdSense for Search, to which you get access when you sign up for AdSense for Content. The Search component lets you add a Google search box to your website. This is a good thing, as it keeps users on your site longer; they don't have to leave your site to conduct a web search.

Keeping visitors on your site longer increases the chances of them clicking through any ad placed on your site. In addition, you now collect a small percentage of the ad revenue when a visitor clicks through an ad on your site's search results page. It's only pennies (or fractions of a penny) per click, but it can add up fast.

AdSense lets you put two different types of Google search boxes on your web pages. You can utilize the standard Google web search box, of course, or you can create a box that lets visitors search within your own website. Either option is free; you can choose either or both.

Getting the search boxes onto your site, is a simple matter of feeding some key information to Google, having Google generate the appropriate HTML code, and then pasting that code into the code for your web page. After the code is inserted, the Google search box automatically appears—and the AdSense ads automatically display on all search results pages thus generated. Every time a visitor clicks one of the ads on the search results page, you receive a percentage of the fee that the advertiser paid to Google. It's that simple.

⊙ Learn more about AdSense for Search in Chapter 4, "Adding AdSense for Search to Your Website."

Understanding Google AdSense for Feeds

You're not limited to placing PPC ads on a full-blown website. You can also place ads on any blog you run, as well as in the blog's RSS feed. If you have a blog, you probably know all about RSS feeds already; it's a way of keeping regular blog readers up-to-date on new blog posts. When a reader subscribes to your blogs feed, he is automatically alerted when new postings are made.

You use the normal Google AdSense for Content program to insert PPC ads into the blog itself. A separate program, called Google AdSense for Feeds, lets you place targeted advertisements in your blog's RSS feeds. As with the other AdSense programs, you control the appearance, positioning, and frequency of these ads—and then collect a portion of all click-through revenues generated.

ⓒ *Learn more about AdSense for Feeds in Chapter 5, "Adding AdSense for Feeds to Your Blog."*

Understanding Google AdSense for Mobile Content

These days, a personal computer is just one way to access the web. Many users are now viewing websites and pages using their iPhones and other mobile devices. To best serve these mobile visitors, you need to optimize your web pages for the smaller screens of these devices; you also need to serve up ads that are specially tailored for this audience and their devices.

To that end, Google offers the AdSense for Mobile Content program. This program optimizes PPC ads for mobile websites, in terms of both appearance and content. It's basically an extension of the AdSense for Content program, tailored for mobile web pages.

If you develop applications for the iPhone or Android phones, Google offers AdSense for Mobile Applications, which lets you integrate PPC ads into your apps. Learn more at www.google.com/ads/mobileapps/.

ⓒ *Learn more about AdSense for Mobile Content in Chapter 6, "Using AdSense for Mobile Content."*

Understanding Google AdSense for Domains

If you happen to own one or more web domains that are currently unused—so-called "parked" domains—you can still use AdSense to earn money from those domains. The Google AdSense for Domains program provides you with links, search results, and, yes, PPC advertising relevant to your parked domain. It's a great way to put up some temporary content until the domain goes live; it's far better than visitors seeing empty pages or "page not found" errors.

ⓒ *Learn more about AdSense for Domains in Chapter 7, "Using AdSense for Domains."*

How Much Money Can You Make?

One of the first questions that most people have about AdSense concerns the money—just how much money can you make from the AdSense program? There's no easy answer to that question, unfortunately.

 TELL ME MORE   Media 2.2—A discussion about making money with AdSense

Access this audio recording through your registered Web Edition at my.safaribooksonline.com/9780131388666/media.

First, you have to know that Google simply doesn't disclose how much money you can make; it doesn't tell you how much it charges its advertisers, nor what percentage of the take you receive. That's right—when you sign up for the AdSense program, you're doing so with absolutely no idea what your earnings will be. It doesn't really sound like a fully informed contractual agreement to me, but that's the way it is.

One of the reasons Google doesn't disclose how much you can make is because the price it charges its advertisers fluctuates literally moment-by-moment. Advertisers bid on keywords, and the final bid price is determined only when a visitor opens a host web page. Google itself doesn't know what it's charging until each ad is served.

That said, we do know in general how the AdSense program works. The ads you display on your pages can be placed on either a cost-per-click (CPC) or cost-per-thousand-impressions (CPM) basis. That is, the advertiser pays either when someone clicks an ad, or when someone simply views the ad. You have no choice on whether you get CPC or CPM ads on your site.

Whenever an advertiser pays Google (for either a click or an impression), you receive a cut of that payment in the form of a commission. How much of a commission you make depends on how much the advertiser is paying Google for that particular ad. The payment varies by advertiser and by quality of content; competition for the most popular content and keywords causes advertisers to bid up the price accordingly.

What does that mean in terms of dollars? It all depends; payments can run anywhere from a few pennies to tens of dollars per click, depending on the type of content you have on your site, and you get a percentage of that (what percentage that is, Google doesn't disclose).

So, the amount you earn is dependent on the price that advertisers are paying, the amount of targeted traffic your site receives, and the number of visitors who view or click the ads on your site. Obviously, the most popular and heavily-trafficked sites command a higher cost per click than those sites with less traffic. It's to your benefit to improve the content of your site to increase site traffic; the more traffic you generate, the more money you can earn from AdSense advertising.

Using AdSense in the Real World

So how do you get started making money with AdSense? We'll discuss the particulars over the next few chapters, but in general, it goes like this:

 **LET ME TRY IT**

How AdSense Works

1. Go to the AdSense website and create a new account. (If you already have a Google account, you're half way there; you just have to add some information about your website or blog, as well as how you'd like to be paid.)

2. Decide what type of ads you want on your site. AdSense offers a variety of ad sizes, formats, and colors.

3. Based on all this information, AdSense will generate a block of HTML code specifically tailored for each page on your site. Copy this block of code and paste it into your web page where you want the ads to appear.

You can display more than one block of ads on a page. For example, you can have ads along the top of your page, along the side, and at the bottom—as well as in between content in the body of your page. The more ads you display, the more opportunities there are to generate click-through revenues.

After the ads start displaying, sit back and wait for your site's visitors to start clicking. You monitor the performance of the ads on your site—and track revenues generated—via AdSense's control panel. You can also use the control panel to change the ads on your site or generate new ads. Google also provides a variety of tools you can use to help optimize your site to generate more ad revenue. (It's in Google's best interest for your site to be as effective as possible, of course.)

 Learn more about tracking performance in Chapter 9, "Monitoring Your AdSense Performance."

3

Adding AdSense for Content to Your Website

When you want to make money from your website, Google AdSense for Content is the way to go. AdSense places content-relevant ads on your site from advertisers both big and small. When your site's visitors click on these ads, you capture a portion of the revenues generated by that ad.

To add AdSense for Content ads to your website, you first have to sign up for the AdSense program. After you've signed up, you then add the AdSense code to your site's HTML—and wait for the money to roll in.

Understanding Google AdSense for Content

Google's AdSense for Content program is one of the best ways to generate revenue from your website. The program is open to any person or company that hosts a website or blog. You don't have to be a big site or a big company; one-page sites run by individuals also qualify.

When you sign up for the AdSense for Content program, Google places one or more small text or image ads on your website. These ads are automatically generated, and automatically selected to be relevant to your site's readers. The advertisers behind these ads range from big international brands to small local businesses, in every category imaginable.

You don't have to worry about inappropriate or undesirable ads appearing, either. AdSense includes a number of safeguards to ensure that you get appropriate and inoffensive ads on your site. These safeguards include filters that let you block ads from competitors or other specific sites; an internal review that judges both ad quality and suitability; and filters that block sensitive or inappropriate content. You can even choose to display a default ad of your choice in the event that Google doesn't find any appropriate ads to display on your web page.

You can also determine how these ads look on your web pages. You can choose from several different ad sizes and configurations; you can even choose the colors used, so that the ads either blend in or stand out from your site's content.

What's virtually guaranteed is that the ads placed on your site will have something to do with your site's content—which makes them more attractive to your site's visitors. If your site content changes, Google changes the ads that appear, as well.

You get paid when a visitor clicks on an ad; if no one clicks, no revenue is generated. By placing the most relevant ads on your site, Google works to increase click-throughs—and increase ad revenues.

Performance is monitored via a number of customizable online reports. You can track the number of page impressions, the number of clicks, and even the click-through rate for the ads on your site. Smart webmasters use these reports to analyze the performance of different ad formats, colors, and such, and then reconfigure their preferences to increase ad performance. And remember, the better performing the ads, the more revenue you generate for your site.

Joining the AdSense for Content Program

Google calls all subscribers to its AdSense program *publishers*, and it's quite easy to get started with the program. You apply online via a simple form, then wait for Google's approval. (Almost all applicants are quickly approved.) Once approved, you're provided with a block of HTML code to insert into your web pages. As soon as the code is inserted, the AdSense ads appear.

LET ME TRY IT

Signing Up for AdSense

1. Go to the main AdSense page (www.google.com/adsense/), shown in Figure 3.1, and click the Sign Up Now button.

2. On the next page you see the AdSense application form. Supply the following information on this form and make the following choices:

SHOW ME   Media 3.1—A video about how to sign up for AdSense
Access this video file through your registered Web Edition at
my.safaribooksonline.com/9780131388666/media.

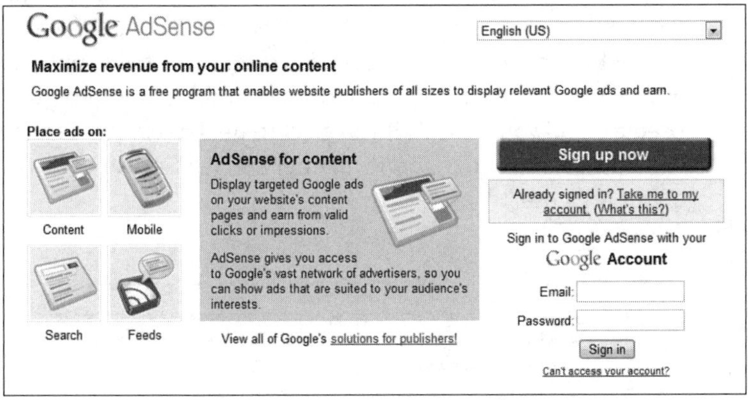

Figure 3.1   *The main page for Google AdSense.*

- **Website Information** (shown in Figure 3.2). Enter the primary URL for your website and then select your site's language. Enter the URL for the top-level domain only; Google will find the other pages on your site itself. You also need to confirm (by checking the option boxes) that your site doesn't provide incentives to click on the ads or offer pornographic content.

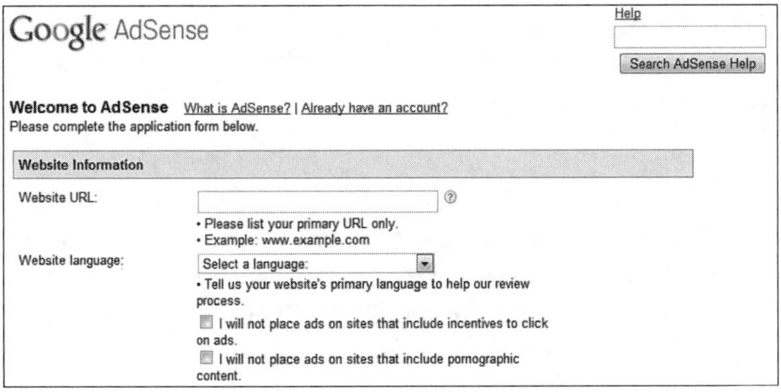

Figure 3.2   *Filling in information about your website.*

🅖 *Providing incentives to click on the ads on your site is a form of click fraud. Learn more about this in Chapter 21, "Dealing with Click Fraud."*

- **Contact information** (shown in Figure 3.3). Start by selecting either an Individual or Business account type. (Select Individual if it's a personal site, or Business if it's a business site.) Then select the country where you live and enter your name and street address; this information is used to send you a check, if you elect to get paid in that fashion. You should also enter your phone number and tell Google how you heard about AdSense.

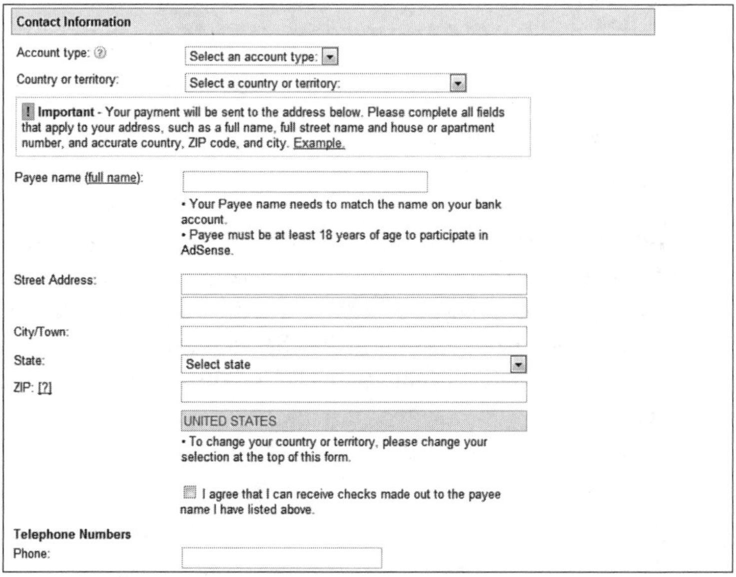

Figure 3.3   *Entering your contact information.*

- **Policies.** You have to agree to abide by Google's various policies—that you won't click on your site's AdSense ads (that's click fraud, again), that you've actually read the policies, and that you don't already have an AdSense account.

3. When you've filled in all the blanks, click the Submit Information button. Google will now verify your email address by sending you a confirmation email.

4. Follow the instructions in the email message and Google will review your application.

5. The review period typically runs two to three days, and then Google will notify you of your acceptance and you'll be ready to log into your AdSense account and get started with the rest of the process.

You can edit your AdSense account information at any time by logging into your account and then selecting the My Account tab.

 LET ME TRY IT

Adding AdSense Ads to Your Website

After your AdSense application has been accepted, you can log into your account from the main AdSense page (www.google.com/adsense/).

 **SHOW ME**   Media 3.2—A video about how to place ads on my website
Access this video file through your registered Web Edition at
my.safaribooksonline.com/9780131388666/media.

Your home page includes a series of tabs; follow these steps to set up your first ad—or create additional ads:

1. Select the AdSense Setup tab, shown in Figure 3.4.

2. Click the AdSense for Content link.

3. When the AdSense for Content page appears, as shown in Figure 3.5, select whether you want to display an ad unit (a block advertisement) or a link unit (a list of linked topics). If you choose to display an ad unit, you also need to pull down the list and select the type of ads you want—text only, image only, or text and image (default). Click the Continue button to continue.

4. When the next page appears, as shown in Figure 3.6, select the ad format you want. Available ad formats include four recommended sizes (medium rectangle, large rectangle, leaderboard, and wide skyscraper), two sizes of horizontal ads, two sizes of vertical ads, and four sizes of square ads. Click the Continue button to continue.

   Ⓖ *Learn more about ad formats in the "Choosing Ad Types and Sizes" section later in this chapter.*

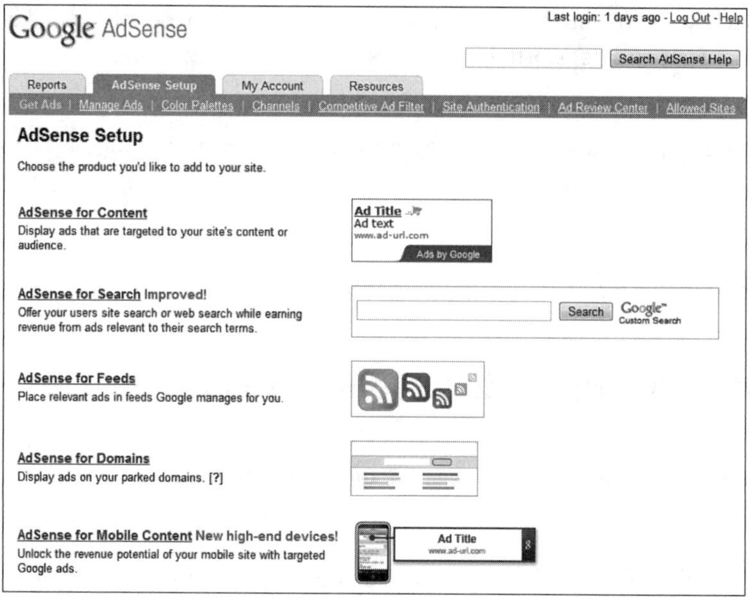

Figure 3.4 *Preparing to set up an AdSense ad.*

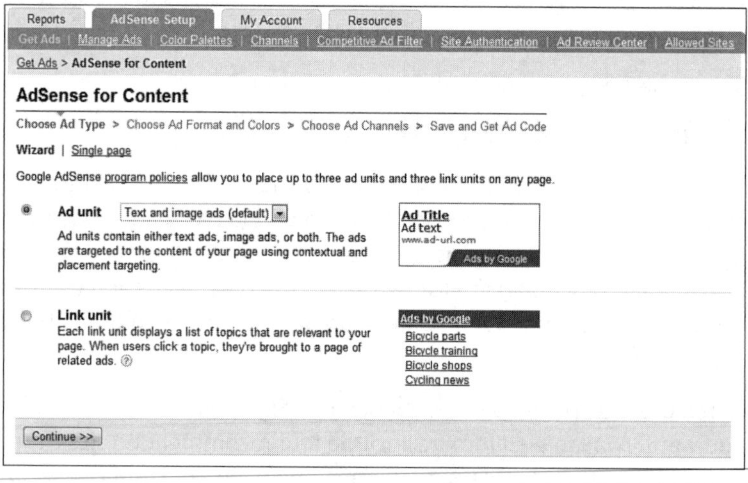

Figure 3.5 *Choosing the type of ad to display—an ad unit or link unit.*

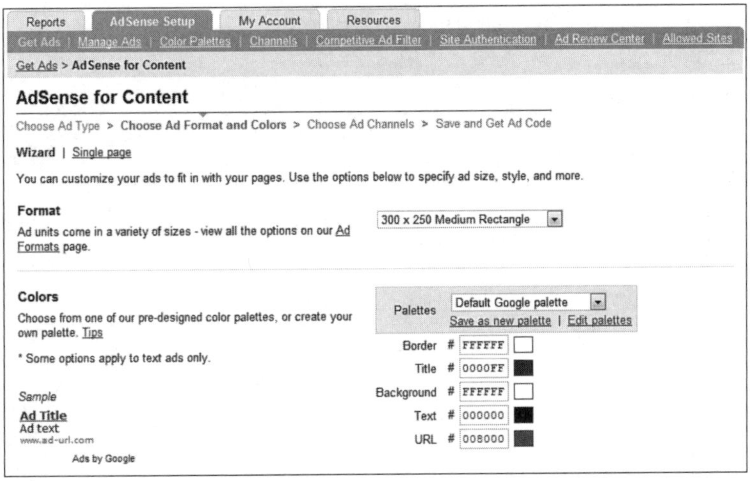

Figure 3.6 *Choosing the ad format and color scheme.*

5. On the same page, select the desired color scheme for the ads. You can choose from a variety of preselected palettes or choose specific colors for various ad elements.

6. Still on the same page, select the fonts and corner style for your ads.

7. At the bottom of this page, select what types of alternate ads you want to display if Google can't find any ads to serve. You can choose to show public service ads, non-Google ads from another URL, or just fill the empty space with a solid color. Click Continue when you're ready to proceed.

8. The next page, shown in Figure 3.7, lets you specify up to five custom channels for your ads; you can create different channels for different pages on your site. Do so if you want (you don't have to) and then click the Continue button.

Ⓖ *Learn more about channels in the "Defining Ad Channels" section later in this chapter.*

9. As shown in Figure 3.8, you're now prompted to name the ad unit you've created. Do so and then click the Submit and Get Code button.

10. The final page, shown in Figure 3.9, displays the code that Google generated for your ad. Copy the code from this page and then paste it into the HTML code for your web page.

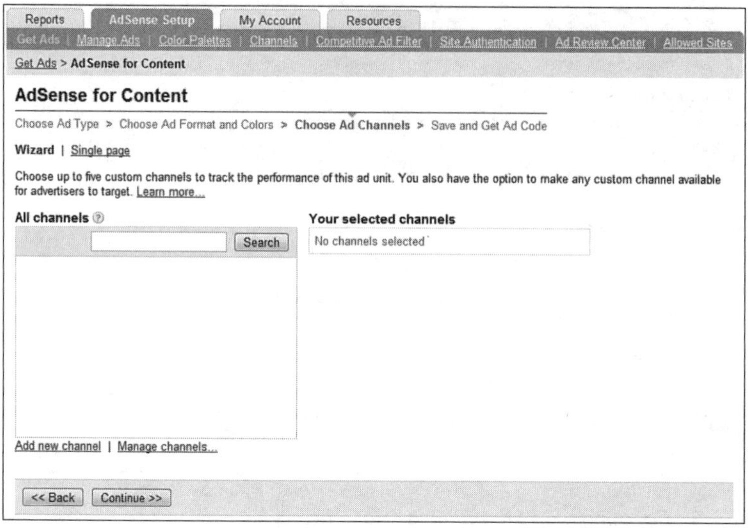

Figure 3.7   *Choosing custom channels for your ads.*

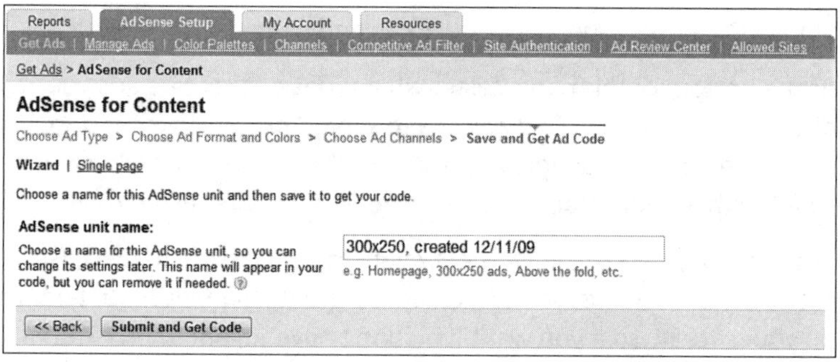

Figure 3.8   *Naming and saving your new ad unit.*

☝ *Learn more about inserting the HTML code in the "Inserting the Ad Code" section later in this chapter.*

There was a lot involved in this deceptively simple process. We'll go through some of the particulars next.

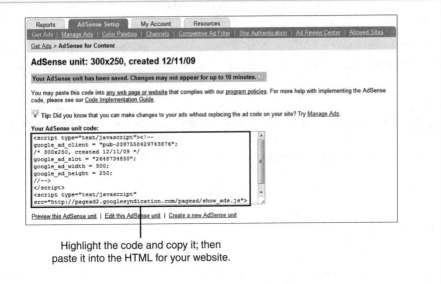

Highlight the code and copy it; then
paste it into the HTML for your website.

Figure 3.9   *The final ad code—copy it into your web page's HTML.*

Choosing Ad Types and Sizes

AdSense lets you place both text and image ads on your site, in a variety of sizes. You can opt to display text ads only, image ads only, or both text and image ads.

What type and size of ad you display depends on how obtrusive you want the ads to be on your site. An image ad looks more like a traditional advertisement than does a text ad, and thus stands out more from your regular page content. Some webmasters feel that this cheapens their sites and results in fewer click-throughs; others feel that it draws attention to the ads and results in more click-throughs. As such, testing might be in order.

Ad size is determined more by the design of your web pages than anything else. Determine the size of the space where you want the ads to appear and then choose the closest ad format. It goes without saying that you shouldn't try to slot a tall ad into a wide space, or vice versa. AdSense offers enough different ad sizes to make this choice relatively easy.

Text Ads

The most common AdSense ads are text ads. These ads typically consist of a title and one or two lines of body text; sometimes the link-to URL appears at the bottom of the ad, and sometimes the title itself is clickable and linked to the advertiser's site.

Google offers text ads in a variety of sizes and formats. Most formats allow for two or more ads from different advertisers; the smallest formats are for single ads only.

SHOW ME   Media 3.3—A video about the differences in text ad types
Access this video file through your registered Web Edition at
my.safaribooksonline.com/9780131388666/media.

Table 3.1 details the available text ad formats.

Table 3.1   Text Ad Formats

Format	Size (in Pixels, Width × Height)	Number of Text Ads Displayed	Description
Leaderboard	728 × 90	4	Displays across the width of a web page
Banner	468 × 60	2	A smaller version of the leaderboard format
Half banner	234 × 60	1	Half of a regular banner ad
Skyscraper	120 × 600	4	A tall and narrow format
Wide skyscraper	160 × 600	5	A slightly wider version of the skyscraper format
Vertical banner	120 × 240	2	A smaller version of the skyscraper format
Button	125 × 125	1	Small, square format
Small square	200 × 200	2	A larger version of the button format
Square	250 × 250	3	An even larger square format
Small rectangle	180 × 150	1	Slightly wider than it is tall
Medium rectangle	300 × 250	4	Slightly larger rectangular format
Large rectangle	336 × 280	4	The largest rectangular format

Figures 3.10 through 3.13 illustrate each of these ad formats.

TELL ME MORE   Media 3.4—A discussion about choosing ad sizes
Access this audio recording through your registered Web Edition at
my.safaribooksonline.com/9780131388666/media.

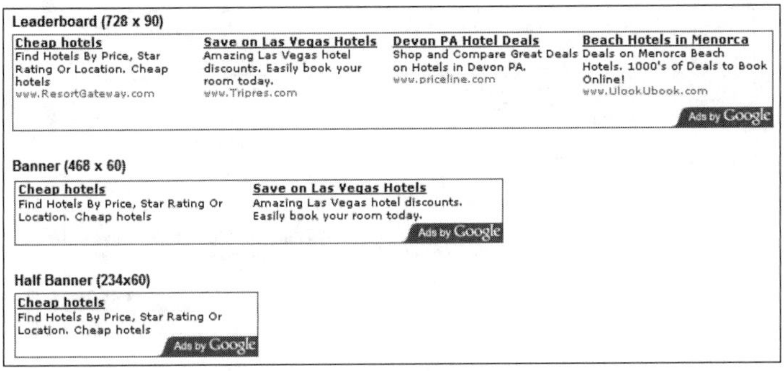

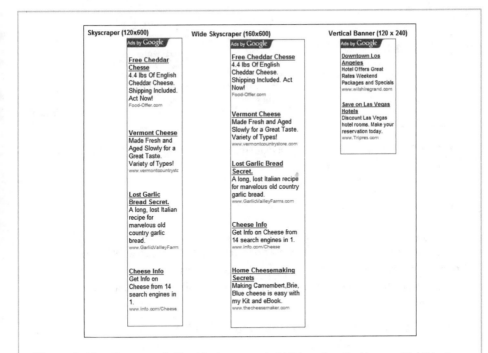

Figure 3.10   *Leaderboard (top), banner (middle), and half banner (bottom) text ad formats.*

Figure 3.11   *Skyscraper (left), wide skyscraper (middle), and vertical banner (right) text ad formats.*

Figure 3.12　*Button (left), small square (middle), and square (right) text ad formats.*

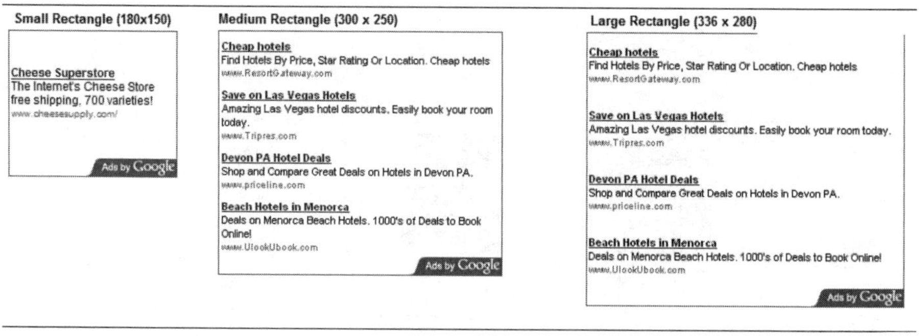

Figure 3.13　*Small rectangle (left), medium rectangle (middle), and large rectangle (right) text ad formats.*

Image Ads

Although text ads are most common, some advertisers prefer displaying their products or brands in a graphical manner. To that end, AdSense offers several image ad formats, each consisting of a single ad from a single advertiser. In these ads, the advertiser's website appears in a text link within the ad; in most instances, the entire ad is also clickable.

There are fewer image ad formats than you find with text ads; because image ads need to be larger to be effective, some of the smaller sizes aren't available. Table 3.2 details the available image ad formats.

Table 3.2　Image Ad Formats

Format	Size (in Pixels, Width × Height)	Description
Leaderboard	728 × 90	Displays across the width of a web page
Banner	468 × 60	A smaller version of the leaderboard format

Format	Size (in Pixels, Width × Height)	Description
Skyscraper	120 × 600	A tall and narrow format
Wide skyscraper	160 × 600	A slightly wider version of the skyscraper format
Small square	200 × 200	A larger version of the button format
Square	250 × 250	An even larger square format
Medium rectangle	300 × 250	Slightly larger rectangular format
Large rectangle	336 × 280	The largest rectangular format

Figures 3.14 through 3.17 illustrate each of these ad formats.

Figure 3.14 *Leaderboard (top) and banner (bottom) image ad formats.*

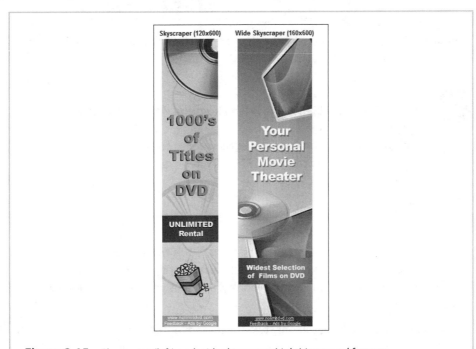

Figure 3.15 *Skyscraper (left) and wide skyscraper (right) image ad formats.*

Figure 3.16   *Small square (left) and square (right) image ad formats.*

Figure 3.17   *Medium rectangle (left) and large rectangle (right) image ad formats.*

SHOW ME   **Media 3.5—A video about the differences between types of image ads**
Access this video file through your registered Web Edition at
my.safaribooksonline.com/9780131388666/media.

Video Ads

If you opt to display image ads on your site, you might be surprised to find that some of these ads are actually *video* ads—that is, ads that display moving videos from the advertisers. You don't have to deliberately opt to display video ads; these ads are rotated with the image ad inventory, and thus will be served along with regular image ads.

That said, video ads display in only two specific ad formats, as shown in Figure 3.18 and detailed in Table 3.3.

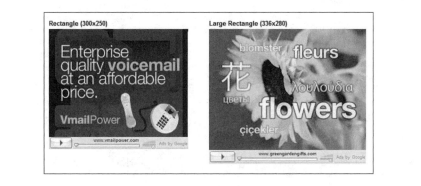

Figure 3.18   *Medium rectangle (left) and large rectangle (right) video ad formats.*

Table 3.3   Video Ad Formats

Format	Size (in Pixels, Width × Height)	Description
Medium rectangle	300 × 250	Perfect for standard 3:2 aspect ratio videos
Large rectangle	336 × 280	Better for widescreen (16:9 aspect ratio) videos

 SHOW ME   Media 3.6—A video about the different types of video ads

Access this video file through your registered Web Edition at my.safaribooksonline.com/9780131388666/media.

In some places on the AdSense site it's implied that video ads are also available in other ad formats—leaderboard, skyscraper, wide skyscraper, square, and small square. It appears, however, that these are just theoretical ads, and that virtually all existing video ads are served in one of the two rectangle formats. This is because videos are not typically shot in extra wide or extra tall formats.

Link Units

You also have the option of displaying *link units* instead of ads. Think of a link unit as a kind of table of contents to related ads. Each link unit displays a list of topics relative to your web page's content; when visitors click a topic link, they're taken to a page full of related ads.

Link units are available in a variety of different sizes, as detailed in Table 3.4. These are *not* the same sizes available for text or image ads; make sure you size your page space accordingly.

Table 3.4　Link Unit Formats

Size (in Pixels, Width × Height)	Number of Links Displayed	Description
728 × 15	4 or 5	Displays across the width of a web page
468 × 15	4 or 5	Displays across half the width of a web page
200 × 90	4 or 5	A rectangular format
180 × 90	4 or 5	A slightly smaller rectangular format
160 × 90	4 or 5	Another rectangular format
120 × 90	4 or 5	The smallest link unit format

SHOW ME　　Media 3.7—A video about the different types of link units
Access this video file through your registered Web Edition at
my.safaribooksonline.com/9780131388666/media.

Figures 3.19 through 3.21 illustrate the available link unit formats.

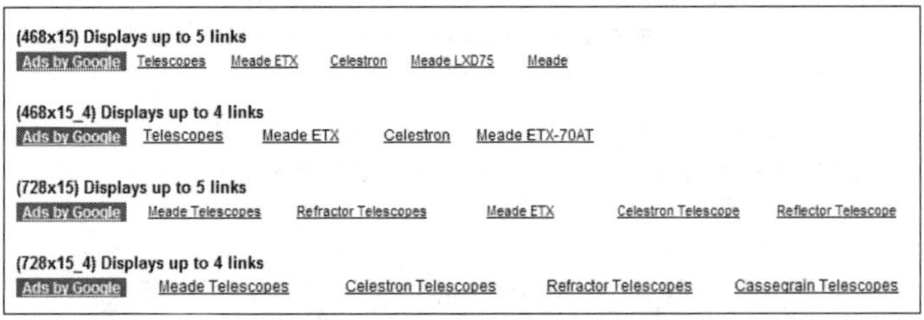

Figure 3.19　*Four- and five-link versions of the 728 × 15 and 468 × 15 link unit formats.*

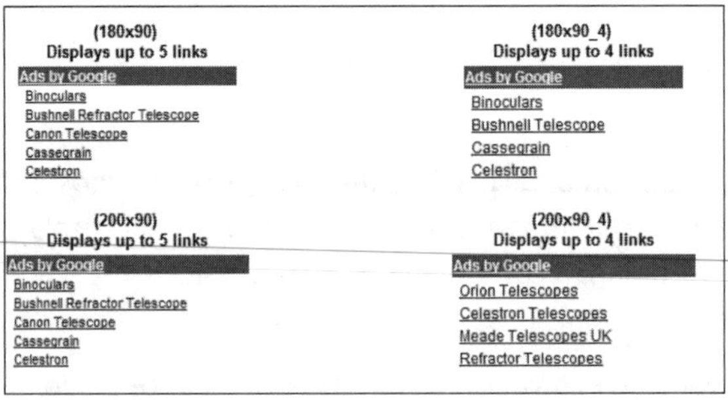

Figure 3.20　*Four- and five-link versions of the 200 × 90 and 180 × 90 link unit formats.*

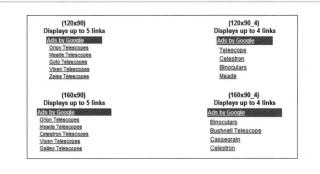

Figure 3.21 *Four- and five-link versions of the 160 × 90 and 120 × 90 link unit formats.*

Inserting the Ad Code

After you've generated the HTML code for a specific type of ad, you then need to insert that code into the underlying HTML code of the pages on your website. If you want the same ad type on each web page, insert the same code onto each page; if you want different types of ads on different pages, insert the code for the appropriate ad type onto those pages where you want that ad type to appear. (You'll also need to insert different code if you create custom channels for your site, as described next in the "Defining Ad Channels" section.)

Even though the code might be the same from page to page, Google generates different ads for the unique content on each page of your site. You only need to create new ad code if the format of the ad (size, type, color, and so on) changes from page to page.

You should insert this AdSense code in the position where you want the ad to appear on your page. For example, if you want the ad to appear at the top of your page, insert the ad code at the beginning of the body code; if you want the ad to appear at the bottom, insert the ad code at the end of the body code. If you have a more sophisticated page design, use the appropriate HTML or CSS tags to position the ad on the page.

If all this code insertion stuff causes your head to spin, just turn the task over to an experienced web designer. He'll know what to do.

By the way, you can regenerate this code at any time by going to the AdSense Setup tab, selecting Manage Ads, and then clicking the Code link (in the Actions column) for any ad unit you've previously saved. You don't have to go through the whole ad creation process every time you need to use the code.

Defining Ad Channels

By default, AdSense tracks all the ads on all the pages of your site in kind of a big lump. If you have multiple pages on your site with different content, you might find it more informative to track the performance of these individual pages so that you can better target the content of those pages. AdSense lets you do this by defining different *channels* within your website; you can then track performance by channel.

You can define each page on your site as a separate channel, or group like pages together in a single channel. In the first example, you create what AdSense calls *URL channels*; each URL is its own channel. In the second example, a site about gardening might have several pages about flowers, other pages about shrubbery, and still more pages about grasses. In this instance, you could create a flowers channel, a shrubbery channel, and a grasses channel, tracking performance for all pages within a category together.

ⓖ *Learn more about tracking performance in Chapter 9, "Monitoring Your AdSense Performance."*

Creating URL Channels

Creating URL channels is relatively easy; you don't have to create separate HTML code for each page. Instead, you simply alert AdSense to each of the pages on your site that you want to track separately.

 **LET ME TRY IT**

Make AdSense Track Web Pages Separately

1. Log onto your AdSense account and click the AdSense Setup tab.

2. Click the Channels sub-tab.

3. On the resulting page, click the AdSense for Content sub-tab.

4. Click the URL Channels link.

5. Click the Add New URL Channels link.

6. In the resulting text box, shown in Figure 3.22, enter the URLs for the pages on your site that you want to track. Enter one URL per line.

| Reports | AdSense Setup | My Account | Resources |

Get Ads | Manage Ads | Color Palettes | Channels | Competitive Ad Filter | Site Authentication | Ad Review Center | Allowed Sites

Channels

Define reporting channels to track and improve your ad performance.

What are Channels? | Guide to Using Channels | Common Questions

| AdSense for Content | AdSense for Search | AdSense for Mobile Content | AdSense for Domains | AdSense for Feeds |

Custom channels | **URL channels**

Actions... ▼ **+ Add new URL channels**   [   ] [Find Channels]

Total URL and Custom Channels remaining: 198

Enter URLs to track, one per line:

[   ]

[Add channels] or cancel

Example URL channels

example.com	track all pages across all subdomains
sports.example.com	track only pages across the 'sports' subdomain
sports.example.com/widgets	track all pages below a specific directory
sports.example.com/index.html	track a specific page

☐ **URL**
☐ curmudgeonspeaks.blogspot.com
☐ mikeandsherrypictures.blogspot.com

Figure 3.22 *Creating a new URL channel.*

7. Click the Add Channels button.

What you enter as the URL depends on the type of page you're tracking:

- To track a regular web page, enter the full URL, like this: **website.com/page.html**

- To track pages generated from a sample script, enter the full path of the script, like this: **website.com/script.asp**

- To track all pages within a certain directory, enter the domain path, like this: **website.com/directory**

- To track pages within a specific subdomain, enter the subdomain name, like this: **subdomain.website.com**

🖱 **LET ME TRY IT**

Creating Custom Channels

If you want to track multiple pages together, you must create a custom channel. To do this, you must inform AdSense of the new channel and then create a custom code to add to each of the pages in that channel.

The first step of the process is creating the channel itself within AdSense. Follow these steps:

1. Log onto your AdSense account and click the AdSense Setup tab.

2. Click the Channels sub-tab.

3. On the resulting page, click the AdSense for Content sub-tab.

4. Click the Custom Channels link.

5. Click the Add New Custom Channels link.

6. On the next page, shown in Figure 3.23, enter a name for your new channel.

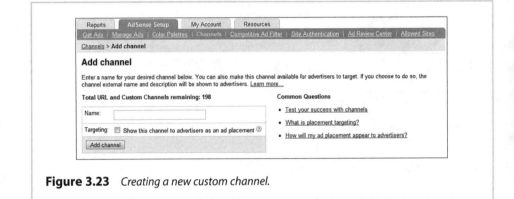

Figure 3.23   *Creating a new custom channel.*

7. If you like, check the option to display this channel to advertisers for more targeted ad placement; if you do so, you'll be prompted to enter additional information about this channel.

8. Click the Add Channel button.

9. Next, you have to generate the channel-specific HTML code. You do this by going through the entire ad setup process, as described in the "Adding AdSense Ads to Your Website" section earlier in this chapter. When you get to step 8, select the channel you're tracking from the Channel list and then click Continue. AdSense now generates the channel-specific code, which you then insert into each of the pages you're tracking as part of this channel.

Adding Pages Behind a Login

If you have a website that's fully open to the public, AdSense does a relatively good job of targeting ads to your pages' content. But what if your pages are behind a password-protected login—pages that Google otherwise can't crawl to determine their content?

Unless you take a special measure, Google simply can't provide targeted ads to those pages it can't otherwise see. This might mean serving up ads unrelated to what's on the page, or just serving up some generic PSAs (public service announcements).

 **LET ME TRY IT**

Display Ads on Password-Protected Pages

If you want to display ads on password-protected pages, you have to create an *authentication rule* that enables Google to crawl these protected pages. It's actually a simple process:

1. Log onto your AdSense account and click the AdSense Setup tab.

2. Click the Site Authentication sub-tab.

3. On the resulting page, scroll down to the Add Your Authentication Rule section, shown in Figure 3.24, and enter the URL for the restricted directory or page into the Restricted Directory or URL field.

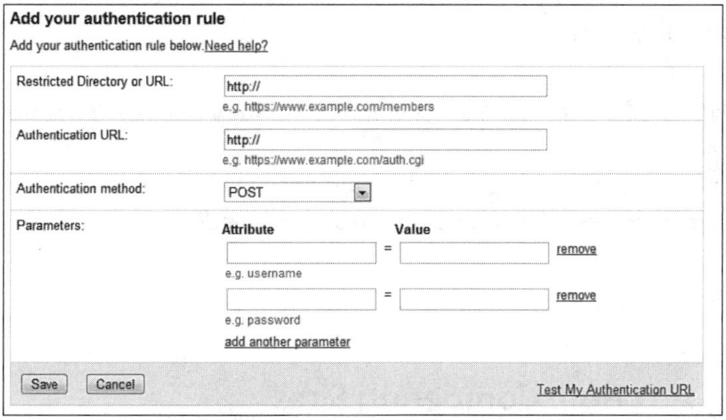

Add your authentication rule

Add your authentication rule below. Need help?

Restricted Directory or URL:	http://
	e.g. https://www.example.com/members
Authentication URL:	http://
	e.g. https://www.example.com/auth.cgi
Authentication method:	POST ▾

Parameters:

Attribute		Value	
	=		remove
e.g. username			
	=		remove
e.g. password			
add another parameter			

[Save] [Cancel]   Test My Authentication URL

Figure 3.24 *Configuring AdSense to work with password-protected pages.*

4. In the Authentication URL field, enter the URL for your authentication or login page.

5. Pull down the Authentication Method list and make the appropriate selection.

6. In the Parameters section, enter the attributes and values for your authentication page. In most instances you enter **username** (or something similar) for the first Attribute, and then assign a user name for Google to use, entering this name into the Value field. You then enter **password** as the second Attribute and assign a password for Google to use, entering this password into the second Value field.

7. Click the Save button.

Filtering Unwanted Ads

Some site owners are uneasy about using AdSense, fearing that Google might display ads from competitors on the site's pages. That's a reasonable fear, and a strategy that benefits some competing sites.

Fortunately, AdSense lets you block ads from specific competitors, as well as all ads within a specific category. This prevents unwanted advertising from appearing on your site.

Blocking Competitive Ads

The most obvious ads you might want to block are those from direct competitors—who would love to share space on your site. To this end, AdSense offers a Competitive Ad Filter that lets you specify, by URL, those sites you don't want advertising on your site.

 SHOW ME   Media 3.8—A video about how to block different types of ads
Access this video file through your registered Web Edition at my.safaribooksonline.com/9780131388666/media.

 **LET ME TRY IT**

Blocking Ads from Competing Sites

1. Log onto your AdSense account and click the AdSense Setup tab.

2. Click the Competitive Ad Filter sub-tab.

3. Select the AdSense for Content sub-tab.

4. In the resulting form, shown in Figure 3.25, enter the URLs for all sites you want blocked. Enter multiple URLs on separate lines.

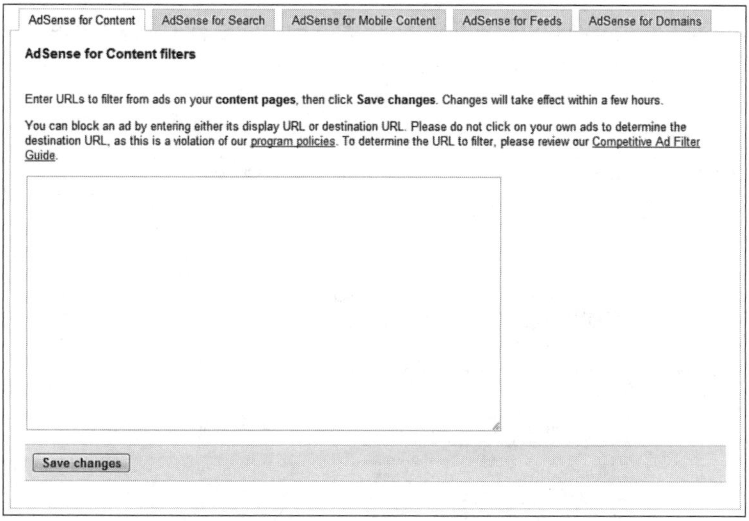

AdSense for Content	AdSense for Search	AdSense for Mobile Content	AdSense for Feeds	AdSense for Domains

AdSense for Content filters

Enter URLs to filter from ads on your **content pages**, then click **Save changes**. Changes will take effect within a few hours.

You can block an ad by entering either its display URL or destination URL. Please do not click on your own ads to determine the destination URL, as this is a violation of our program policies. To determine the URL to filter, please review our Competitive Ad Filter Guide.

[Save changes]

Figure 3.25 *Filtering ads from competing sites.*

5. Click the Save Changes button.

How precisely you filter a site depends on what you enter for the site's URL:

- To filter ads linking to all pages in a domain, enter the domain address like this: **website.com**

- To filter ads linking to a subdomain on the site, enter the subdomain address like this: **subdomain.website.com**

- To filter ads linking to a specific page on the site, enter the page address like this: **website.com/page.html**

 **LET ME TRY IT**

Blocking Ads by Category

You can also block entire categories of ads from appearing on your pages.

Blocking ads by category is helpful if you want to avoid all competitive ads without having to identify specific competitors. Follow these steps:

1. Log onto your AdSense account and click the AdSense Setup tab.

2. Click the Ad Review Center sub-tab.

3. In the Category Filters section, shown in Figure 3.26, check those categories you don't want displayed on your site.

Ad Review Center

Select a Client-ID: [▼]

Helpful Links

- What is the Ad Review Center?
- What is category filtering?
- How does AdSense work with Google certified ad networks?
- What happens if I allow or block a single ad or advertiser from a Google certified network?
- Video overview of Google certified networks

Category Filters

Category filters allow you to block ads in certain ad categories from appearing on your site, regardless of how they're targeted. We've provided the percentage of total earnings and impressions recently generated by ads for each category below to help you decide which categories, if any, to filter.

Filtered categories will block ads in all languages supported by category filtering. ⓘ

Filtered Categories:

Category Show category details	% Recent Earnings ⓘ	% Recent Ad Impressions ⓘ
☐ Cosmetic Procedures & Body Modification	0.0%	0.6%
☐ Dating	0.0%	0.5%
☐ Drugs & Supplements	0.0%	0.6%
☐ Get Rich Quick	4.0%	2.9%
☐ Politics	0.0%	0.6%
☐ Religion	0.0%	1.2%
☐ Ringtones & Downloadables	0.0%	0.6%
☐ Sexual & Reproductive Health	0.0%	0.1%
☐ Sexually Suggestive	0.0%	2.3%
☐ Video Games (Casual & Online)	9.5%	5.6%
☐ Weight Loss	0.0%	0.6%

Categories you filter will no longer display Recent Earnings or Ad Impressions estimates.

[Submit] [Cancel]

Figure 3.26 *Filtering ads by category.*

4. Click the Submit button.

 **LET ME TRY IT**

Allowing Ads from Specific Sites Only

You can also go the other direction and specify a list of sites that you want displayed on your pages.

When you specify a list of sites, only ads from these sites will be displayed; all other ads will be blocked. Here's how to do it:

1. Log onto your AdSense account and click the AdSense Setup tab.

2. Click the Allowed Sites sub-tab.

3. When the next page appears, select the Only Allow Certain Sites to Show Ads for My Account option.

4. This expands the page, as shown in Figure 3.27. Enter the URLs for those sites you want to allow, one URL per line.

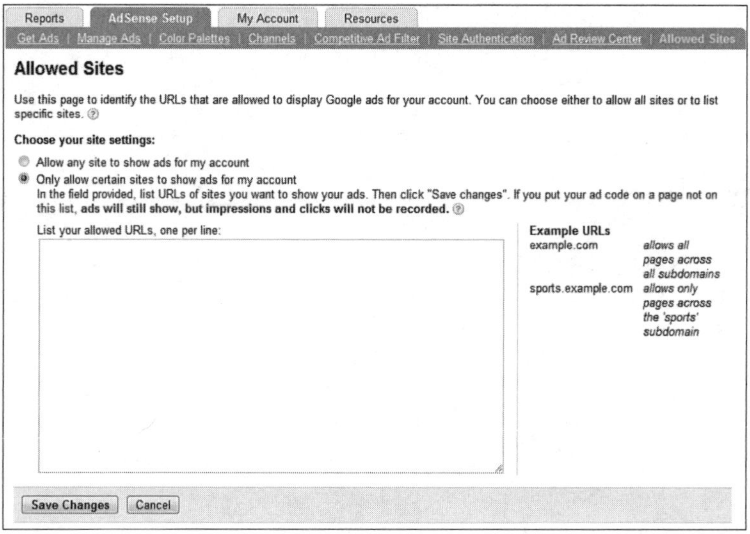

Figure 3.27 *Creating a list of approved sites to display ads on your pages.*

5. Click the Save Changes button.

Creating a short list of allowed sites could result in a lack of suitable ads appearing on your pages—or force AdSense to display PSAs instead of ads. In either instance, this could result in significantly decreased ad revenues for you.

4

Adding Google AdSense for Search to Your Website

Aside from the simple PPC ads provided by AdSense for Content, there's another way to generate ad revenue from your website. If your site is large enough that visitors could benefit from searching the site for the information they want, you can add a Google search box to your site and generate revenue from the ads that appear on the subsequent search results pages.

You do all this via Google's AdSense for Search program. And when you place a search box on your site, you not only generate ad revenue, you also improve the experience of your site's visitors. It's a win-win for everybody.

Understanding AdSense for Search

Google AdSense for Search is another way for you to generate ad revenue from your website. The AdSense for Search program is a subset of Google's AdSense for Content program that lets you insert a search box on your site, like the one in Figure 4.1. Depending on how you configure it, visitors can use this search box to either search your website or to search the entire web. The search results pages display typical AdSense PPC ads; you generate revenue when visitors click on these ads.

 SHOW ME   Media 4.1—A video about how AdSense for Search works
Access this video file through your registered Web Edition at my.safaribooksonline.com/9780131388666/media.

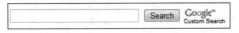

Figure 4.1   *A Google search box displayed on a typical website.*

Even better, you can customize to some degree the results from these on-site searches—both the matching pages and how they're displayed on the results pages. And, of course, you can customize how the PPC ads are displayed on the search results pages.

For starters, you can specify just where your visitors can search. AdSense lets users search your site only, a collection of sites you choose, or the entire web. You can also prioritize and restrict visitors' searches to specific sections of these sites.

Obviously, the PPC ads that appear alongside the search results, like the ones shown in Figure 4.2, are targeted to the user's search query. It's the same content-sensitive advertising that you're used to with AdSense for Content, but displayed alongside users' search results. You can opt to display these ads along the top and right sidebar of the search results page, or at the top and bottom of the page. Naturally, you can also customize the color scheme of the ads to make them look more like organic search results, or to stand out from the results.

AdSense for Search uses the same search technology used on the Google search site itself, so you know the results will be good—both fast and relevant to users' queries. In fact, the results should be identical to those obtained on the main Google site, at least before you do any customization.

No revenue is generated from merely searching from the Google search box, or from the display or search results. As with AdSense for Content, revenue is generated only when users click on the ads displayed on the search results pages.

TELL ME MORE   Media 4.2—A discussion about why Google AdSense for Search makes sense for your site
Access this audio recording through your registered Web Edition at my.safaribooksonline.com/9780131388666/media.

Figure 4.2   *A typical search results page with AdSense for Search ads displayed in the right column.*

Adding a Google Search Box to Your Site

Google AdSense for Search is part of the AdSense for Content program, so you first need to join that program.

 SHOW ME   Media 4.3—A video about how to add a search box to my site

Access this video file through your registered Web Edition at my.safaribooksonline.com/9780131388666/media.

Learn more about signing up for AdSense for Content in Chapter 3, "Adding AdSense for Content to Your Website."

 **LET ME TRY IT**

Join the AdSense for Search Program

After you're signed up, follow these steps to add a Google search box to your pages and get going with AdSense for Search:

1. Log into your AdSense account and select the AdSense Setup tab.

2. Click the AdSense for Search link.

3. When the AdSense for Search page appears, as shown in Figure 4.3, select whether you want to search only the sites you select or search the entire web. If you want to limit the search to your own website, select Only Sites I Select and proceed to Step 4. If you want visitors to be able to search the entire web, select The Entire Web and proceed to Step 5.

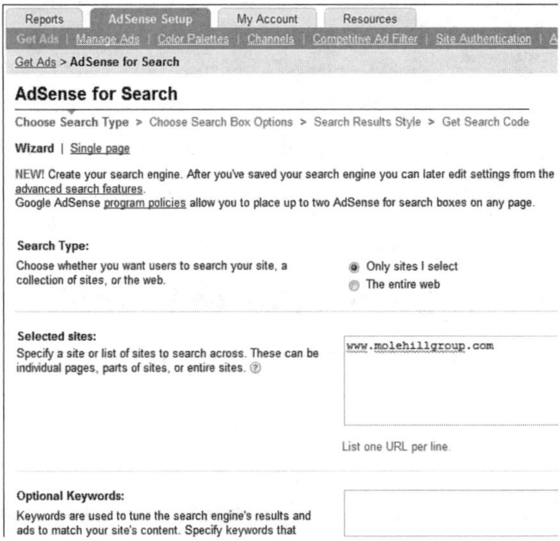

Figure 4.3   *Adding Google search to your site.*

4. If you opted to search only selected sites, enter the URLs for those sites into the Selected Sites box; enter multiple URLs on separate lines. If you want to limit the search to your site only, enter only the URL for your site. If you want to limit the search to a subdomain or directory within your site, enter the URL for that subdomain or directory.

5. To fine-tune the search results, enter one or more keywords that describe the subject and content of your site into the Optional Keywords box. Use spaces to separate multiple keywords.

 Learn more about using keywords in the "Fine-Tuning Search Results with Keywords" section later in this chapter.

6. Scroll down to the More Options section of this page and verify your site's language, encoding, and country.

7. If you want to specify a reporting channel for your AdSense for Search ads, check the Automatically Create a New Channel box and either select an existing channel or let AdSense create a channel for you.

 Learn more about channels in Chapter 3.

8. If you want to prevent inappropriate sites from appearing in the search results, check the Use SafeSearch option.

9. Click the Continue button.

10. The next page, shown in Figure 4.4, lets you determine how the Google search box will appear on your site. Select the desired look and feel, enter a length for the text box (in characters), and then click the Continue button.

11. On the next page, shown in Figure 4.5, select how you want the search results page to display. You can open the search results on the Google site in the same browser window, on the Google site in a new browser window, or within your own site. If you opt to display results on your own site, you'll need to enter the URL for the page where you want the results displayed.

 Learn more about how to display results in the "Displaying Search Results on Your Own Site" section later in this chapter.

12. On the same page, in the Ad Location section, select where you want the ads to appear on the search results page—Top and Right, Top and Bottom, or Right.

13. Still on the same page, select a color palette for the ads, or choose custom colors for specific ad elements.

14. If you opted to display search results on Google's pages, you'll see the section shown in Figure 4.6, which lets you optionally "brand" the search results with your own logo. Enter the URL for your logo image file, and the URL for where you want visitors directed when they click the logo.

15. Click the Continue button to proceed.

16. On the next page, agree to Google's terms and conditions, enter a name for this specific search engine, and then click the Submit and Get Code button.

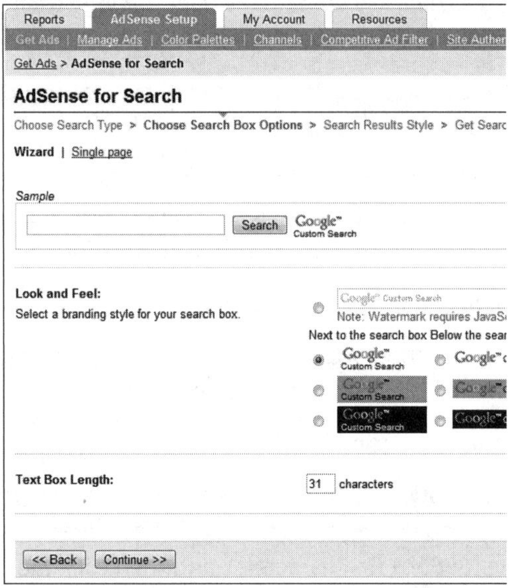

Figure 4.4 *Configuring the look and feel of your Google search box.*

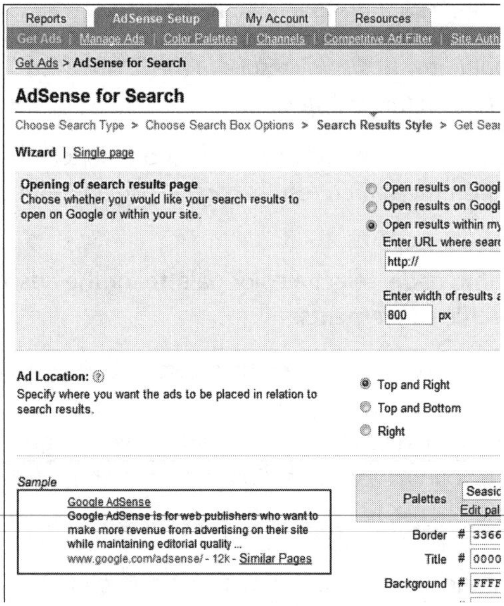

Figure 4.5 *Configuring how the search results page—and the AdSense ads—will appear.*

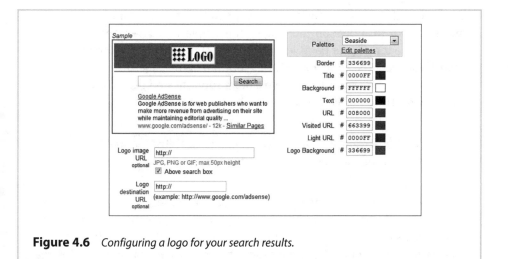

Figure 4.6   *Configuring a logo for your search results.*

17.   The final page, shown in Figure 4.7, displays the code that Google generates
      for the search box. Copy the code from this page and then paste it into the
      HTML code for your web page.

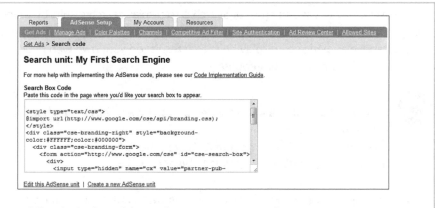

Figure 4.7   *The final search box code—copy it into your web page's HTML.*

Inserting the Search Box Code

After you've generated the HTML code for your new search box, you then need to
insert that code into the underlying HTML code of the pages on your website
where you want the search box to appear. You can insert the search box into just
one or into multiple pages on your site; the same code is used wherever you want
the box inserted.

Enter this code into your page's underlying HTML in the position where you want the search box to appear on your page. For example, if you want the search box to appear at the top of your page, insert the code at the very beginning of the body code; if you want the ad to appear at the bottom of the page, insert the ad code at the end of the body code. If you have a more sophisticated page design, use the appropriate HTML or CSS tags to position the ad on the page.

If all this code insertion stuff causes your head to spin, just turn the task over to an experienced web designer. He'll know what to do.

After the code is inserted and the web page saved, the search box will appear on the designated pages on your website. Visitors can now use the search box to search your site or the web, as you previously determined, and see the results of their searches either on a Google page or on a special page on your site. The search results page also displays PPC ads; whenever someone clicks on one of these ads, revenue is generated.

Displaying Search Results on Your Own Site

The easiest way to use AdSense for Search is to display search results on a Google page. This, however, takes visitors away from your site; you might prefer to keep a more captive audience by displaying search results on your own web page. If this is your want, Google can accommodate you.

SHOW ME   Media 4.4—A video about how to have search results shown on your site
Access this video file through your registered Web Edition at
my.safaribooksonline.com/9780131388666/media.

When you opt to display search results on your own page, you first have to create a page on your site for the search results. The results of user searches then appear in a frame on this page. This keeps visitors on your site, rather than kicking them out to Google.

To do this, start by creating the page where the search results will display. Then follow the steps to create a new search, outlined in the "Adding a Google Search Box to Your Site" section earlier in this chapter. When you get to Step 11, select Open Results Within My Own Site. This expands the page, as shown in Figure 4.8. Enter the URL for the search results page you created and then enter the width of the frame for the results area in pixels. Complete the rest of the process as normal.

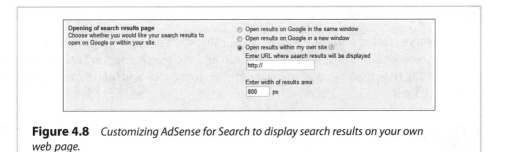

Figure 4.8   *Customizing AdSense for Search to display search results on your own web page.*

When you're done creating the search, Google displays two pieces of code. The first is the code for the search box, as described previously, which should be inserted where you want the search box to appear. The second, labeled Your Search Results code, should be copied and pasted into the HTML source code of the search results page you created. Save all your web pages and you're ready to go.

Fine-Tuning Search Results with Keywords

By default, Google displays search results and PPC ads relating to the queries entered by your site's visitors. You can tweak these results, however, to better promote the content of your site by including your own keywords; Google will then consider both your keywords and your visitors' keywords when constructing search results.

You should use keywords to describe the topic of your search engine and the content of the pages you're promoting. A keyword can literally be a single word or it can be a multiple-word phrase; in either instance, the keyword or phrase should be descriptive of what your site is about.

You can also use keywords to remove any ambiguity from your visitors' searches. Google uses the example of the word "tiger," included in a user search. The keywords you enter influence what type of "tigers" are found in the search results. Add the keyword *golf* and your search results will display sites relating to Tiger Woods; add the keyword *wildlife* and your search results will display sites relating to the wild animal; add the keyword *apple* and your search results will display sites relating to the Mac operating system.

You enter keywords for a given search box when you create the search box. Follow the steps to create a new search, outlined in the "Adding a Search Box to Your Site" section earlier in this chapter. When you get to Step 5, enter one or more descriptive keywords into the Optional Keywords box. Use a space to separate multiple keywords. When you're done, continue with the rest of the search creation process as normal.

Editing Your Website Search

After you've created a specific search for your site, you can easily go back and edit any of the search settings. This is useful if you find the search returning results that aren't quite to your liking, or if you want to change the look and feel of the search results pages.

LET ME TRY IT

Editing Search Settings

1. Log into your AdSense account and select the AdSense Setup tab.

2. Click the Manage Ads sub-tab.

3. When the Manage Ads page appears, as shown in Figure 4.9, find the name of the search you want to edit in the list and click the Edit Settings link.

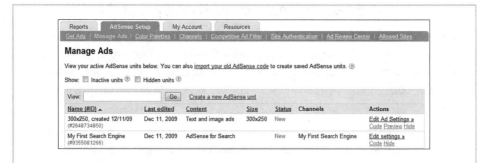

Figure 4.9   *Managing your AdSense ads and searches.*

4. Proceed through the ad setup pages and then save your updates.

⊙ *Learn more about tracking AdSense for Search performance in Chapter 9, "Monitoring Your AdSense Performance."*

5

Adding AdSense for Feeds to Your Blog

Blogging is a big deal; many companies and individuals forgo the whole website experience and instead offer their opinions via personal or corporate blogs. If you have your own blog, you can use AdSense to generate revenue from it, just as you would with a website. You can place AdSense for Content ads on the blog itself, and use Google's new AdSense for Feeds service to place ads in your blog's RSS feed. Many bloggers find that they can generate significant revenue by placing these types of ads on their blogs and feeds.

Adding AdSense for Content Ads to a Blogger Blog

Let's start by examining how to place PPC ads on your main blog page. This is especially easy if your blog is hosted by Blogger (www.blogger.com), which, like AdSense, is run by Google. In this instance, Google makes sure that its two services work smoothly together.

    ☝ *Before you enable AdSense for your Blogger blog, you must first open an AdSense account. Learn more in Chapter 3, "Adding AdSense for Content to Your Website."*

Learn more about creating a Blogger blog in my companion book, *Using Blogger* (Michael Miller, Que, 2010).

 TELL ME MORE   Media 5.1—A discussion about blogs
Access this audio recording through your registered Web Edition at
my.safaribooksonline.com/9780131388666/media.

 **LET ME TRY IT**

Activating AdSense: The Easy Way

If you have a Blogger blog, it's quite easy to add AdSense ads as part of the basic page that hosts all your blog posts.

 SHOW ME Media 5.2—A video about how to activate AdSense
Access this video file through your registered Web Edition at
my.safaribooksonline.com/9780131388666/media.

You can insert ads in the blog's sidebar, as shown in Figure 5.1; at the bottom of your blog; or between every blog post. Here's how to do it:

1. From within Blogger, open the Blogger Dashboard, shown in Figure 5.2.

2. Click the Monetize link to the right of your blog's name.

3. When the Make Money with AdSense page appears, as shown in Figure 5.3, select where you want ads to appear. You can opt to display ads in the sidebar and below each post, in the sidebar only, or below each post only.

Figure 5.1 *A Blogger blog with AdSense ads in the sidebar.*

Figure 5.2   *The Blogger dashboard.*

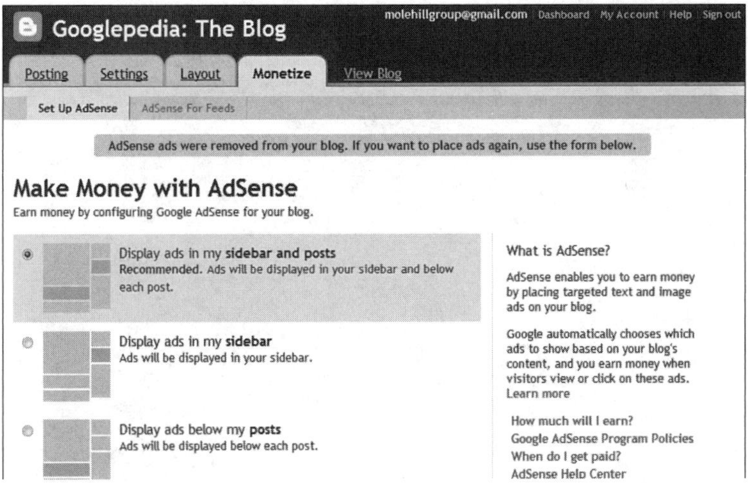

Figure 5.3   *Activating AdSense ads for a Blogger blog.*

4. Click Next.

That's it—AdSense is now activated for your blog, and ads will appear where you specified.

 **LET ME TRY IT**

Activating AdSense: Custom Placement

There's another way to add AdSense ads to your blog, however, that enables more targeted ad placement. With this method, you can display ads at the bottom of your blog, as well as multiple places within the sidebar. Just follow these steps:

 SHOW ME   Media 5.3—A video about how to place ads on my blog

Access this video file through your registered Web Edition at
my.safaribooksonline.com/9780131388666/media.

1. From within Blogger, open the Blogger Dashboard.

2. Click the Layout link next to your blog name.

3. When the Add and Arrange Page Elements page appears, as shown in Figure 5.4, click the Add a Gadget link in the sidebar or in the space at the bottom of the blog.

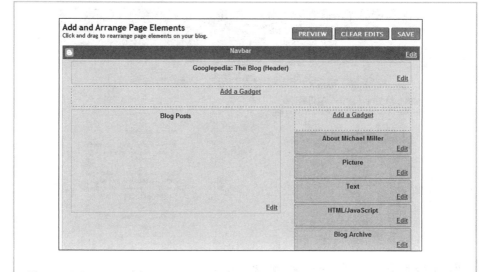

Figure 5.4   *Customizing the placement of your AdSense ads.*

4. When the Add a Gadget window appears, scroll down to the AdSense section and click the + button.

5. When the Configure AdSense window appears, as shown in Figure 5.5, select a format for the ads, and determine whether you want to display text-only ads or text and image ads.

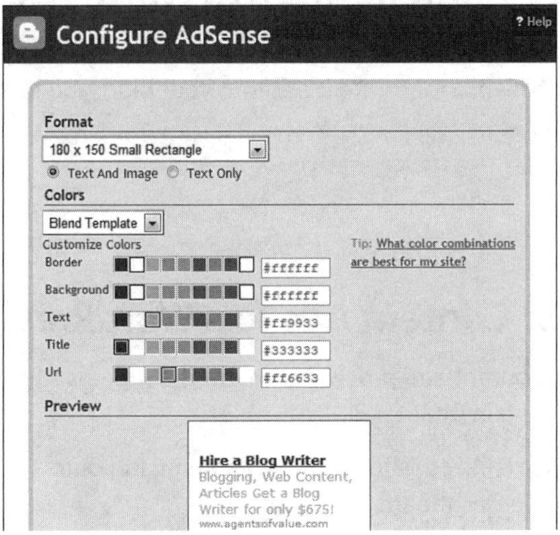

Figure 5.5 *Configuring an AdSense gadget for your blog.*

6. Still in the Configure AdSense window, select a color template or custom colors for the ads and then click the Save button.

7. An AdSense module is now added to the sidebar or below your blog. To reposition an ad within the sidebar, simply click and drag it to a new position.

AdSense automatically uses the ID previously assigned to your Google Account. If you want to assign your ads to a different ID, click the Switch to a Different Publisher ID link in the Configure AdSense window.

After you've activated AdSense for your blog, you can view your ad activity in the standard AdSense console (www.google.com/adsense/). This console tracks your click-through activity. You can also select the AdSense Setup and My Account tabs to manage the details of your account and ads.

Although it's relatively easy to add AdSense ads to a Blogger or WordPress blog, you can't add ads to your Facebook or MySpace pages. The terms of service of these social networks prohibit such third-party advertising, and the coding of the pages doesn't allow the script technology necessary to enable ad insertion. (Facebook, however, does have its own AdWords-like PPC advertising system; learn more at www.facebook.com/advertising/.)

Adding AdSense for Content Ads to a WordPress Blog

If your blog is hosted by WordPress (www.wordpress.com) or a similar blog hosting service, you can still insert AdSense for Content ads into your blog; you just have to do so manually.

 **LET ME TRY IT**

Adding AdSense for Content Ads to a WordPress Blog

1. Log into AdSense for Content and proceed through the process to create a new ad unit, as described in Chapter 3.

2. After you generate the HTML code for your new ad unit, log onto WordPress and open the Dashboard.

3. Click the Appearance link and select Widgets.

4. Select the Text widget and click Add.

5. A new Text widget appears; click the Edit link for this widget.

6. When the new form appears, as shown in Figure 5.6, enter a name for this widget.

Archives GAT	Add		Recent Articles GAT	Edit
Blogroll GAT			Meta GAT	Edit
Meta GAT			Mortgage Calculator	Edit
Pages GAT	Add		Text	Cancel
Pages	Add	Your blog's WordPress Pages	AdSense Widget	

```
<div style="padding-left:5px; padding-right:5px;
padding-bottom:5px; padding-top:5px; ">
<script type="text/javascript"><!--
google_ad_client = "pub-8325072546567078";
google_ad_width = 160;
google_ad_height = 600;
google_ad_format = "160x600_as";
google_ad_type = "text_image";
google_ad_channel ="";
google_color_border = "E8E7D0";
google_color_bg = "FFFFFF";
google_color_link = "B96F17";
google_color_url = "B96F17";
google_color_text = "000000";
```

Calendar	Add	A calendar of your blog's posts
Archives	Add	A monthly archive of your blog's posts
Links	Add	Your blogroll
Meta	Add	Log in/out, admin, feed and WordPress link
Search	Add	A search form for your blog
Recent Posts	Add	The most recent posts on your blog
Tag Cloud	Add	Your most used tags in cloud format
Categories	Add	A list or dropdown of categories

Done   Remove

Save Changes

Figure 5.6 *Pasting AdSense code into a WordPress widget.*

7. Paste your AdSense code into the text area for this widget.

8. Click the Done button.

9. When prompted, click the Save Changes button.

Several WordPress plug-ins make the AdSense insertion process easier and provide greater flexibility in terms of ad placement. The most popular of these include AdSense Deluxe (www.acmetech.com/blog/2005/07/26/adsense-deluxe-wordpress-plugin/) and Advertising Manager (www.wordpress.org/extend/plugins/advertising-manager/).

Adding AdSense Ads to Your Site Feeds

When you add an AdSense module to your blog, the ads appear only on your blog—not in the syndicated blog feed. Obviously, the more exposure for the ads, the more revenue you can generate, so it's probably a good idea to include AdSense ads within your site feed, as shown in Figure 5.7. This isn't hard to do.

Figure 5.7   *AdSense ads displayed in a blog feed.*

A *site feed* is an automatically updated stream of a blog's contents, enabled by a special XML file format called *RSS* (Really Simple Syndication). When a blog has an RSS feed enabled, any updated content is published automatically as a special XML file that contains the RSS feed; this syndicated feed is then picked up by RSS feed reader programs and aggregators, so that subscribers are automatically informed of new posts.

SHOW ME   Media 5.4—A video about how to add advertising to my site feeds

Access this video file through your registered Web Edition at my.safaribooksonline.com/9780131388666/media.

LET ME TRY IT

Adding Advertising to a Site Feed

1. Log into your AdSense account and select the AdSense Setup tab.

2. Click the AdSense for Feeds link.

3. When the AdSense for Feeds page appears, as shown in Figure 5.8, go to the Ad Type field and determine the type of ad you want—text ads only, image ads only, or both text and image ads.

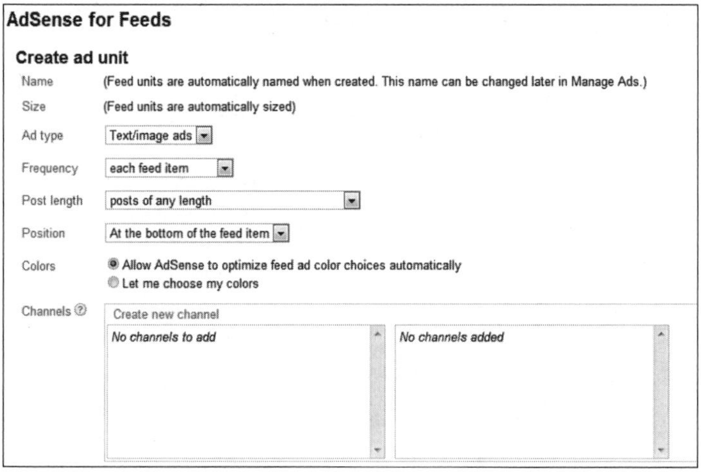

AdSense for Feeds

Create ad unit

Name	(Feed units are automatically named when created. This name can be changed later in Manage Ads.)
Size	(Feed units are automatically sized)
Ad type	Text/image ads ▾
Frequency	each feed item ▾
Post length	posts of any length ▾
Position	At the bottom of the feed item ▾
Colors	⦿ Allow AdSense to optimize feed ad color choices automatically ○ Let me choose my colors
Channels ⓘ	Create new channel No channels to add No channels added

Figure 5.8   *Enabling AdSense for Feeds.*

---

4. In the Frequency field, determine how frequently you want the ads to appear—after each feed item or after every second, third, or fourth item.

5. In the Post Length field, select the length of posts where you want ads selected. The default is for posts of any length, but other options are available.

6. In the Position field, select where you want the ads to appear—at the bottom or at the top of each feed item.

7. In the Colors field, opt to let AdSense determine the ad colors or select the Let Me Choose My Colors option. If you select the latter option, you'll then need to pick colors for each ad element.

8. If you want to track your ads by channel, either select an existing channel in the Channels section or click the Create New Channel link to create a new channel.

☉ *Learn more about channels in Chapter 3.*

9. In the Feeds section, click the Add link beside each feed you want to activate. If a given blog feed isn't listed, click the Burn New Feed link and, when prompted, enter the URL for your blog.

10. Click the Save button.

AdSense will now display ads on the selected blog feeds, in the manner specified.

☉ *Learn more about tracking AdSense for Feeds performance in Chapter 9, "Monitoring Your AdSense Performance."*

6

Using AdSense for Mobile Content

If your website is optimized for mobile devices, or if you include alternate mobile pages, you can generate revenue by placing PPC ads on those mobile pages. When mobile visitors click those ads, you make money.

Google runs a separate AdSense for Mobile Content program that places PPC ads on web pages optimized for mobile viewing. It's a lot like the normal AdSense for Content program, but with fewer and more mobile-friendly ads per page.

Understanding Google AdSense for Mobile Content

If you have an iPhone or similar mobile device, you're familiar with surfing the web from your phone. Viewing normal web pages on a small screen can be a pain, with all the normal content squished together appearing smaller and harder to see (and click). For that reason, many webmasters are creating alternate versions of their sites that are optimized for mobile viewing, with all page elements resized and rearranged for the dimensions of mobile screens.

 TELL ME MORE   Media 6.1—A discussion about the mobile web
Access this audio recording through your registered Web Edition at
my.safaribooksonline.com/9780131388666/media.

If you have mobile-optimized pages on your site, you can use Google's AdSense for Mobile Content to add PPC ads to those pages. AdSense for Mobile Content works just like AdSense for Content, matching ads to your site's content; you earn money when mobile visitors click those ads.

 SHOW ME   Media 6.2—A video about how AdSense for mobile content works
Access this video file through your registered Web Edition at
my.safaribooksonline.com/9780131388666/media.

Google AdSense for Mobile Content is not available in all locales. As of January 2010, it's available in the following countries only: Australia, Austria, Belgium, Canada, China, Denmark, Finland, France, Germany, Greece, India, Ireland, Italy, Japan, Korea, the Netherlands, Norway, Poland, Russia, Singapore, South Africa, Spain, Sweden, Switzerland, Taiwan, the United States, and the United Kingdom.

Because mobile pages are different from normal web pages, the ads serviced by AdSense by Mobile Content are a bit different, as well, containing just 24 to 36 characters of text, followed by the advertiser's destination URL. Figure 6.1 shows a sample mobile text ad.

Figure 6.1   *An AdSense for Mobile Content text ad at the bottom of the screen.*

Mobile advertisers also have the option of allowing customers to directly connect via phone. In this instance, a "call" link appears next to the destination URL. Customers press this link to automatically call the advertiser's number.

In addition to traditional text ads, AdSense also serves mobile image ads, such as the one in Figure 6.2. Clicking one of these ads can either open the advertiser's website or dial the advertiser's phone number, at the advertiser's discretion.

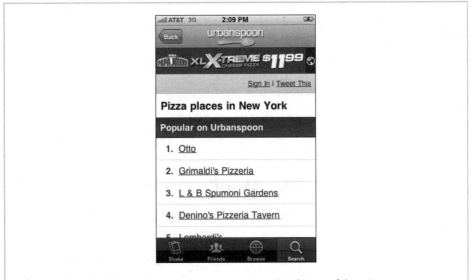

Figure 6.2   *An AdSense for Mobile Content image ad at the top of the screen.*

You can display just one mobile ad unit per mobile page. This can be a single or double ad; if you opt to display the double ad unit, it can be placed only at the bottom of each page.

You can use AdSense for Mobile Content only if you have a mobile-compliant web page. Adding AdSense for Mobile Content code to a standard web page does not display any ads.

If you don't yet have mobile-friendly pages on your site, you can create such pages by rewriting your existing pages in a mobile markup language, such as XHTML, WML, or CHTML. You'll also need to employ server-side scripting, such as ASP or PHP; this enables Google to properly serve its AdSense ads. Naturally, you'll also need to revamp your page layout to show properly on mobile phone displays.

If you're a developer of applications for the iPhone, Android, and other mobile platforms, Google's AdSense for Mobile Applications lets you insert PPC ads in your mobile apps. Learn more at www.google.com/ads/mobileapps/.

Adding AdSense Ads to Mobile Pages

If you have mobile-friendly web pages, it's easy to add AdSense advertising.

SHOW ME   Media 6.3—A video about how to place AdSense ads
on mobile pages
Access this video file through your registered Web Edition at
my.safaribooksonline.com/9780131388666/media.

 **LET ME TRY IT**

Activating AdSense for Mobile Content

Start by signing up for the overall AdSense program and then following these
steps:

1. Log onto your AdSense account and select the AdSense Setup tab.

2. Click the AdSense for Mobile Content link.

3. On the Choose Ad Type page, shown in Figure 6.3, pull down the Device
    Type list and select the type of device for which your site is optimized.

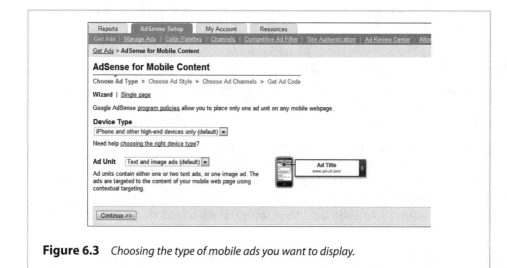

Figure 6.3   *Choosing the type of mobile ads you want to display.*

When choosing a device type, the default setting of iPhone and Other High-End
Devices Only is best if your site is designed primarily for Apple's iPhone and
other smartphones. If your site supports a wider variety of phones, select the All
Phones option.

4. On the same page, pull down the Ad Unit list and select what types of ads you want to display: Text ads only, image ads only, or both text and image ads.

5. Click the Continue button.

6. On the Choose Ad Style page, shown in Figure 6.4, pull down the Format list and select one of the available ad formats.

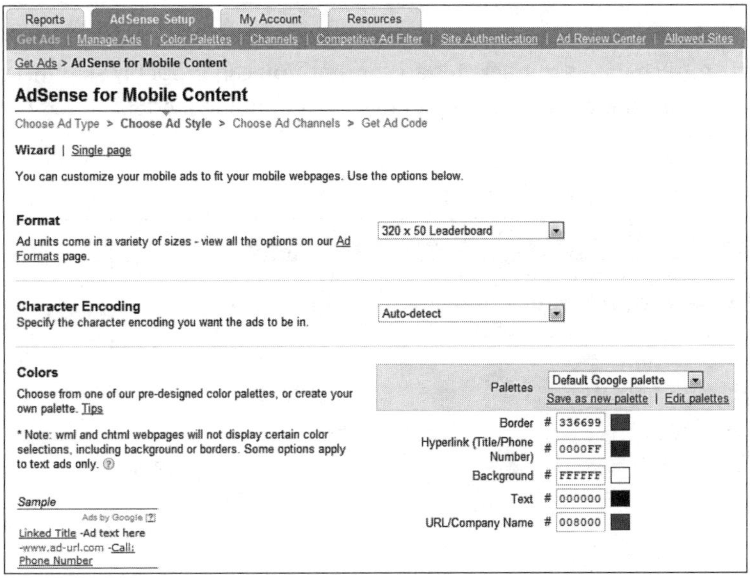

Figure 6.4 *Selecting a style for your mobile ads.*

If you select All Phones as your device type, you have two ad styles to choose from: Single and Double, with the latter displaying two text ads stacked. If you selected iPhone and Other High-End Devices Only as your device type, four ad styles are available: 320 × 50 leaderboard, 250 × 250 square, 200 × 200 small square, and 300 × 250 small rectangle.

7. If you selected All Phones as your device type, you now need to specify the markup language used to create your web page. Choose from WML (WAP 1.x), XHTML (WAP 2.0), or CHTML. (This option isn't available if you selected iPhone as your device type; the markup language is already known.)

8. On the same page, select the appropriate character encoding; in most instances, Auto-Detect is the best option.

9. Still on the Choose Ad Style page, select the desired color palette for your ads, or define custom colors for specific ad elements.

10. Scroll down to the More Options section and select what you want to display if relevant ads aren't available—public service ads, non-Google ads from another URL, or a solid color to fill the space.

11. Click the Continue button.

12. On the Choose Ad Channels page, shown in Figure 6.5, choose up to five custom channels to track this ad content. You can probably skip this step, as mobile ads are tracked separately from traditional AdSense ads by default.

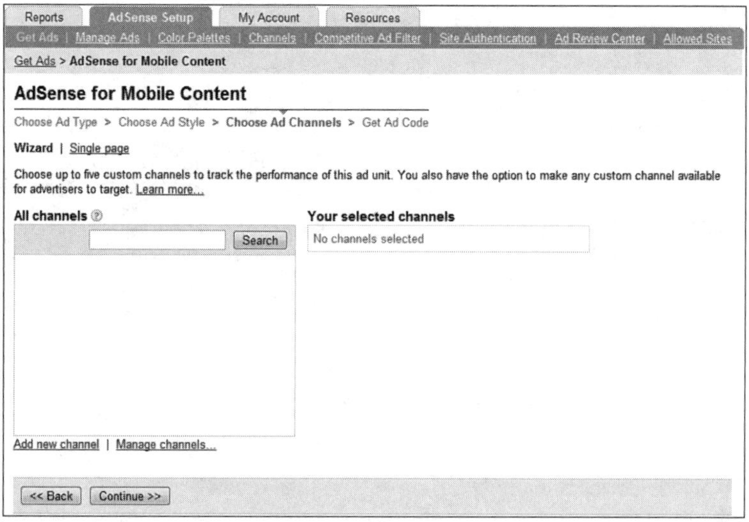

Figure 6.5   *Selecting channels to use to track the performance of your mobile ads.*

⊕ *Learn more about channels in Chapter 3, "Adding AdSense for Content to Your Website."*

13. Click the Continue button.

14. On the final page, if you selected All Phones as your device type, you need to select the scripting language you use on your web page—PHP, CGI/Perl, JSP, or ASP. This option isn't available if you select iPhone as your device type.

15. In all instances, the final page now displays your AdSense code, as shown in Figure 6.6. Copy this code and paste it into the underlying code of your mobile web page where you want the ad to appear.

Figure 6.6 *The final code for your mobile ads—copy and paste into your mobile web pages.*

Unfortunately, you can't preview your mobile ads on your computer's web browser. You can view AdSense mobile ads only on a mobile phone or other similar device.

Unlike AdSense for Content ads, which appear on your web pages almost immediately, it takes a while for AdSense for Mobile Content ads to appear. Allow about 48 hours for ads to start displaying on your mobile web pages.

⏺ *Learn more about tracking AdSense for Mobile Content performance in Chapter 9, "Monitoring Your AdSense Performance."*

7

Using AdSense for Domains

Here's an interesting notion: You can actually make money from web domains that don't have any content—so called "parked" or unused domains. Although it might seem counterintuitive to think that people would visit a site without any content, Google's AdSense for Domains programs helps you put content on otherwise empty sites, and then serves up PPC ads related to that content. Visitors stumbling across your parked domain thus find some content (mainly links to other sites) and are enticed to click on the related ads that accompany those links.

Although this probably isn't a way to get rich, it is a way to generate some much-needed cash flow from any domains you've registered but not yet developed. Read on to learn more.

Understanding Google AdSense for Domains

Google AdSense for Domains is both similar to and different from Google's other AdSense programs. It's similar in that it places PPC ads on a site that you designate. It's different in that it also places actual content on that site. In that regard, AdSense for Domains is a one-stop solution when you have an undeveloped domain.

How AdSense for Domains Works

A parked domain is essentially a web address you've purchased and registered but not yet created pages for. Normally, when visitors access this type of undeveloped address, they see some sort of "page under construction" message or a 404 error message. AdSense for Domains lets you fill this blank space, however temporarily, with links, search results, and other content—including PPC ads. This way visitors find *something* when they enter your domain's URL, and might even be persuaded to click on some of the ads, thus generating revenue from an otherwise fallow site.

TELL ME MORE   Media 7.1—A discussion about domain parking
Access this audio recording through your registered Web Edition at
my.safaribooksonline.com/9780131388666/media.

How does AdSense determine what type of content to put on a parked page? It uses Google's semantic technology to target content to the domain name. The more descriptive the domain name, the better focused the content. It's that simple.

Let us say that you've registered the domain www.blogstarawards.com (a real example). AdSense analyzes the domain name and serves up content related to blogs and blogging. This way, visitors find something related to what they entered as the site's URL.

What does one of Google's AdSense for Domains pages look like? Figure 7.1 provides a glimpse, using the www.blogstarawards.com example. The page's content consists solely of "sponsored listings," essentially links to related advertisers; visitors clicking on any of these listings generate PPC revenue. Clicking one of the "related topics" links displays a similar page with "sponsored listings" pertaining to that topic.

Figure 7.1   *A typical AdSense for Domains page on a parked domain.*

When a visitor uses the search box, Google returns a typical search results page, such as the one shown in Figure 7.2. On this page, the PPC ads (also called "sponsored listings") are displayed on the right side of the page; the organic searches on the main part of the page do not generate PPC revenue.

SHOW ME   Media 7.2—A video about how AdSense for domains work
Access this video file through your registered Web Edition at
my.safaribooksonline.com/9780131388666/media.

You searched for: templates

[Search]

Web Search Results

Templates - Microsoft Office Online
EasySubmit **templates** available from Microsoft Corporation ... Looking for **templates**? Find what you need
quickly and easily with our **Template** collections ...
office.microsoft.com

Web **Templates**, Flash **Templates**, Website **Templates** Design ...
Template Monster offers professional web **templates**, flash **templates** and other web design products
available for immediate download.
www.templatemonster.com

Templates | Website **Templates**
Templates of all kinds. Website **Templates**, 3D Models, Illustrations, etc. We combine fun with
professionalism!
www.templates.com

Free Web **Templates** - Free website **templates**, web **templates**, page ...
We have a collection of 5641 Free **Templates** available for download created by designers ... Free business
and hosting website **templates**. Instatn download. ...
www.freewebtemplates.com

Office 2008 **Templates**
The **template** features categories for food descriptions, calories, and fat grams. It'll even calculate your totals
over a week-long period. ...
www.microsoft.com

Template - Wikipedia, the free encyclopedia
Template (file format), a standardized file type used by computer software as a pre-formatted example on
which to base other files, especially documents ...
en.wikipedia.org

Web **Templates** - Flash Website **Templates** - Logo Design - **Templates** Box

Sponsored Listings

Business Card Templates
80% Off Full-Color Business Cards.
Includes Free UV or Stock Upgrade.
www.Vistaprint.com

eProject is now Daptiv
The Leader in OnDemand Business
Software Has a New Name!
www.Daptiv.com

Design Business Cards
10,000+ Designs. High Quality
Printing. Low Online Prices.
www.123Print.com/Business-Cards

Newsletter Templates
Create impressive email newsletters
in minutes. 400+ template designs
www.ConstantContact.com

Free Resume Templates
Create Custom Resumes Quickly.
Templates Based on Your Occupation
www.PongoResume.com

Business Card Templates
100's of Free Templates.
Glossy Upgrade. Browse & Design Now
www.OvernightPrints.com/FreeGlossy

Figure 7.2   *The results of a search on an AdSense for Domains page.*

Program Restrictions

It goes without saying that AdSense for Domains is designed solely for sites without any existing content. If you've already added legitimate content to your site, you should use the regular AdSense for Content program instead.

⊙ *Learn more about AdSense for Content in Chapter 3, "Adding AdSense for Content to Your Website."*

Beyond that no-brainer condition, know that any domain you register with AdSense for Domains must adhere to Google's policies. In essence, these policies prohibit the following:

- **Artificial click generation (also known as click fraud).** Clicks on Google's PPC ads must result from genuine user interest; you can't use any manual or automated method that artificially generates clicks on those ads.

⊙ *Learn more about click fraud in Chapter 21, "Dealing with Click Fraud."*

- **Click encouragement.** You can't encourage users to click the ads on your site; this prohibits using text such as "click these ads" or "visit these links." You also can't pay users to click on the ads.

- **Spam advertising.** You can't promote your AdSense for Domains site via unsolicited mass emails (spam) or advertisements on third-party websites.

- **Inappropriate URLs.** Sexy or provocative URLs can draw a lot of traffic, but Google doesn't like them. You can't include URLs that include pornographic, adult, mature, profane, violent, or racially intolerant terms. You also can't include URLs that reference illegal drugs, prescription drugs, gambling, weapons, alcoholic beverages, tobacco, tragedies or other sensitive current events, or any illegal activity.

- **Infringing URLs.** In addition, you can't register URLs that violate any trademark, copyright, patent, or other intellectual property rights.

- **Disputed URLs.** You have to own the domain name free and clear; Google won't let you register any domains that are currently in dispute.

There are other restrictions, as well. You can't deceptively drive traffic to an AdSense for Domains site; you can't frame an AdSense for Domains site on another site, or include it in a pop-up window; you can't use redirects; and you can't include any scripts that modify visitors' browser settings or otherwise interfere with site navigation. In addition, the keywords you use to target the site must be relevant to the domain name.

And, lest you think that running a massive ring of parked sites is the road to riches, know that Google restricts the number of domains you can register with the AdSense for Domains program. At present, a single publisher can register only 1,500 domains—which, come to think of it, isn't that big a restriction. Go for it, if you want.

Why Use AdSense for Domains?

The AdSense for Domains program is unique in that it creates dummy content pages for empty websites, thus enabling publishers to earn money from essentially doing nothing. It's an odd little program—who uses it?

 SHOW ME   Media 7.3—A video about who uses AdSense for domains?
Access this video file through your registered Web Edition at
my.safaribooksonline.com/9780131388666/media.

There appear to be two primary types of AdSense for Domains users. The first is the publisher who has purchased a domain name, but as yet hasn't had time to build a website for that domain. In this instance, AdSense for Domains is a temporary solution, enabling the publisher to put something on the site and generate a bit of revenue before the main site goes live.

The second type of AdSense for Domain user is the professional "parker," a publisher who buys a truckload of unused domains in the hopes of generating a tiny bit of revenue from each—and thus multiplying that revenue by hundreds, if not thousands, of sites. With little or no effort involved in building a site, AdSense's PPC ads present a high revenue-to-cost ratio opportunity.

These parked domains typically have URLs that are close to the URLs of other popular sites. The goal is to benefit from users' misspellings and mistypings; a user mistypes the URL for a popular site and instead is taken to the parked domain, complete with ads and sponsored links just waiting to be clicked.

Let it be known that I'm not a big fan of parked domains as a business strategy. I'm a firm believer in fair pay for real work, and parking domains in this fashion is not real work at all; it's lazy and opportunistic at best, and overtly fraudulent at worst. Still, money can be made this way, and AdSense for Domains makes it relatively easy to do.

How much money can you make from a parked domain? It depends on the domain itself, and how many visitors purposefully or accidentally surf to the site. You probably will never generate as much ad revenue from a parked domain as you would from a legitimate website with valuable content, but then again, you don't have to put in much effort with the parked domain. AdSense for Domains is certainly worth doing if you just don't have the time to put together real content for a domain you've purchased, but don't expect any single parked domain to be a huge revenue generator.

Enabling AdSense for Domains

 SHOW ME   Media 7.4—Another video about AdSense for domains
Access this video file through your registered Web Edition at
my.safaribooksonline.com/9780131388666/media.

 **LET ME TRY IT**

Filling a Parked Domain with Content

Presuming that you've already registered a domain and left it empty, here's how you fill it up with content from the AdSense for Domains program. Just follow these steps:

1. Log into your AdSense account and select the AdSense Setup tab.

2. Click the AdSense for Domains link.

3. The first time you access AdSense for domains, you're prompted to review the terms of service; check the appropriate box and then click the I Accept button.

4. When the AdSense for Domains page appears, as shown in Figure 7.3, click the Add New Domains link.

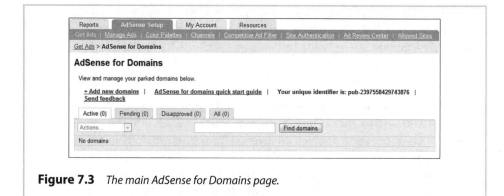

Figure 7.3   *The main AdSense for Domains page.*

5. On the Add Parked Domains page, shown in Figure 7.4, enter one or more domain names, one per line. You also need to select a language for these domains. When you're finished, click the Add Domain(s) button.

> If you have a ton of domains to enter, you can add them all at once by saving the domain names to a CSV file and then using the Bulk Add Domains option.

6. The domains you just added are now added to the Pending sub-tab on the AdSense for Domains page. You now need to modify the settings for these domains at your domain registrar. In general, you need to create a CNAME alias that refers to your AdSense ID and A (host) records that point to specific Google addresses. Instructions for doing this with several major

registrars, such as GoDaddy and Network Solutions, are located at www.google.com/adsense/support/bin/answer.py?answer=76049. After you've changed these domain settings, it should take about 48 hours for your domains to move from the Pending sub-tab to the Active sub-tab.

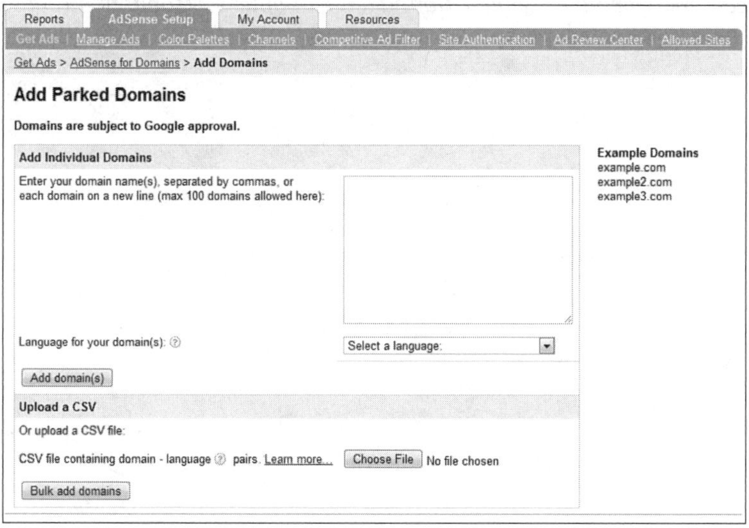

Figure 7.4 *Adding a parked domain to your account.*

If your domain moves to the Disapproved sub-tab instead of the Approved sub-tab, it's likely that your site violates Google's terms of service. Learn more online at www.google.com/adsense/support/bin/answer.py?answer=96830.

7. After your domain is active, you can customize certain elements of the resulting AdSense for Domains page. Return to the AdSense for Domains page, select the Active sub-tab, select the domain you want to edit and then pull down the Actions list and select Edit Settings.

8. Select a color palette for your page, or choose custom colors for specific page elements, and then click the Save Colors button.

9. Enter one or more keywords that help define the site's content into the Optional Keyword Hints box and then click the Save Keyword Hints button.

To track the performance of this domain via channels, return to the AdSense for Domains page, select the domain, pull down the Actions list, select Change Channel, and select a channel from the resulting list. Learn more about channels in Chapter 3.

The main page of your domain will now go live, formatted as you specified. You can return to the AdSense for Domains page at any time to edit the page's settings; use AdSense's standard tracking tools to track the performance of this domain.

Learn more about tracking performance in Chapter 9, "Monitoring Your AdSense Performance."

8

Earning Sales Commissions from the Google Affiliate Network

There's one more way that Google helps you make money from your website, and it doesn't involve advertising. The Google Affiliate Network is a way for you to earn commissions from items that your site visitors purchase—not from you, but from online merchants that are part of Google's network. You link to these merchants and their merchandise on your site; when a site visitor clicks a link and then purchases a product, you earn a sales commission.

Understanding the Google Affiliate Network

The Google Affiliate Network is all about affiliate marketing. The network connects websites (you) with retailers with goods for sale. When you select a given retailer to partner with, you earn either a referral bounty or a percent of all sales generated from your site.

First, you choose one or more advertisers that you want to feature on your site. Second, you place on your site links or ads for the affiliate retailers. Then, when someone clicks the ad on your site and continues to the retailer's website, and eventually purchases the product advertised, you receive a commission on the sale.

The Google Affiliate Network is the new name for the DoubleClick Performics Affiliate program, which was acquired by Google in 2008.

TELL ME MORE   Media 8.1—A discussion about affiliate advertising
Access this audio recording through your registered Web Edition at
my.safaribooksonline.com/9780131388666/media.

Who Advertises on the Google Affiliate Network?

What kinds of advertisers are we talking about? The Google Affiliate Network is host to major retailers such as Armani Exchange, Barnes & Noble, Blue Nile, Cabela's, Kohls, OfficeMax, Sears, Shoes.com, and Target, as well as countless smaller retailers. In terms of goods and services offered, they run the gamut from apparel to sporting goods, with everything in-between.

As you can see, these are trusted retailers offering a variety of valued products. You're sure to find at least one advertiser offering products that will appeal to your site's visitors.

How Much Can You Earn?

As noted, you make money when a visitor clicks through an ad on your site and proceeds to purchase something from the advertiser. In general, you earn a percentage of the purchase price—in effect, a sales commission.

Commissions vary greatly from advertiser to advertiser, but tend to run in the 5% to 25% range. In general, you find lower commission rates from those advertisers with higher response rates, and higher commission rates from those with lower response rates. That is, the more likely an advertiser is to generate a sale, the less they'll pay per sale. Big volume equals lower commission rates, while lower volume equals higher commission rates. It all kind of evens out in the end.

What Do the Ads Look Like?

Ads from the Google Affiliate Network are more often graphical rather than the text-based ads typical of the AdSense program. They can be banner ads, such as the one in Figure 8.1, or smaller, squarish ads, such as the one in Figure 8.2. Some ads promote specific products, while others promote a brand or the retailer in general. When visitors click the ads, they go directly to the retailer's site, typically to a special landing page that corresponds to the ad displayed. From there they can get more information and place an order.

Joining the Google Affiliate Network

The Google Affiliate Network, while linked to Google AdSense, operates separately from AdSense. This means you have to apply separately to be a part of the Affiliate Network.

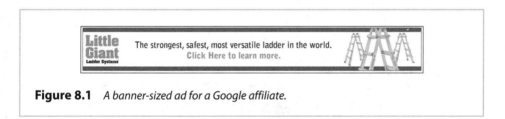

Figure 8.1   *A banner-sized ad for a Google affiliate.*

Figure 8.2   *A smaller, squarish ad for a Google affiliate.*

 **LET ME TRY IT**

Applying for the Google Affiliate Network

1. Go to www.google.com/ads/affiliatenetwork/.

2. Click the Publishers Learn More button.

3. When the next page appears, click the Sign Up link.

4. On the next page, click the Yes, I Have an AdSense Account (assuming you have an AdSense account, of course; if not, select the No, I Don't Have an AdSense Account option).

5. You now will be prompted to supply your AdSense email and publisher ID; enter these in the blanks provided.

6. Click Submit & Continue.

7. You now see the application screen shown in Figure 8.3. You'll need to fill in the following information:

    • Website URL

    • Display name (the title of your site)

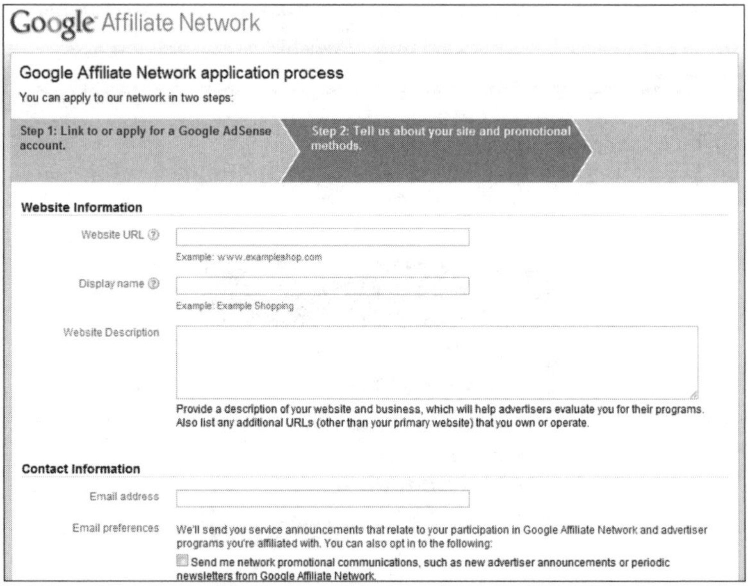

Figure 8.3   *Applying to the Google Affiliate Network.*

- Website description—advertisers use this to evaluate whether you'd be a good fit with their product mix

- Contact information—your email address and contact preferences

- Promotional methods—the ways you promote your site, including website/content, search engine marketing, incentives/loyalty programs, email marketing, and software application/toolbars

8. After you've provided all this information, check the various boxes to tell Google you've read and agree with its program policies and then click the Submit button.

9. Google now processes and evaluates your application. You should hear back from Google within 24 hours or so, informing you that your application has (or hasn't) been accepted.

Applying to Advertiser Programs

After you've been accepted into the Google Affiliate Network, you have to apply to specific advertiser programs to display ads from those retailers on your site. This isn't like AdSense, where Google automatically serves the ads; you have to choose which advertisers you want to partner with, and then ask them for permission to do so.

 SHOW ME   Media 8.2—A video about how to apply for advertiser programs
Access this video file through your registered Web Edition at my.safaribooksonline.com/9780131388666/media.

Viewing a List of Advertisers

To view a list of advertisers and apply to partner with an advertiser, follow these steps:

1. From your Google Affiliate Network page, select the Advertisers tab.

2. Click the Join sub-tab.

3. This displays a list of all network advertisers, as shown in Figure 8.4; you can filter this list by category or name. For each advertiser, you see information about its primary product category, average earnings per click (EPC), its payout rank (where it ranks compared to other network advertisers), the duration of the commission, whether there's a product feed available, and the company's payment terms—how long it takes you to get paid. To view more information about the advertiser and its commission structure, pull down the View menu for that advertiser and select either View Ad Planner Profile, Advertiser Info, Commissions, or Advertiser Specific Terms to learn more about that advertiser and the potential commissions you can earn.

4. To sign up with an advertiser, check the box for that advertiser and then click the Apply to Selected button. (You can apply to more than one advertiser at once.)

Your application will now be reviewed by the advertiser(s) you selected. You'll be contacted via email when your application is accepted (or rejected).

Inserting Ads on Your Site

After you're approved by an advertiser, you now have to add that retailer's ads to your website. Here's how you do it:

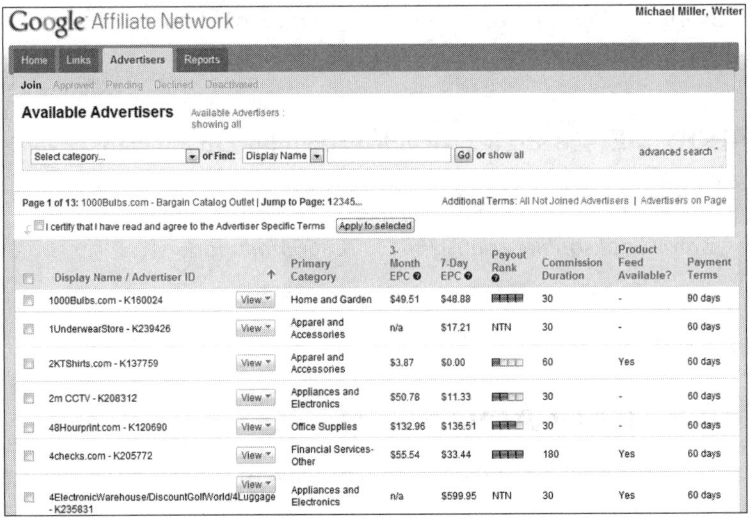

Figure 8.4　*Viewing advertisers in the Google Affiliate Network.*

 SHOW ME　Media 8.3—A video about activating affiliate network ads
Access this video file through your registered Web Edition at
my.safaribooksonline.com/9780131388666/media.

LET ME TRY IT

Adding a Retailer's Ads to a Website

1. From your Google Affiliate Network page, select the Links tab.

2. Select the By Advertiser sub-tab.

3. When the next page appears, as shown in Figure 8.5, go to the selected advertiser, click the Actions button, and select Get Links.

4. You now see a selection of different ads you can use, like the one shown in Figure 8.6. Click Get HTML for the ad you want.

5. Google now generates the HTML code necessary to display the selected ad, as shown in Figure 8.7. Copy this code and paste it into your web page where you want the ad to appear.

Some advertisers offer both image and text ads. Click the Image Links or Text Links tabs to view the different types of available ads.

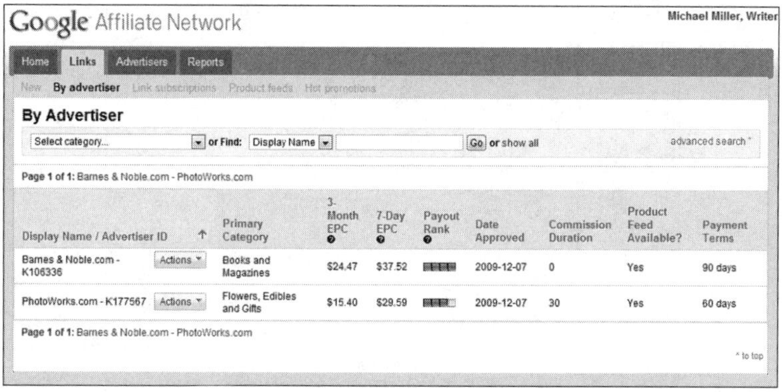

Figure 8.5 *Getting ready to create ad code for a selected advertiser.*

Figure 8.6 *Selecting ads to display on your site.*

Obviously, you can insert more than one ad on your site, and even have multiple ads on a single page. (Figure 8.8 shows the home page of my website, with two ads from different advertisers.) You can even, depending on the terms of each advertiser, display ads from multiple advertisers. Just remember, you want to display ads from advertisers that will most appeal to your site's visitors—so choose wisely!

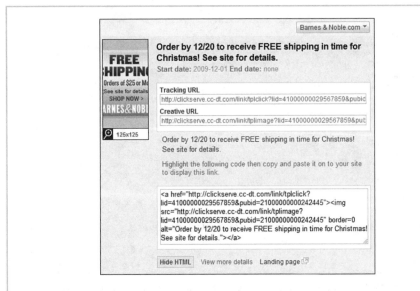

Figure 8.7   *Copy the HTML code into your own web page.*

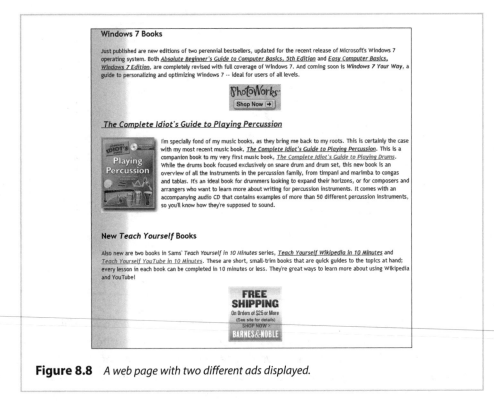

Figure 8.8   *A web page with two different ads displayed.*

Viewing Reports

Various reports are available from your main Google Affiliate Network page. These reports help you track all activity on your account—including orders placed by your site's visitors.

To run various reports, click the Reports tab and then click the appropriate report sub-tab. You can then select a date range, advertiser, and view for the report, as shown in Figure 8.9

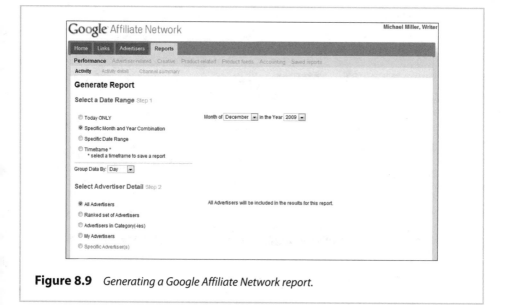

Figure 8.9 *Generating a Google Affiliate Network report.*

What reports are available? Here's a sampling:

- **Performance**, including activity and activity detail reports (visits, sales, transactions, and so forth), as well as channel summary reports

- **Advertiser-related**, including performance by advertiser and by product category

- **Creative**, including reports that track performance by both links and creative size

- **Product-related**, including products detail, order item detail, and product category revenue reports

- **Product feeds**, which displays clicks, sales, and commissions by product data feed link

- **Accounting**, which displays earnings accrued from each of your advertisers

- **Saved**, which displays any customized reports you've previously saved

After you've selected a report and specified the information you want displayed, click the Generate Report button to display the report onscreen, as shown in Figure 8.10. Alternatively, you can click the Export to Excel button to generate a file you can import into Excel and work with offline.

Activity Results Overview Data | Revenue Data | Action/Transaction Data | Search Data

Details
- Dec. 1, 2009 to Dec.11, 2009
- All Advertisers, Michael Miller, Writer, Confirmed Orders Only

Page 1 of 1 : 2009-12-01 - 2009-12-11   Total Rows: 11   Export to Excel

Date ↑	Advertisers	Links	Imp.*	Visits	Actions	Action Conv. %	Trans.	Trans. Conv. %	Total Conv. %	Amount	Avg. Amount	Publisher Fee
2009-12-01	0	View Links	0	0	0	0%	0	0%	0%	$0.00	$0.00	$0.00
2009-12-02	0	View Links	0	0	0	0%	0	0%	0%	$0.00	$0.00	$0.00
2009-12-03	0	View Links	0	0	0	0%	0	0%	0%	$0.00	$0.00	$0.00
2009-12-04	0	View Links	0	0	0	0%	0	0%	0%	$0.00	$0.00	$0.00
2009-12-05	0	View Links	0	0	0	0%	0	0%	0%	$0.00	$0.00	$0.00
2009-12-06	0	View Links	0	0	0	0%	0	0%	0%	$0.00	$0.00	$0.00
2009-12-07	0	View Links	0	0	0	0%	0	0%	0%	$0.00	$0.00	$0.00
2009-12-08	0	View Links	0	0	0	0%	0	0%	0%	$0.00	$0.00	$0.00
2009-12-09	0	View Links	0	0	0	0%	0	0%	0%	$0.00	$0.00	$0.00
2009-12-10	0	View Links	0	0	0	0%	0	0%	0%	$0.00	$0.00	$0.00
2009-12-11	0	View Links	0	0	0	0%	0	0%	0%	$0.00	$0.00	$0.00
GRAND TOTALS			0	0	0	0%	0	0%	0%	$0.00	$0.00	$0.00

Page 1 of 1 : 2009-12-01 - 2009-12-11   Total Rows: 11   Export to Excel

Figure 8.10   *Viewing an Activity Performance report.*

Getting Paid

The Google Affiliate Network pays members on a cost-per-action (CPA) basis. That is, you get paid when one of your site visitors actually purchases something through an ad on your site. You don't get paid just for someone viewing the ad, or even for someone clicking the ad; there has to be a verifiable action involved, in the form of a product purchase.

Although most affiliate sites pay a commission based on a percentage of an item's purchase price, some affiliates pay a referral bounty. This is essentially a click-through payment; the site pays when a user visits them from an ad on your site.

Payment is handled via Google AdSense. As noted previously, advertisers generate commissions on varying schedules; some pay monthly, some pay every 60 days, and so forth. Google will pay you within 30 days of when the advertiser generates the commission. Payments are placed directly in your AdSense account, and disbursed according to your choices there.

 Ⓖ *Learn more about Google AdSense payments in Chapter 3, "Adding AdSense for Content to Your Website."*

Optimizing Google Affiliate Network Performance

The Google Affiliate Network can be a good supplement to your normal AdSense revenues. (They're not mutually exclusive, remember.) But for these affiliate ads to pay off, you have to take a few things into account.

First, remember that you only get paid when a visitor buys something after clicking the affiliate ad; you don't get paid for the clicks themselves. This means that curious visitors, who can generate nice revenue in the AdSense program, don't earn you a single penny. You have to have *serious* visitors—that is, visitors serious about purchasing what is advertised on your site.

To that end, it's imperative that you choose your advertisers carefully. To inspire actual purchases, you have to advertise products or services that are of interest or value to your site's visitors. This means matching advertisers with your site's topic; you need to promote items that make sense given your site's content. If you have a site dedicated to photography, for example, you're better off choosing an advertiser that specializes in photo services or digital cameras than one that pushes lingerie or flowers.

Along the same lines, don't assume that so-called mass merchants, such as Target or Walmart, will appeal to all of your visitors. Yes, they'll have some appeal—they carry a little bit of everything, after all—but general-interest advertisers will typically generate lower sales than targeted advertisers. Of course, if your site is more general-interest, going with a mass merchant might make sense; but if your site has tightly focused content, choosing an advertiser that mirrors that content probably makes more sense.

That said, you don't have to limit yourself to a single advertiser. Maybe you'll choose one special-interest advertiser and one general-interest one, to cover multiple bases, or perhaps you'll mix-and-match advertisers by the page, specific to each page's content.

Another thing you can—and should—do is change the ad units on a regular basis. Each advertiser offers several different ad units, often targeted to specific promotions. Change the ads on your pages every few weeks so that they remain fresh to your regular visitors. Switch to different ads from the same advertisers, or switch to different advertisers. It helps to have a pool of advertisers and ads you can choose from.

Finally, with all this ad and advertiser switching, know that testing is important. Try a certain type of ad for a week or two and then try something different for the next few weeks; see which ad or advertiser generates the most sales. You can even experiment with different ad sizes and placements. Test, test, test until you find a combination that pulls the best. That's the way the pros do it.

9

Monitoring Your AdSense Performance

No matter which version of AdSense you're using—Content, Search, Feeds, Mobile Content, or Domains—Google offers a variety of reports to help you monitor the performance of the ads on your site or blog. These reports show you how many clicks you're generating and how much that means in terms of earnings.

Smart webmasters use these reports not just to determine how much ad revenue they're generating, but also to increase the amount of that revenue. That requires reading between the lines in these reports, analyzing *why* your current ads are performing as they are, and then fine-tuning your site so that you generate more click-throughs per ad.

Viewing Overview Reports

You access all available AdSense reports from the main AdSense page (www.google. com/adsense/). Select the Overview tab and you have a variety of reports available.

Displaying Overview Information

The most basic—and, for many users, the most useful—reports are found on the Overview sub-tab. The primary overview, shown in Figure 9.1, details a variety of performance-related information for all your AdSense programs—AdSense for Content, AdSense for Domains, AdSense for Search, AdSense for Mobile Content, AdSense for Feeds, and the Google Affiliate Network. It also details your total earnings for any selected period.

 SHOW ME   Media 9.1—A video about how to display overview information
Access this video file through your registered Web Edition at
my.safaribooksonline.com/9780131388666/media.

Figure 9.1 *Viewing an overview of your AdSense performance.*

The Referrals line in this report refers to the now-defunct AdSense Referrals program, which was discontinued back in 2008.

The information presented for each of these programs includes the following:

- **Page impressions**, or the number of people you have viewing your web pages. This doesn't measure anything about the ads on your pages, just the number of visitors your pages receive.

- **Clicks.** This measures the actual number of clicks that the ads on your pages receive. Each click represents a source of revenue.

- **Page CTR**, or the click-through-rate per page. This measures the number of ad clicks divided by the number of impressions per page—in other words, the percentage of people who visit your pages who click on the AdSense ads. Naturally, the higher the CTR the better, as it means that more of your visitors are clicking on the ads—and generating revenue for you.

- **Page eCPM**, or the effective cost-per-thousand impressions per page. This represents your estimated earnings for every 1,000 impressions you receive; it doesn't represent what you've actually earned. This metric is derived by dividing your total estimated earnings by total page impressions.

Effective CPM is useful for estimating future revenue if you increase (or decrease) the amount of traffic to your pages. For example, if your eCPM is $1.50 and you currently have 1,000 visitors to your site, you're earning $1.50 in income. But if your eCPM stays the same and you increase site traffic to 10,000 visitors, you'll earn $15; increase traffic to 100,000 visitors and you'll earn $150.

- **Estimated Earnings.** This final column details the actual money you've earned for the selected period.

In addition, you can view performance data for your top AdSense for Content channels. Just click the Top Channels link and you'll see this same information for your top channels; click the further View All AdSense for Content Channels to see data for all the channels you've created.

By default, this information is displayed for the current day only. You can, however, view data for other time periods—Yesterday, Last 7 Days, This Month, Last Month, Since Last Payment, and All Time. Just pull down the View list and select the desired time frame.

What's the most important information in this overview? The earnings number is important, of course, as that's the amount of money the ads on your site have generated for the given period. But I also find the click-through rate (CTR) valuable, as it tells you just how effective those ads are; it describes the percent of visitors who click on the ads. A low CTR indicates that the ads just aren't working—possibly because they're not as targeted or relevant as they should be. This is a sign that you might need to tighten the focus of your pages, to help AdSense better target the ads it serves.

Any messages sent to you from the Google AdSense team are displayed in the Recent Messages section of the Overview sub-tab. Click any message header to read the full message.

Generating Quick Reports

The Overview sub-tab also lets you generate a series of quick reports that show ad performance on a day-to-day basis for specific periods. You can then customize, to some degree, these quick reports to display more specific information.

 SHOW ME   Media 9.2—**A video about how to create quick reports**
Access this video file through your registered Web Edition at
my.safaribooksonline.com/9780131388666/media.

Let's start with the quick reports themselves. Scroll down to the Quick Reports section of the Overview sub-tab, as shown in Figure 9.2, and you see the automatically generated reports for each of the AdSense programs. For each program, you see the following reports:

- This month, by day

- This month, by channel and day

- Last month, by day

- Last month, by channel and day

- Since last payment, by day

- Since last payment, by channel and day

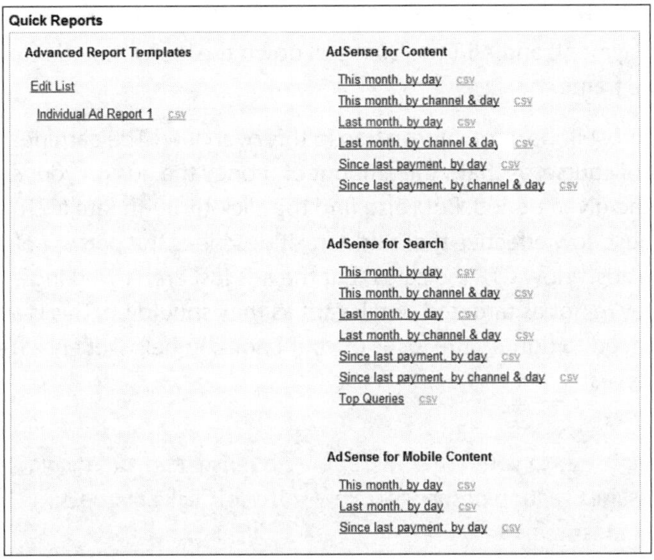

Figure 9.2   *Available AdSense quick reports.*

Click any link to display that quick report. If you'd rather download the raw data to work with in Microsoft Excel, click the CSV link instead; this downloads the data as a comma-separated value file, which imports cleanly into an Excel spreadsheet.

Figure 9.3 shows a typical "by day" report. Each day of the reporting period gets its own row, while you see the by-now familiar columns for Page Impressions, Clicks, Page CTR, Page eCPM, and Estimated Earnings. Click the link at the top of any column to resort the data by that metric.

| December 1, 2009 - December 12, 2009 | Save as Report Template: ⊙ Enter new name... [Save] |
| ⊙ Replace report... [▼] CSV |

Totals		2,875	13			$1.21
Date	Page impressions	Clicks	Page CTR	Page eCPM [?]	Estimated earnings
Tuesday, December 1, 2009	244	1	0.41%	$0.13	$0.03
Wednesday, December 2, 2009	335	1	0.30%	$0.49	$0.16
Thursday, December 3, 2009	266	4	1.50%	$2.99	$0.80
Friday, December 4, 2009	295	0	0.00%	$0.00	$0.00
Saturday, December 5, 2009	249	0	0.00%	$0.05	$0.01
Sunday, December 6, 2009	245	7	2.86%	$0.83	$0.20
Monday, December 7, 2009	267	0	0.00%	$0.00	$0.00
Tuesday, December 8, 2009	220	0	0.00%	$0.00	$0.00
Wednesday, December 9, 2009	194	0	0.00%	$0.00	$0.00
Thursday, December 10, 2009	218	0	0.00%	$0.00	$0.00
Friday, December 11, 2009	244	0	0.00%	$0.01	$0.00
Saturday, December 12, 2009	98	0	0.00%	$0.03	$0.00
Totals	2,875	13			$1.21
Averages	239	1	0.45%	$0.42	$0.10

Figure 9.3   *Viewing a "by day" quick report.*

You can fine-tune the report by changing the parameters displayed at the top of the report page. These parameters are the same as those found on the Advanced Reports sub-tab, which we'll discuss next.

Viewing Advanced Custom Reports

In addition to the basic overview and canned quick reports, AdSense lets you create your own custom reports. You can cut the AdSense data just about any way you'd like, within reason.

Creating a Custom Report

To create a custom report, go to the Advanced Reports sub-tab under the Reports tab. As you can see in Figure 9.4, AdSense lets you specify a number of parameters that affect the data display, including the following:

- **Choose product.** Select which AdSense program you want to analyze.
- **Choose date range.** Select a range of dates that you want to analyze.
- **Show data by** page, ad unit, or individual ad.

SHOW ME   Media 9.3—A video about how to create custom AdSense
reports
Access this video file through your registered Web Edition at
my.safaribooksonline.com/9780131388666/media.

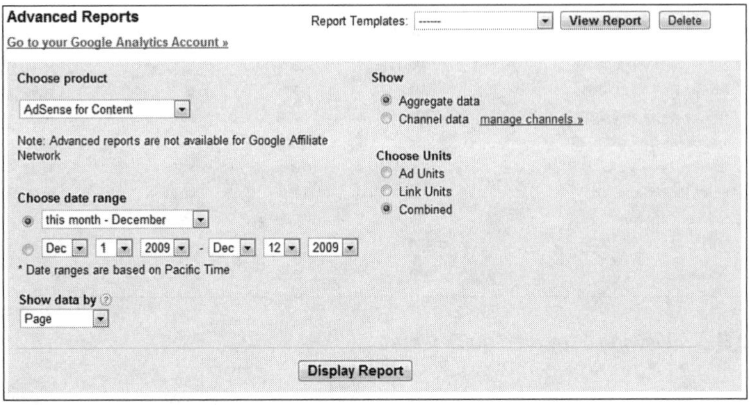

Advanced Reports   Report Templates: ⎢----- ⎢▾⎢ ⎢ View Report ⎢ ⎢ Delete ⎢
Go to your Google Analytics Account »

Choose product   **Show**
⎢ AdSense for Content   ⎢▾⎢   ⦿ Aggregate data
                                          ○ Channel data manage channels »
Note: Advanced reports are not available for Google Affiliate
Network   **Choose Units**
                                          ○ Ad Units
Choose date range   ○ Link Units
⦿ this month - December   ⎢▾⎢   ⦿ Combined

○ ⎢Dec⎢▾⎢ ⎢1⎢▾⎢ ⎢2009⎢▾⎢ - ⎢Dec⎢▾⎢ ⎢12⎢▾⎢ ⎢2009⎢▾⎢
* Date ranges are based on Pacific Time

Show data by ⓘ
⎢Page   ⎢▾⎢

⎢ Display Report ⎢

Figure 9.4   *Creating a custom report.*

If you elect to show data by individual ad, you can also show data by targeting
type—either contextual ads or direct ad placements.

- **Show** either aggregate data or data for each channel you've previously created.

- **Choose units.** Select to display ad units, link units, or both (combined).

Make your selections and then click the Display Report button. A report is now
generated and displayed at the bottom of the page.

Saving Your Custom Report

After you've created a report that does what you want it to do, you can save it for
future use—as a custom report template. To save a report, enter a name for the
template into the Save As Report Template box and then click the Save button.

To review a saved report, pull down the Report Templates list at the top of the
Advanced Reports sub-tab and then click the View Report button. That report is
now displayed at the bottom of the page.

To delete a custom report, select it from the Report Templates list then click the Delete button.

Using the Report Manager

All your saved reports, as well as your most recently viewed reports, can be quickly recalled using AdSense's Report Manager. Select the Report Manager sub-tab under the Reports tab and you see the list of reports shown in Figure 9.5. Your most recently generated reports are listed at the top of the page; your saved reports are listed at the bottom.

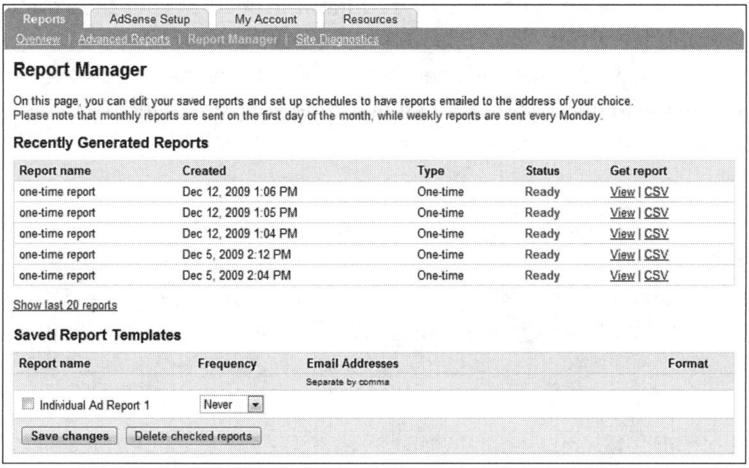

Figure 9.5 *Managing and automating reports with the Report Manager.*

Click the View link next to any recent report to view that report again. Display more reports by clicking the Show Last 20 Reports link.

You can configure AdSense to automatically run any of your saved reports and then email the results to you. Pull down the Frequency list next to a saved report and select either Daily, Weekly, or Monthly. Enter your email address in the next column and then select what file format you want—plain CSV (comma-separated values) or CSV-Excel, which works even better with Excel. Click the Save Changes button and your reports will be emailed per your request.

Linking Google AdSense with Google Analytics

You can generate even more detailed analysis by linking your Google AdSense account with Google Analytics, a free service offered by Google that generates detailed statistics about visitors to any subscribing website. Google Analytics tracks visitors from all referring websites, including search engines, pay-per-click (PPC) advertising networks (such as Google AdSense and AdWords), display advertisements, email marketing, and other sources.

 TELL ME MORE   Media 9.4—A discussion about web analytics
Access this audio recording through your registered Web Edition at
my.safaribooksonline.com/9780131388666/media.

You can use Google Analytics to analyze various aspects of your site's traffic—how many people are visiting, which pages they're visiting, how long they stay, where they came from, where they visit next, where they leave the site, and so forth. With this information in hand, you can then fine-tune your site to increase traffic and generate higher AdSense ad revenues.

Google Analytics tracks only AdSense for Content ads. It does not track any other AdSense programs, including AdSense for Search, AdSense for Mobile Content, or AdSense for Feeds. In addition, Analytics only tracks the performance of AdSense ad units; it does not track the performance of link units.

Learn more about using Google Analytics to track your site's performance in my companion book, *Sams Teach Yourself Google Analytics in 10 Minutes* (Michael Miller, Sams, 2010).

Integrating with Google Analytics

To link your AdSense account with Google Analytics, go to the Overview sub-tab under the Reports tab and click the Integrate Your AdSense Account with Google Analytics link. When the next page appears, select Create My Free Google Analytics Account if you don't yet have an account; select I Already Have a Google Analytics Account if you already have an account. Click the Continue button to proceed and then follow the onscreen instructions from there.

When you first create your Google Analytics account, Google generates a piece of code you'll need to insert in your page's underlying HTML code. This code lets Google track your site's visitors; follow the onscreen instructions to generate and insert this code into your pages.

Viewing AdSense Information in Google Analytics

Once linked, information about your AdSense ads now appears in the Google Analytics Dashboard. You access the Dashboard by going to the main Google Analytics page (www.google.com/analytics/), shown in Figure 9.6, and then clicking the View Report link for your website.

When you open the Dashboard for your website, click the Content link in the left panel, as shown in Figure 9.7, and then click AdSense. This displays the AdSense Overview report shown in Figure 9.8, which contains all sorts of information.

 SHOW ME Media 9.5—A video about how to view AdSense information in Google Analytics

Access this video file through your registered Web Edition at
my.safaribooksonline.com/9780131388666/media.

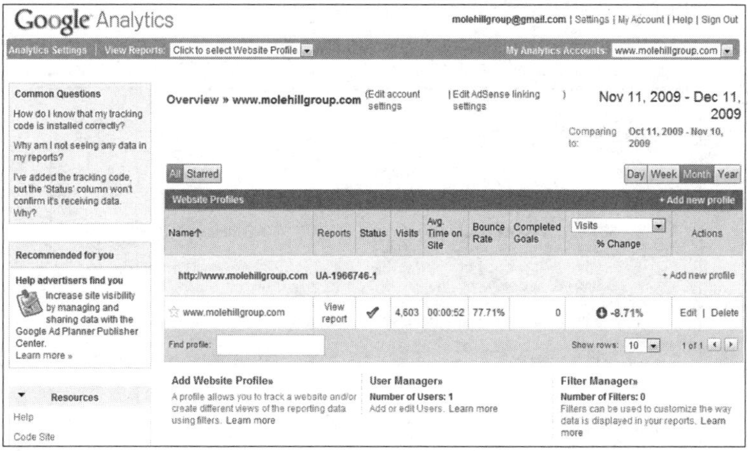

Figure 9.6 *Accessing Google Analytics.*

Figure 9.7   *Accessing AdSense data from the Google Analytics Dashboard.*

Figure 9.8   *Viewing the AdSense Overview report in Google Analytics.*

We'll start at the top of the page, which displays a graph that shows revenue per day for the past 30 days. Pull down the list at the top right side of the page to select a different date range.

The overview table in the middle of the page displays a variety of useful data. Some of this data mirrors that found in the normal AdSense dashboard, but some of it is unique to Google Analytics:

- **AdSense Revenue**, which tracks the revenue generated from your AdSense for Content ads.

- **AdSense Revenue/1000 Visits**, which calculates the revenue generated per 1,000 user visits. It's calculated by dividing the total revenue for the period by 1,000; it's a good way to compare revenue between sites or pages with varying traffic levels.

- **AdSense Ads Clicked**, which tracks the total number of AdSense ads clicked through by site visitors.

- **AdSense Ads Clicked/Visit**, which tracks the number of AdSense ads clicked per customer visit. This is a good metric for estimating how your total clicks might increase if you were to increase site traffic.

- **AdSense CTR**, which calculates the click-through rate for the ads on your site.

- **AdSense eCPM**, which calculates the effective cost-per-thousand impressions per page—essentially, your estimated earnings for every 1,000 impressions you receive.

- **AdSense Unit Impressions**, a useful metric which tracks the number of times ad units are shown on your site.

- **AdSense Unit Impressions/Visit**, which tracks the number of times ad units are shown per customer visit.

- **AdSense Page Impressions**, which tracks the total number of pages viewed by site visitors.

- **AdSense Page Impressions/Visit**, which measures the number of pages viewed per customer visit.

Click any of these items to view a daily graph and table for that metric. For example, Figure 9.9 shows the AdSense CTR graph and table.

At the bottom of the AdSense Overview page is the AdSense Details section, which displays two pieces of information. The Top AdSense Content report displays details revenue information about specific pages on your site; the Top AdSense

Referrers report tracks revenue by the top traffic sources coming to your site. Click the View Full Report beneath each of these summaries to view the full reports.

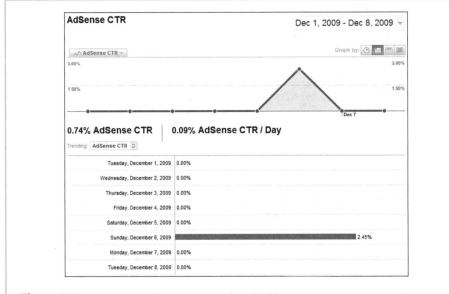

Figure 9.9   *Viewing the AdSense CTR graph and table.*

All Google Analytics reports are highly customizable. You can change the reporting period by using the pull-down list at the top right of every page; most reports also let you graph by day, week, and month, using the buttons beneath the pull-down list. In addition, many reports include different views, such as Table, Percentage, Performance, Comparison, and Detail. (Available views vary by report.)

If you're a heavy AdSense user, it makes sense to link your AdSense account with Google Analytics. The data and reports available in Google Analytics will make it much easier for you to pinpoint performance issues on your site, and make the necessary changes to increase ad performance.

Viewing Site Problems

Ever wonder how Google determines what types of ads it displays on your pages? Well, Google tries to figure out the content of your site by sending a *crawler* to your pages. This is an automated program that literally crawls your site, examining the keywords specified both in the page's content and in the underlying HTML code. The crawler then reports its findings back to Google, which uses the data to serve related ads to your site.

Google's crawler can be somewhat controlled by commands embedded in a special ROBOTS.TXT text file found on many websites. Webmasters use the ROBOTS.TXT file to provide sitemaps for larger sites, as well as to prohibit certain crawlers from indexing their site.

If Google's crawler has trouble accessing or analyzing your site, this information is noted on the Site Diagnostics sub-tab under the Reports tab. As you can see in Figure 9.10, any blocked URLs are noted, as is the reason for any specific problem.

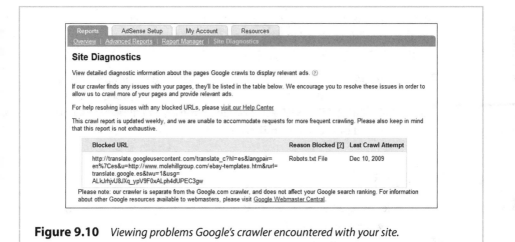

Figure 9.10 *Viewing problems Google's crawler encountered with your site.*

There are two main reasons for most crawler problems, as indicated in the Reason Blocked column:

- **Robots.txt File.** This indicates that the specified page is marked as disallowed in your ROBOTS.TXT file; you'll need to edit the file to change this. It's also possible that said file doesn't yet exist and needs to be created.

- **URL Not Found.** This indicates that your server might have been down when Google's crawler tried to visit. It could also indicate that the permissions for your server are set to disallow Google's crawler; if this is the case, you'll need to contact your web hosting service to get this changed.

Managing Account Information

You can also use the Google AdSense dashboard to manage your AdSense account. Select the My Account tab and you see the following sub-tabs:

- **Account Settings.** This displays your basic account settings—email address, password, payee information, and such. To edit any individual item, click the Edit link next to that section.

- **Account Access.** The top part of this page lists those users who have access to your AdSense account. The bottom part of this page lists third-party services, such as Blogger, that access your account. You can block access for any third party by clicking the Disable Access link.

- **Payment History.** This displays your AdSense earnings and payments for a specified period—Last 3 Months, Last 12 Months, or All Time. Click the Details link to view more details for any given period.

- **Tax Information.** Google reports all of your AdSense earnings to the U.S. government for tax purposes. As part of the registration process you will be required to submit a Form W-9 to Google; in return, you'll receive a Form 1099 at the end of the tax year. This page details your W-9 status.

Getting Paid

If you haven't yet entered your payment information, now is as good as any to do so. You need to enter this info for Google to pay you any revenues generated as part of the AdSense program.

 LET ME TRY IT

Entering Payment Information

1. Log onto your AdSense account and select the My Account tab.

2. Select the Account Settings sub-tab.

3. Scroll down to the Payment Details section and click the Edit link.

4. When the Choose Form of Payment page appears, as shown in Figure 9.11, select how you want to be paid. If you want funds deposited automatically in your bank account, select the Add a New Bank Account option in the Electronic Funds Transfer section. If you want to receive a paper check, select one of the two Check options.

5. Click Continue to proceed.

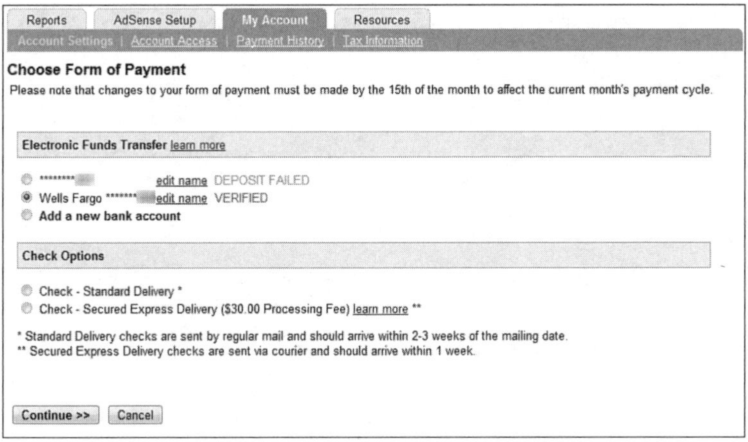

Figure 9.11   *Selecting payment options.*

6. If you opt for Electronic Funds Transfer, you're prompted to provide the necessary information about your bank account—account number, check routing number, and so forth. Follow the onscreen instructions and Google proceeds with an account verification procedure. This entails depositing a small amount into your bank account, and then you verifying the amount of the deposit. The entire process takes several days, at the end of which you're set up for direct deposit.

7. If you opt for payment via check, you see a Confirmation screen. Click Save Changes to verify your selection.

Payment via Electronic Funds Transfer is faster and safer than payment via check. Choose this option to get your money quicker.

Google typically sends payments the last week of each month for the prior month's activity. So, you should receive a check the last week of February for your January earnings.

The exception to this is if you don't earn enough money to meet Google's payment threshold. In the U.S., there's a $100 minimum; different levels apply in different countries and currencies.

Google will hold and accrue all earnings until you reach the minimum payment threshold. Any earnings at or above this level will be paid the following month.

Ten Tips for Increasing Your AdSense Revenue

Just putting AdSense ads on your website doesn't guarantee that you'll make a lot of money from them. The key to generating significant earnings is to get a lot of visitors to click through the ads—that means both increasing your site traffic and the visibility and appeal of the ads themselves.

To that end, in this chapter I offer a number of things you can do to improve the earnings potential of your AdSense ads. Following these tips won't guarantee increased ad revenue, but it's a good start for maximizing your AdSense potential. It's a must read!

 SHOW ME   Media 10.1—A video about tips for increasing AdSense revenue
Access this video file through your registered Web Edition at
my.safaribooksonline.com/9780131388666/media.

Tip #1: Give Your Ads Prominent Position

The number one tip for increasing AdSense revenues is to make the AdSense ads more visible on your site. And the easiest way to do that is to position them prominently on your pages.

Why Position Matters

Now, some webmasters are a bit shy when it comes to advertising. They want to generate ad revenue, yes, but they don't want to "compromise the integrity" of their sites. Maybe they're afraid that visitors will be turned off by too-prominent advertising; maybe they're just reluctant to cede content space to advertising.

TELL ME MORE   Media 10.2—A discussion about site integrity
versus AdSense revenue

Access this audio recording through your registered Web Edition at
my.safaribooksonline.com/9780131388666/media.

Whatever the reason, any webmaster who doesn't play up advertising front and center is going to be disappointed in the ad revenue his site generates. It's simple, really. If you hide your AdSense ads, no one will see them. And if no one sees them (or clicks them), you won't generate any earnings.

Conversely, when you place AdSense ads in a prominent position on your web pages, your earnings will increase. You want to do everything within your power to make sure that all your site visitors see some advertising. Don't be afraid of offending or annoying your visitors; to be effective, ads have to intrude.

All that said, you might have reservations about imposing advertising on your site's visitors. If that's the case, you might need to reconsider the whole AdSense thing. If you take the approach of having your ads blend into the background, you may create a more pleasant user experience but you're darned sure to generate fewer click-throughs and less ad revenue. Maybe that's a compromise you want to make; you'll accept less revenue to create a cleaner user experience. If you opt for this approach, don't gripe about AdSense not working. If you want higher revenue, you have to force visitors to see those ads. Yes, some visitors will find it annoying, but it's tough to find a site these days that doesn't feature in-your-face advertising. Everybody wants to make a buck, and this is how you do it.

What's the Best Position?

So what's the best place to put AdSense ads on your site? In a nutshell, the best position for an ad is one nearest your page's core content and that a visitor can see without scrolling. That means near the top-middle of your page, either above, to the left, or below the main content of your page.

In general, ads perform better on the left side of a page than on the right. That's because we all read from left to right, and see the left-side content before we do that on the right.

Google put together a "heat map" of possible ad positions, and ranked the different positions in terms of click-through potential. Figure 10.1 shows that page map. Place your ads in one of the slots marked 1 or 2 to get the best results; avoid those slots with higher numbers.

SHOW ME Media 10.3—A video about how to choose the best ad positioning
Access this video file through your registered Web Edition at
my.safaribooksonline.com/9780131388666/media.

As you can see from this map, it's important to place your ads near important content; you want visitors to see the ads when they view must-read content. That points out another good position for ads—directly after the end of an article, blog post, or other editorial content. You also get a good bang for your buck by positioning ads *between* other elements, such as between articles or blog posts. Also good is placement near navigational elements, such as menus and back/up buttons.

Even better, take a look at your pages from the viewpoint of one of your site's visitors. Where does your eye go? What's the most important content on the page? That's where you want to place your ads—somewhere around this key content or focal point. Yeah, it might be a little intrusive, but it will get noticed—and that results in more clicks and more income for you.

Bottom line: Top is better than bottom, left is better than right, and butting up against important content is best of all.

Positioning Link Units

If you opt to display link units in place of or in addition to normal PPC ads, the art of positioning is a little different. That's because some users will view these link units as navigation links—they are somewhat general category topic titles, after all.

Some webmasters and site visitors view the use of link units in this fashion as misleading at best and unethical at worst, as they trick some users into thinking they link to legitimate content on your site. If this is a concern of yours, you shouldn't employ this tactic.

With this in mind, you'll get a good response from choosing a horizontal link unit design and placing it at either the very top or very bottom of your pages. Positioned at the top of a page, as shown in Figure 10.2, these links look like header-based menu or navigation links. Positioned at the bottom of a page, as shown in Figure 10.3, they look like footer-based navigation. In either spot, some users will think that they're links to other content on your site—which, of course, they're not. But when confronted with the resulting list of related sites, some users will click through and generate ad revenue for you.

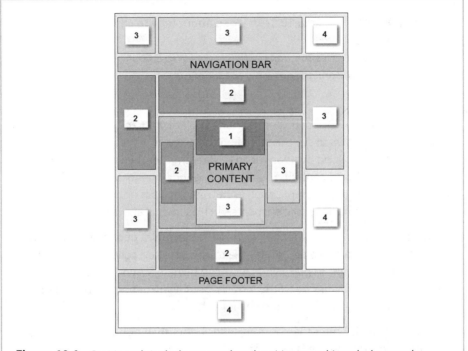

Figure 10.1   *Position ads in the lower-numbered positions to achieve the best results.*

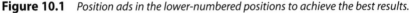

Figure 10.2   *A horizontal link unit positioned at the top of the page—it looks like a menu to content on your site.*

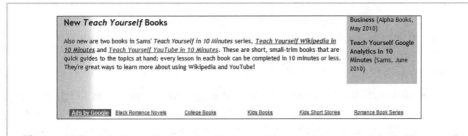

Figure 10.3   *A horizontal link unit position at the bottom of the page—it looks like a set of navigational links.*

Tip #2: Format Your Ads to Look Like They're Part of the Page

Here's a test: What type of ad performs best—one that stands out from your regular page template or one that blends in? Contrary to what you might initially think, it's the ad that blends in that performs best; visitors tend to view such an ad as part of the page content, rather than as an ad.

That's right, just getting an ad noticed isn't enough; visitors also have to be enticed to click on the ad. Apparently, ads that stand in stark contrast to the underlying page look too much like ads and not enough like valuable content. Visitors are more likely to click on content than they are on obvious ads.

When it comes to choosing ad colors, then, go with a color scheme that is similar to your page's color scheme. Avoid colors that contrast too much with your page's colors.

So, if your page has simple black text against a white background, *don't* choose a color scheme with a colored background and bright type. Instead, go with a simple white background and black text. Likewise, if your page has a dark blue background with white type, choose that same (or a similar) color scheme for your ads. You want visitors to think that the ads are part of your content, not something separate.

Similarly, if you want to increase click-throughs, don't surround your ad with a border. A border signals visitors that this is something that can (or even should) be avoided; ads without borders blend better into the page's background.

Figures 10.4 and 10.5 demonstrate how this works. Note how the ad block in Figure 10.5 looks more organic, more like it's a continuation of the other content on the page. In contrast, the ad in Figure 10.4 looks like... well, it looks like an ad. You might notice it, but you probably don't want to click on it.

A poorly formatted ad
that doesn't fit the page

Figure 10.4   *An ad formatted in sharp contrast to the underlying page—bad.*

Tip #3: Choose a Large Ad Format

When it comes to advertising effectiveness, bigger is better. It should come as no surprise that wider ad formats tend to outperform narrower formats—even if the narrower ad is also taller. It's all about readability—visitors can read more text at a glance with a wider ad than they can with a taller one.

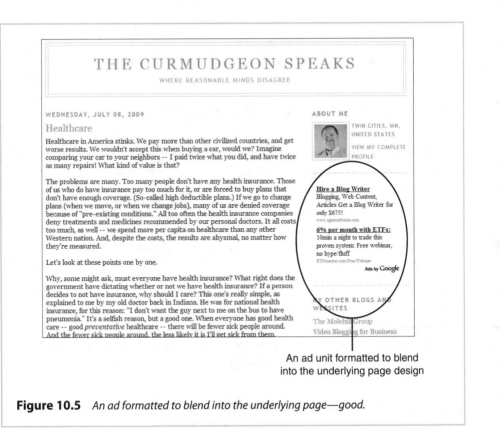

Figure 10.5 *An ad formatted to blend into the underlying page—good.*

Google says that the most effective formats are the 336×280 large rectangle, the 300×250 medium rectangle, and the 160×600 wide skyscraper. These are all largish ad units, and thus are dominant on the underlying page.

Along the same lines, many sites have had good luck with wide ads, such as the 728×90 leaderboard and 468×60 banner. Obviously, you should experiment with different ad sizes, as well as ad positions, to find the ones that work best with your site.

Tip #4: Display Both Text and Image Ads

When you create an AdSense ad unit for your site, you have a choice of a text ad, image ad, or both. Don't get so enamored of the typical text ad that you dismiss the image ad option; it's best to display both types of ads.

You might not be aware of this, but not all advertisers go the text-only route; some advertisers choose the text format only and others choose only the image format. When you opt to display both types of ads, you have a wider pool of potential advertisers who can display their ads on your page. And more potential advertisers mean better targeted ads—and a higher click-through rate.

That said, some visitors might be turned off by overly intrusive image ads—especially those of the video variety. If you feel that image ads detract too much from your site's content, stick with text ads only; it is a safer bet, overall.

Tip #5: Surround Your Ads with Images

One reason some people don't like image ads is that they're too attention-getting; given the choice of looking at words or pictures, most of our eyeballs drift to the pictures. But that preference provides a means of increasing the performance of text-based ads on your site, if you know the trick.

And here's the trick: You can draw more attention to a text ad if you surround it with images—attractive images that your visitors would want to look at, anyway. This means putting an image above or below (or both above and below) the AdSense module.

It's even better if the images have something to do with the ad content. For example, if you have a page about notebook PCs, and you're fairly sure that AdSense will serve up an ad related to notebook PCs, then surround that ad with pictures of notebook PCs. This approach not only draws attention to the ad, but it actually makes the ad appear to be more integrated into your page's content.

Tip #6: Put Multiple Ads on Your Page

If you have a large web page (one with a lot of scrolling content), you have room to put more than one ad on the page. Google lets you put up to three ad units on each page, in addition to three link units and three referral units.

The more ads you include, the more earnings you can generate.

That said, just because you can put multiple ads on your page doesn't mean you should. If you make your page too ad-heavy, you'll turn off visitors who might think your site has nothing but ads, without enough content. Use good judgment here—although three ads per page shouldn't be overly intrusive, given a large enough page.

By the way, the three-ads-per-page limitation applies only to websites. If you have a Blogger blog, you can configure blogger to insert ads between each and every one of your posts. That's a good deal, and gets more ads in front of your blog readers.

🅖 *Learn more about configuring Blogger for AdSense in Chapter 5, "Adding AdSense for Feeds to Your Blog."*

Tip #7: Use Section Targeting

Google tries to figure out the key content on your page and target its ads to that content. But if Google is having trouble separating the wheat from the chaff, content-wise, you can give things a little nudge by telling Google's crawlers what content you want targeted.

You do this by performing something called *section targeting*, using some simple HTML tags. All you have to do is surround the key content on your web page with these tags, and Google will look here—and only here—to determine what ads to display on your page.

Here are the tags to use—essentially an "on/off" pair of comment tags. Just insert the "on" tag before your primary content and the "off" tag after the content, like this:

```
<!-- google_ad_start -->
Important content here
<!-- google_ad_end -->
```

The content surrounded by these tags will be crawled by Google and used to specify targeted advertisements. And here's the best thing—you can use this trick as many times as you want on your page. So if you have multiple sections that should be targeted, surround each section with the appropriate tags; there's no limit as to how many sections you can target.

By the way, there's also a set of tags you can use to tell Google to ignore when doing the ad targeting thing. Use the following set of tags to lower the importance of a block of content:

```
<!-- google_ad_start(weight=ignore) -->
key page content here
<!-- google_ad_end -->
```

As with the previous tags, you can use the "ignore" tags as many times as you want on a page.

> Google says that it might take up to two weeks for a change in content targeting to be taken into account by AdSense.

Tip #8: Utilize Third-Party Tools to Track Your AdSense Performance

Google's AdSense tracking tools are good, but they're not the only tools at your disposal. There are a variety of third-party tools you can use to track your AdSense performance—and improve your click-through rate and ad revenues.

Here's a short list of some of the more popular such tools.

• **AdsBlackList** (www.adsblacklist.com, free or paid). This is a web-based service that lets you identify and block low-return advertisers from your site. The basic service is free; a Premier account, which generates a full list of 200 poor-performing advertisers, costs about $4 per month.

• **AdSense Earnings Tool** (www.freedownloadsarchive.com/Internet/ Tools_and_Utilities/Adsense_Earnings_Tool_31570.html, free). This utility monitors AdSense earnings in real time, without having to log onto the Google AdSense site.

• **Google Ads Preview** (googleadspreview.blogspot.com, free). A web-based tool, shown in Figure 10.6, that lets you see what specific ad types will look like on Google (text ads, image ads, and link units) and on competing services (Yahoo! and Chitika).

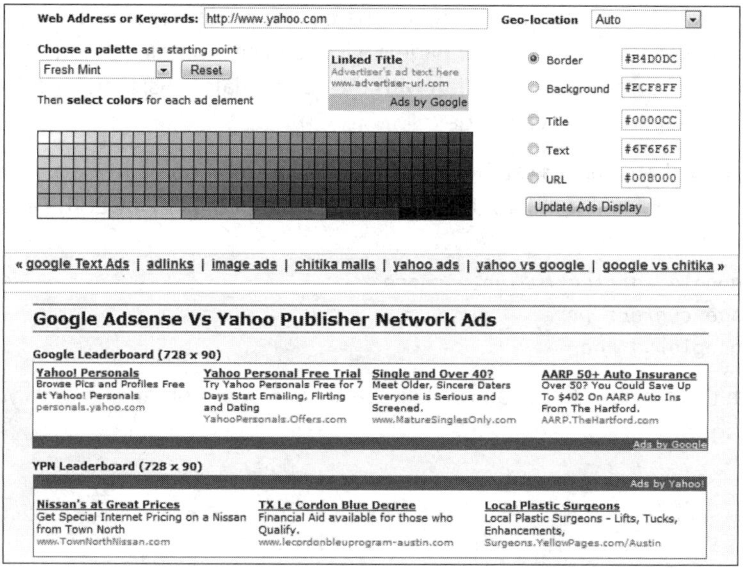

Figure 10.6 *Comparing ad types from competing advertising networks on the Google Ads Preview website.*

• **Google AdSense Calculator** (www.tutorials-db.com/tools/Adsense_ Calculator/, free). A quick-and-easy web-based calculator you can use to predict changes in earnings if you improve your page impressions, click-through rate, or cost-per-click.

- **Google AdSense Preview Tool** (www.labnol.org/google-adsense-sandbox/, free). This is a web page you can use to see what ads Google is serving up for various keywords or web page addresses. As you can see in Figure 10.7, simply enter a keyword or URL into the first box, select your location from the Country list, and then click the Show Google Ads button. The current ads being served for that URL or keyword will be displayed on the following page.

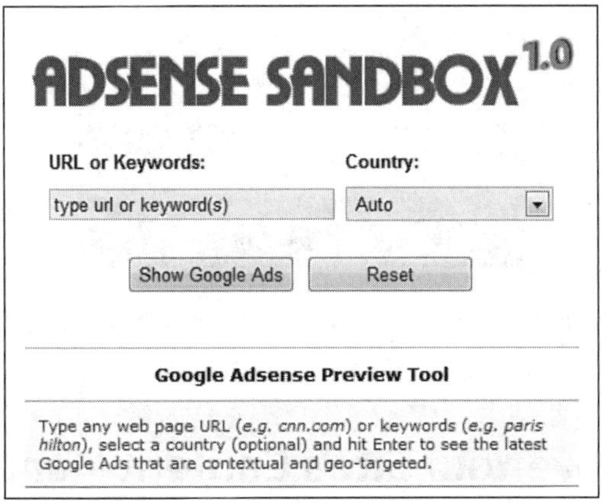

Figure 10.7   *Previewing ads with the Google AdSense Preview Tool.*

- **QuickSense** (http://www.quicksenseapp.com, $3.99). This is a mobile application, shown in Figure 10.8, that lets you track your AdSense earning on your Apple iPhone or iPod Touch. It lets you track performance wherever you are, any time of the day; just pull out your iPhone and see how things are going. In addition to earnings, QuickSense also tracks impressions, clicks, CTR, eCPM, and more.

QuickSense is just one of several AdSense apps for the iPhone. Other similar applications include iEarn (iearn.anxer.com, $1.99); iAdSense (iadsense.alexandre-gomes.com, $1.99); SenseEarn (www.hans-schneider.de/senseearn/, $3.99); and SimpleSense (www.ketacode.com/keta/simplesense/, free).

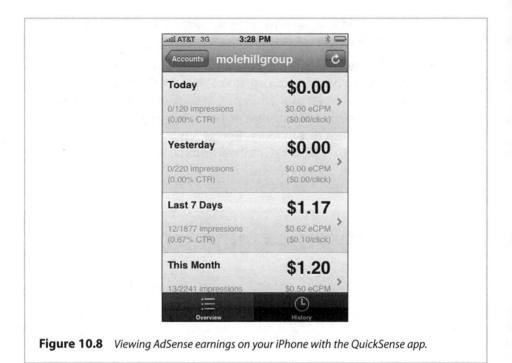

Figure 10.8   *Viewing AdSense earnings on your iPhone with the QuickSense app.*

Tip #9: Improve Your Site's Content—and Increase Your Traffic

So far I've provided a lot of little tricks that you can use to increase your AdSense ad revenues. Not to belittle any of these tricks, some of which work better than others, but there's really only one sure-fire way to increase your ad revenue: Improve the content of your website. Here's why.

The better and more timely your site's content, the more visitors you'll attract. The more visitors you have, the more click-throughs your ads will receive. And, it goes without saying, the more click-throughs you get, the more ad revenue you generate.

So to increase your ad revenue, improve your site. It's as simple as that.

Providing quality and targeted content is step one in optimizing your site for search. This process, dubbed *search engine optimization* or *SEO*, fine-tunes your site so that it shows up higher in Google search results. Because most new visitors find a site by searching, ranking higher in the search results delivers increased traffic levels.

You always want your site to rank on the first page of Google's search results. Most users don't bother to click to the second page of search results; not appearing on the first page will dramatically decrease your site's traffic.

It's really quite simple: Provide a high-quality, content-rich site, and Google will rank it highly. When visitors search for that particular topic, they see your site in Google's search results and click to visit. After they're on your site, they see your AdSense ads and some percentage of those visitors click the ads, generating revenue for you. It's a multi-step process, but better content ultimately results in higher ad revenues.

Content improvement is just one part of the SEO process; you also have to choose and feature high-performance keywords, include the appropriate HTML code, and more. Learn all about the process in my companion book, *The Complete Idiot's Guide to Search Engine Optimization* (Michael Miller, Alpha Books, 2009).

Let's face it—people don't visit your site because of the ads, they visit because of the content. If your content is lacking, users either don't visit or quickly leave when they do find your site. In either case, they don't stick around long enough to click on any ads. On the other hand, when you provide interesting and useful content, you not only attract visitors but you also keep them—and the longer they stay on your pages, the more likely they are to click on your ads.

It also bears repeating that Google targets its ads to your site's content. So the better and more focused your content, the more appropriate the ads that Google serves. If your content is weak or unfocused, the ads Google serves won't be nearly as appealing. It's all about the content—both to attract visitors and to serve up the most effective ads.

Tip #10: Test, Test, Test

There's one last AdSense tip that you need to take to heart. Success with the AdSense program doesn't come quickly or easily. It takes a lot of hard work to optimize your site for AdSense and thus optimize your AdSense revenue. You need to try various approaches before you find the one that generates the most revenue.

That's right, using AdSense is a trial-and-error process. You need to try different site content, different ad types, different colors, and different placements to find the most effective combination. That means trying different things—changing this element or that and seeing how that affects your click-through rate and revenues.

Successful publishers are constantly trying new things, tweaking their sites and settings to see what works and what doesn't.

It's all about testing. Don't ever assume that the one way you're doing things is the best way—or that what worked in the past will continue to work in the future. Change things up, try this thing or that, and then see how that change affects performance. Find something that works and do more of it; discover something that isn't working and change it.

When you make a change to your site or AdSense settings, leave the new ads in place for at least a week. It takes this long to determine whether the change has substantial impact on your clicks and revenues.

As you can see, making money with AdSense takes time. Don't expect the riches to start flowing from day one; it might take months or even years to find just the right combination of content and placement to make your site profitable. It takes time to generate traffic, and it takes time for that traffic to result in measurable advertising revenues. It's a long build but one worth waiting for. Just be a little patient; good things will come if you work hard and smart.

Bonus Tip: What *Not* to Do

We'll end this chapter and our discussion of AdSense with a bit of a bonus tip. This tip isn't about what you need to do to increase revenue, but rather about those things you *shouldn't* do.

To that end, here is a short list of things you should avoid doing if you want to maximize your AdSense revenues—and keep from getting kicked out of the AdSense program altogether!

Don't Mix AdSense with Other Ad Programs

Google AdSense isn't the only PPC ad network out there, and you don't have to be 100% loyal to Google, but you shouldn't put AdSense ads side-by-side with ads from other programs on the same page. You can mix and match Google and other networks throughout your site, but any given page should be devoted to ads from a single ad network only.

Don't Overdo It

Along the same lines, you don't want the advertising on your site to overwhelm the actual content. If you have a short page, that means not placing multiple ads on the page. And even if you have a longer page, limit yourself to the three ad units that Google says you can have, no more. If the ad-to-content ratio gets too high, visitors will start getting turned off—and quit clicking completely.

Don't Put Ads on Your Registration or Sign-In Pages

You can put AdSense ads on just about any page on your site. But Google won't let you put their ads on your registration, confirmation, sign-in/log-in pages. I'm not sure why, but them's the rules.

Don't "Beg" for Clicks

Google wants all clicks generated by its ads to be organic—that is, motivated by the ads themselves, and not by any outside influences. To that end, you're not allowed to encourage or entice site visitors to click on the ads displayed on your site. That goes as far as not including text that says "Help keep my site running by clicking on these ads" or "Please support the advertisers on my site." To be safe, just make sure your site's content pretty much ignores the ads on the page.

Don't Click on Your Own Ads

This is a biggie. You should never—and I repeat, *never*—click the ads that Google serves to your own site. Doing so constitutes click fraud, which is both a violation of Google's terms of service and a crime. Again, Google wants all clicks to be both organic and legitimate; you artificially inflating your ads' click-through rate is neither. It doesn't matter if it's just a click or two or if you hire a gang of teenagers with lots of time on their hands to click en masse; any form of deliberate clicking of this sort will get you banned from the AdSense program, at the very least.

Similarly, you should never join a program that promotes reciprocal click fraud—that is, you promise to click another site's links in return for them clicking yours. Even if it's not you doing the clicking, it's still click fraud, in that the clicker has no interest in or intention of purchasing the advertised goods and services. It's all fraudulent activity, and you should not engage in it.

Ⓖ *Learn more about click fraud in Chapter 21, "Dealing with Click Fraud."*

Don't Create "Made for AdSense" Sites

Some webmasters create websites designed solely to host ads and generate advertising revenue. These "made for AdSense" sites have little to no original content; what content there is exists only to draw traffic from Google and other search sites to view the ads displayed thereon. These parasitic websites contain nothing of real value to visitors.

One such type of site is called a *doorway page*. This is a web page that is low in actual content, but is instead stuffed with repeating keywords and phrases designed to increase the page's search rank. As you might suspect, doorway pages contain little or no original content; they're typically optimized for a number of terms that aren't connected to the site's primary content.

Doorway pages often require visitors to click a "click here to enter" link to enter the main website. In other instances, visitors to a doorway page are quickly redirected to another page.

Another approach is the so-called *link farm*, a group of web pages that all link to one another. The purpose of a link farm is to increase the number of links to a given site; because Google's PageRank is at least partially driven by the number of linked-to pages, using a link farm can make it appear as though a large number of sites are linking to a given site.

Then there are *scraper sites* that "scrape" results pages from Google and other search engines to create phony content for a website. There is no unique original content, and thus no reason for someone to actually visit this site; the scraped content is used solely to increase the site's Google search ranking.

What doorway pages, link farms, and scraper sites have in common is that they're all typically full of clickable ads. They exist to draw traffic to these ads and hopefully trick some of these visitors into clicking the ads. These sites add no value at all to the Internet; they're brazen attempts to make money by doing virtually nothing.

If this is how you intend to make your online fortunes, I'd appreciate it if you quit reading this book now; I'd rather not contribute to this activity in any way, shape, or form. This is nothing more than leeching off the Internet community, and is deservedly banned by Google and most of the major ad networks.

III

Using Google AdWords

11

Creating an Online Advertising Plan and Determining Your AdWords Budget

The first section of this book dealt with pay-per-click advertising from the website publisher's point of view, as a source of revenue. The second section of this book looks at PPC advertising from the advertiser's point of view, as a way of advertising your website, product, service, or brand.

If you run a website or blog, there are many ways to draw traffic to your site. You can optimize your site so that it ranks higher in Google search results; you can conduct email campaigns; you can roll out the public relations apparatus; and you can advertise.

When it comes to this last approach, there are many different types of advertising you can do, from display ads to video ads to pay-per-click ads—the same type of ads you can display on your website to generate revenue. PPC advertising is perhaps the most popular type of web-based advertising, and Google AdWords is the largest PPC advertising program.

Many companies and websites combine PPC advertising with search engine marketing and other online marketing in a holistic online marketing campaign. All these types of advertising are closely connected, after all—and the combination of the various approaches increases your chances of reaching potential customers and increasing site traffic.

Getting to Know Google AdWords

Google AdWords is the flip side of Google AdSense. It's a network for web advertisers, where Google sells all the AdSense ads it places—both on users' sites and on its own search results pages. In this respect, AdWords essentially serves as an ad broker, arranging ads from individual advertisers and then placing those ads on their own and on third-party websites.

Just as Google is the largest search engine, Google AdWords is far and away the largest PPC ad network. Google claims that its AdWords program reaches more than 80% of all Internet users; most advertisers confirm that AdWords generates the overwhelming majority of PPC traffic to their sites.

The relationship between AdWords and AdSense works like this:

1. An advertiser purchases one or more keywords via Google's AdWords program.

2. That ad is displayed on websites that subscribe to Google's AdSense program—if the site's content matches the keywords purchased. (The ad is also displayed on Google search results pages when someone searches for the purchased keywords.)

3. The advertiser pays Google (AdWords) when someone clicks on the ad.

4. Google (AdSense) pays the host website a portion of the ad revenues collected from the advertiser.

PPC Advertising: A Quick Review

We've discussed pay-per-click advertising a lot in the first part of this book, in relation to Google's AdSense programs for website publishers. But just in case you skipped the first ten chapters, here's a quick overview of what PPC advertising is and how it works—from the advertiser's perspective.

PPC advertising isn't like the traditional display advertising you might do in newspapers or magazines. At its core, PPC ads aren't about display space to promote a brand or product, but rather about placing a targeted message in front of the customers who are most interested in the topic. The ads are, more often than not, text ads rather than image ads; you don't pay for the space, but rather when a customer clicks on the ad.

It all starts when a PPC advertiser purchases a particular keyword or phrase from the ad network—in this instance, Google AdWords. The advertiser then creates a small text ad that relates to this keyword. That text ad is displayed in two different places.

Learn more about PPC keywords in Chapter 16, "Choosing the Right Keywords."

The display of the PPC ad occurs when a user enters a query on Google's search engine. The advertiser's ad is displayed on the first page of the search results, in the "sponsored links" section, either on the top or side of the page. As you can see in

Figure 11.1, the ad is designed to look kind of like an organic search result; it kind of blends into the search results.

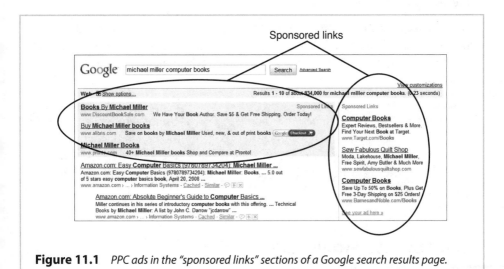

Figure 11.1   *PPC ads in the "sponsored links" sections of a Google search results page.*

The second place the ad appears is on third-party sites that belong to Google's AdSense network. (As you can see, AdSense and AdWords are related programs, the first displaying ads sold by the second.) The ad is placed on specific pages that have content that relates to the purchased keyword. These ads, primarily text-only (as you can see in Figure 11.2), can appear anywhere on the given page; the ad placement is up to the owner of the web page.

Figure 11.2   *PPC ads on a third-party web page, courtesy of Google's AdSense network.*

Learn more about the AdSense program for web publishers in Part 2 of this book, "Using Google AdSense."

To serve these content-focused ads, Google employs the same search technology it uses to provide its own search results. For advertisers, this means that the ads you place will be displayed alongside content (either search results or page content) that relates to the keywords you purchased. This is a good thing, as an ad that is somehow related to the content of a web page reaches a more targeted audience than a more broadly focused display ad—and results in higher click-throughs and presumably more sales.

As you'll recall, the reason these are called pay-per-click ads is that the advertiser pays Google only when customers click on the link in the ad. If no one clicks, you don't pay Google anything; of course, the more clicks that are registered, the more you pay.

Here's something important to know about PPC advertising—your ad probably won't appear on every search engine results page for the keyword you purchase. The page inventory is limited, while advertisers are theoretically unlimited. Google rotates ads from multiple advertisers on its search results and third-party pages.

What You Can Advertise

Okay, you know how PPC advertising works. You also know how you can use it to make money from your website. But how can you use PPC advertising as an advertiser—that is, what exactly can you advertise with PPC ads?

The answer is simple: You can advertise just about anything using PPC ads. Here's the broad list:

- **Your website.** Probably the most common purpose for PPC advertising is just to drive traffic to a website. The target website may or may not have products or services available for sale; conversion typically isn't the goal—increasing traffic is.

- **Products you have for sale.** If you have products for sale, PPC advertising can drive potential customers to your site, where they can purchase those products. In this instance, conversion (from clicks to direct sales) is the goal.

- **Services you offer for sale.** Just as you can use PPC advertising to sell products, you can also use it to sell services on your website. This includes, by the way, subscription services, whether they be website subscriptions or subscriptions to other types of services.

- **Sales leads.** Some websites don't sell products directly, but rather collect email or postal addresses to use as sales leads. Just as you can use PPC advertising to sell products, you can also use it to drive potential customers to your website and then capture their contact information.

- **Your company or brand.** Although PPC advertising is arguably better suited for traffic building and direct sales, many companies use PPC advertising as brand or image advertising. In this instance, the ads entice interested consumers to click to a website where the company's message is presented, in various ways.

As I said, you can use PPC advertising for just about any promotional purpose. And the largest PPC advertising network is Google AdWords—which places ads on Google's search results pages.

 LET ME TRY IT

How AdWords Works

Google AdWords embraces the now traditional PPC ad model. As an advertiser, you pay for (actually bid on) one or more keywords. Your ads appear on Google search results pages when those keywords are searched for, or on third-party pages that contain content related to those keywords. You pay for each click on your ads; if nobody clicks, you don't pay anything. (Of course, you also don't generate any traffic—which means your advertising isn't working.)

The process is actually quite easy, and it goes something like this:

1. Sign up for the AdWords program.

2. Write the ad (a title line and a few lines of text).

3. Enter the URL of the page on your site that you want to link to.

4. Choose the keyword(s) you want to purchase—up to 20 keywords or phrases (you can add more keywords and phrases after you create your ad).

5. Set the maximum you're willing to pay per click.

6. Set your monthly AdWords budget—Google recommends a $50 monthly minimum.

 SHOW ME   Media 11.1—A video about how AdWords works
Access this video file through your registered Web Edition at
my.safaribooksonline.com/9780131388666/media.

After your ad campaign is started, you can monitor performance from the AdWords dashboard. From here you can view your campaign's performance, generate various reports, create new ads, and access Google Analytics for additional performance tracking.

How Google Makes Money

If you follow Google at all, you might wonder how this multi-billion-dollar company makes all its money, given that its primary site (the Google search site) is free for all to use. The answer is that Google doesn't intend to make money from search, at least directly; it makes its money by selling advertising, through the AdWords program.

It should come as no surprise that the three top PPC ad networks are run by the three top Internet search engine companies—Google, Yahoo!, and Microsoft. All of these companies give away search but charge for advertising on their search results pages (and on other sites, of course). In this regard, the search engines are merely containers for revenue-generating advertising, much as the articles in traditional magazines and newspapers are just filler between the advertisements that actually pay the rent.

So Google makes virtually all its money from the AdWords program, one click at a time. Its namesake search engine is there primarily to host these ads. All of which makes Google more like a traditional media company than a true technology company; everything it does is in service to its ad network.

How does that affect you? Well, it's important to know with whom you're dealing. In the case of Google AdWords, you're dealing with the Internet's largest ad network, as well as with the largest host site for Internet advertising—Google's main search site. Google devotes its rather substantial resources to finding new places to display advertising—which gives it more advertising space to sell. And while you could advertise with one of the smaller PPC ad networks, advertising with AdWords gets you placement on www.google.com—the Internet's number-one website, period.

 TELL ME MORE   **Media 11.2—A discussion about how Google makes money**
Access this audio recording through your registered Web Edition at
my.safaribooksonline.com/9780131388666/media.

Developing an Online Marketing Plan

PPC advertising is an important part of any online marketing campaign—but it isn't the only marketing you can or should do. It's only one component of a well-rounded online marketing plan; you need to construct a marketing plan that recognizes the impact of PPC advertising while still mining the benefits of other types of marketing.

What we're talking about, of course, is creating an online marketing plan for your organization that revolves around PPC advertising but doesn't depend solely on it. That's a challenge for any marketer today, especially with new and exciting channels to exploit.

Understanding the Components of an Online Marketing Plan

How do you market your business online? You can't just put up a website and hope that potential customers will trip over it. No, you have to reach deep into your bag of marketing tricks to attract customers online, sway them in your direction, and persuade them to purchase whatever it is you're selling. (Or simply increase your brand awareness, if that's your game.)

Fortunately, there are many tools you can use to promote your business online—some you're no doubt familiar with, others that might be new to you. Let's see what you have to work with.

 SHOW ME   Media 11.3—A video about how to get started developing an online marketing plan
Access this video file through your registered Web Edition at
my.safaribooksonline.com/9780131388666/media.

Pay-Per-Click Advertising

We'll start with the marketing tool that drove you to read this book—pay-per-click advertising. There are three primary PPC advertising networks today, all connected with the web's largest search engines:

* Google AdWords (adwords.google.com)

* Yahoo! Sponsored Search (advertising.yahoo.com/smallbusiness/ysm)

* Microsoft adCenter (adcenter.microsoft.com)

Most companies devote a large part of their online marketing budget to this popular form of advertising. But how much of *your* mix should you devote to PPC advertising?

It depends. Although it's unlikely that PPC ads will drive as much traffic to your site as will organic search engine results, which we'll discuss next, it can still be an effective part of your mix. There is always some percentage of searchers who will either confuse paid results with organic results, thus benefiting PPC advertisers, or who trust the paid results much the same way they trust display ads in traditional Yellow Pages directories.

PPC advertising can also be beneficial if you compete in a niche with some very influential targeted websites. Find out which ad networks those sites use, and place your ads with those networks. Purchasing the right keywords will almost guarantee placement for your ads on those sites, which should generate some very targeted traffic.

Display Advertising

PPC ads are small, targeted, text ads, which should not be confused with more traditional display ads. Display ads, such as the one in Figure 11.3, are those banner ads that you see at the top (and sometimes along the sides) of web pages. These banner ads combine text and graphics (and sometimes videos and Flash animations), much the same way that display ads work in printed media.

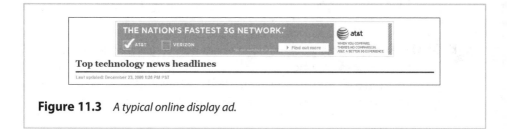

Figure 11.3   *A typical online display ad.*

Although most display ads are clickable, thus facilitating the type of direct marketing common with all-text PPC ads, they're most often used for brand-building purposes, or to reinforce aspects of a larger marketing campaign. As such, you tend to see large national advertisers go the display ad route, instead of engaging in the guerrilla marketing common with text ads.

The problem with display advertising, as compared to search engine marketing or PPC advertising, is that the click-through rates are much, much lower. Most people see a display ad and move right past it. Even if the ad registers, they don't bother to click through, which results in click-through rates in the low single digits. Of course, if you purchase space on enough high-traffic websites, even that low click-through rate can generate significant traffic. And, let us not forget, users can still receive your ad message even if they don't click the ad.

That said, display advertising is one of the fastest-growing parts of the online marketing mix, especially as big national advertisers slowly but surely move onto the Internet. If you have a message for a mass audience, and the corresponding budget, this might be a way to go.

Search Engine Marketing

Advertising aside, the most effective online marketing tool for most businesses is search engine marketing. In a nutshell, search engine marketing is the art (or science) of driving traffic to your site from Google and the other major search engines.

Unlike traditional advertising (including PPC advertising), search engine marketing doesn't purchase results. A marketer doesn't pay the search engines anything to get listed, nor for specific results. You don't pay for space or rank or clicks.

Technically, PPC advertising is part of search engine marketing. That is, search engine marketing includes both optimizing organic search results and paying for "sponsored" listings in those search results—both activities that drive traffic to your site from the major search engines.

Instead, search engine results occur organically. If you do your job right designing your website, users searching for the right topic will see your website among the top search results. That results in click-throughs to your site, which you ideally convert into customers, revenues, and profits.

The key to effective search engine marketing, then, is ensuring that your site ranks high enough in the search results to get noticed by potential customers—higher, most certainly than your competitors. The higher your site's search ranking, the more traffic you create—and the more effective your search engine marketing.

You improve your site's search ranking by employing search engine optimization techniques. In essence, you want to optimize your site so that it appears as high as possible in the search engine rankings. Because you can't directly buy your way to the top of the results, you have to improve your rankings organically, by making your site as authoritative and relevant as possible.

You see, the majority of traffic for most websites comes not from direct URL entry, links from other websites, or even PPC advertising. Instead, the bulk of new traffic comes from queries made at Google, Yahoo!, and the other search engines. For this reason, most companies devote a large part of their marketing budget to search engine optimization. It's not the only thing you should do to market your business online, but it might be the most important thing.

⊕ *Learn more about search engine marketing and SEO in Chapter 18, "Combining PPC Advertising with Search Engine Marketing."*

Email Marketing

Many firms also find success with email marketing. An email marketing campaign involves the sending of targeted email messages to a company's existing customer base; these emails can advertise upcoming promotions, new products, and the like.

> Don't confuse email marketing with spam emails. Legitimate email marketing is sent only with prior approval by the customer; spam is unsolicited and typically unwanted email.

Most email marketing is a form of direct marketing. You're using the emails not to increase brand awareness or simply drive traffic to your website, but rather to solicit direct sales of a particular product or service. As such, email marketing has appeal to many types of companies, especially those with aggressive direct sales operations. It's relatively low-cost (especially compared to traditional postal-based direct marketing), it's fast, it's targeted, and it's easily trackable.

Successful online merchants use email marketing to entice more sales from their existing customer base. If you offer goods or services for sale over the web, email marketing should be an essential part of your marketing mix.

Blog Marketing

Blogs are becoming more important to savvy online marketers—especially those that recognize that a company blog can be an effective channel of communication between a company and its customers. In this regard, blogs let companies talk to and with their customer base; they can use the blog to convey the company's message, or to solicit input from interested customers. It's a great way to research what's on the minds of your most active customers.

Because hosting and posting to a blog are relatively inexpensive (the biggest expense is the time to manage the blog), company blogs are especially valuable to small and budget-conscious organizations. As such, an internal blog can be a valuable component of a company's overall online marketing mix.

Of course, you can also use public relations techniques to market your products and services through third-party blogs. The goal here is to get your company or product in front of influential bloggers; when a well-read blogger mentions your company or product, that's like free advertising to all of that blog's readers.

Social Media Marketing

The newest type of online marketing is social media marketing—exploiting social networks and social bookmarking services to bring visibility to your company, brand, or product. We're talking communities like Facebook (www.facebook.com), MySpace (www.myspace.com), and Twitter (www.twitter.com)—huge communities of interconnected users.

Although you can place display ads on all these sites, a more effective approach is to create a profile page for your business and use that page to announce upcoming products, promotions, and events. Naturally, your profile page should include links back to your company's website—or, even better, a landing page customized for your "friends" on that social network.

Marketing to social networks is low-cost but resource-intensive. To be effective, you have to spend lots of time on the social network sites, participating in various communities and actively seeking new friends. If you don't work the community, this type of effort is likely to fail.

Online PR

Which brings us to the topic of online public relations. In some aspects, online PR is no different from traditional PR; you're trying to get as many outlets as possible to mention your latest product or service. But online PR involves many new and different channels you need to address, from blogs and social networks to topic-oriented communities and message boards. It's not as simple as sending out a hard copy press release.

To that end, blog and social media marketing are just different types of online PR. When you cultivate relationships with influential bloggers, for example, you're engaging in a public relations activity. You get your best results not by sending out an electronic press release, but by making friends with individual bloggers and actively participating in targeted online communities.

It goes without saying that public relations is always a key part of a company's marketing mix. That remains so when we're talking about the online marketing mix—which has to include online PR.

Making All the Elements of Your Online Marketing Plan Work Together

For most companies, PPC advertising will not be the only component of their online marketing plan. Most companies will also engage in some combination of search engine marketing, online display advertising, email marketing, blog marketing, social media marketing, and online public relations.

Knowing this, it's important that all components of your marketing mix mesh with each other. They should all carry the same message; you don't want to present one image to the search engines, another to customers viewing display ads, and yet another to blogs and social media through your PR activities. Your message should be consistent, no matter where customers encounter that message.

What does that mean, in reality?

First, it means that the way you define your business has to be consistent. The keywords you choose as part of your website's search engine optimization should also be the keywords you purchase for your PPC advertising, should also be key words in the copy for your display ads, should also be highlighted in the promotional emails you send to customers, should also be talking points when you communicate with influential bloggers, and should also be present in the electronic press releases you send to online news organizations. You can't describe your business one way in press releases, another way in advertisements, and yet another way to the search engines—you must have a consistent message.

That extends to using themes and images from your display advertising on your website—especially in the landing pages you create for your search engine and email marketing campaigns. When someone clicks the URL in a promotional email, they should land on a page that not only repeats the message of the email, but also mirrors the look and feel of your display advertising. Again, consistency is the key.

The need for consistency between different types of advertising doesn't mean that you can't adapt the message for the medium. PPC ads, for example, demand much less copy than do promotional emails and landing web pages. Your message and image have to reflect how they're being delivered; given the unique qualities of each online medium, you can't be a slave to consistency.

The point is, all of your online media need to work together. They have to convey a consistent message and image, and should not send conflicting messages to your customer base. Your online marketing mix should be a consistent whole that is greater than the sum of its parts.

Driving your consistent message is your intimate knowledge of the market and your customers—your ability to *think like the customer*. This insight helps you select the right keywords for your PPC advertising and search engine marketing, as well as informs the messages and images you send in your display advertising and public relations efforts.

Determining Your AdWords Budget

Now that you know that PPC advertising should be just one element of your online marketing place, how much of your budget should you devote to PPC advertising? As with all marketing-related activities, it depends.

Understanding CPC and CPM

Advertising with Google AdWords isn't like a traditional advertising buy; there are no contracts and deadlines and such. You pay a one-time $5 activation fee, and then are charged either on a cost-per-click (CPC) or cost-per-thousand-impressions (CPM) basis. (You can choose either payment method.) You control your costs by specifying how much you're willing to pay (per click or per impression) and by setting a daily spending budget. Google will never exceed the costs you specify; if you give Google a $100 budget, it will run only $100 worth of ads.

How much does AdWords cost? That's up to you, really. If you go with the CPC method, you can choose a maximum CPC price—anywhere from $0.01 to $100 per click. If you go with the CPM method, there is a minimum cost of $0.25 per 1,000 impressions. Your daily budget can be as low as a penny, up to whatever you're willing to pay.

With the CPC option, the rate is determined by the popularity of and competition for the keyword purchased, as well as the quality and quantity of traffic going to the site hosting the ad. As you can imagine, popular keywords have a higher CPC, while less popular keywords can be had for less.

If you go the CPC route, Google uses special technology, dubbed AdWords Discounter, to match the price you pay with the price offered by competing advertisers for a given keyword. The AdWords Discounter automatically monitors your competition and lowers your CPC to one cent above what they're willing to pay.

As is now apparent, this process is actually a form of auction, and advertisers are essentially bidding on the most popular keywords. For example, you might say you'll pay up to $5 for a given keyword. If you're the high bidder among several advertisers, your ads will appear more frequently on pages that contain that keyword. If you're not the high bidder, you won't get as much visibility—if your ad appears at all.

You can opt to prepay your advertising costs, or to pay after your ads start running. With this last option (the most popular way to pay), Google charges you after 30 days or when you reach your initial credit limit of $50, whichever comes first. Even small advertisers can participate, as Google accepts payment via credit card, debit card, direct debit, or bank transfer.

Determining Your Total Budget

So how much money should you devote to PPC advertising? Perhaps the better question is, how much can you afford?

First, know that AdWords requires you to submit a *daily* budget—that is, how much money you're willing to spend per day. Because you probably don't budget per day, you'll have to take your normal monthly or yearly budget and divide it by the appropriate number of days. This is your daily AdWords maximum. (For example, if you have a $1,500 monthly advertising budget, divide $1,500 by 30 days to get a $50 daily budget.)

Second, know that more is better than less. Now, you'd expect Google to say this; they make more money when you have a larger budget. But it's really a matter of exposure. If you have a large budget, your ads will show up on a larger number of search results and third-party pages; the more often your ad appears, the more traffic you'll generate. In addition, you'll be creating additional exposure; even if users don't click on your ad the first time they see it, by the third or fourth exposure, you've created some brand awareness. If your ads appear only a total of a few times per day, you just won't gain any traction.

When you create your campaign, Google will suggest a budget for you. Believe it or not, this isn't a bad number. The key point is if you budget *under* Google's recommended number, your ads will display only occasionally. It's best to budget at or above Google's suggested level.

And remember, if your ads are working—that is, if they're generating an acceptable click-through rate—you'll make more money the more ads you run. There should be a direct correlation between the number of ads, and thus your ad budget, and your sales level. Up your budget and you up your sales. It's really that simple.

Of course, you probably don't want to take this to an illogical extreme. If you're generating $1,000 in sales from $100 in advertising, don't immediately up your budget to $1,000,000 in expectation of generating $10,000,000 in sales. There are a lot of other factors involved; besides, you probably couldn't handle that sort of sales level, at least not overnight. Starting slow and seeing what happens is always a good strategy.

Your AdWords budget and your actual "spend" probably won't be the same. That is, you could budget $100 a day but Google might only place $50 (or $10) worth of ads. This is a factor of bidding against other companies for keywords (you don't always win the bidding) and the popularity of the keywords themselves; if no one is searching for a given keyword, there won't be any ads to display.

Having said all this, if you're budgeting less than $10 per day, you're probably wasting your money. You need to budget at least that much to make any impression whatsoever; spend less than that and you won't have any visibility. For example, if you budget $2 per day and bid $0.50 per click, Google will display only four ads maximum—which are likely all to be displayed early in the day. (That's right, you can use up your budget in the morning, with no money left to fund ads later in the day.)

In fact, this is the biggest trap for new AdWords advertisers—setting too low a daily budget. Remember, your ads appear when people search on a keyword you've purchased; if hundreds or thousands of people are searching for that keyword, a $2 budget won't go far at all. Choose a bigger budget (and a lower CPC) and you'll run more ads throughout the day.

In reality, $10 per day might not be enough. Some experts recommend spending at least $100 per day—although that would put AdWords beyond the reach of many small advertisers.

Still, you can't spend more than you can afford. Determine how much money you can afford to spend on advertising and set your AdWords budget accordingly. You can always ramp up your spending if and when your sales increase. What you can't do is spend money you don't have.

12

Creating Your AdWords Account

If you want to advertise with AdWords, the first stop is to create your AdWords account. There's a bit involved with this, as AdWords offers two types of accounts—Starter and Standard editions. Choosing the right edition is important, as is understanding AdWords' account structure and organizing your account accordingly.

So read on to learn how to get started with AdWords. It's something everybody has to do—once.

Signing Up for AdWords

Everything you do with AdWords takes places on the AdWords website, located at adwords.google.com. As you can see in Figure 12.1, until you sign up or sign in, this home page is a gateway to everything about AdWords, and contains links to a lot of useful information; you should feel free to click around and learn more before you get started.

After you've created your AdWords account, you can sign into that account from the adwords.google.com page. Just enter your email address and password into the appropriate blanks, and then click the Sign In button.

 TELL ME MORE   Media 12.1—A discussion about why you should advertise your website
Access this audio recording through your registered Web Edition at
my.safaribooksonline.com/9780131388666/media.

Google AdWords   Change Language: English ▾

Advertise your business on Google
No matter what your budget, you can display your ads on Google and our
advertising network. Pay only if people click your ads.

Start now »

Your ads appear beside
related search results...

People click
your ads...

...And connect
to your business

Sign in to Google AdWords with your
Google Account

Your ad here
See your ad on Google
and our partner sites.
www.your-company-site.com

Email:
Password:

☑ Stay signed in
Sign in

Can't access your account?

Learn about AdWords

How it works

Reach more customers

Costs and payment

For local businesses

Success stories

You create your ads
You create ads and choose keywords, which are words
or phrases related to your business. Get keyword ideas

Your ads appear on Google
When people search on Google using one of your
keywords, your ad may appear next to the search
results. Now you're advertising to an audience that's
already interested in you.

Keywords are what people search
for on Google.

Figure 12.1   *The AdWords gateway page.*

 **LET ME TRY IT**

Create an AdWords Account

Creating an AdWords account is an involved process, but it's something you'll have
to do only once. Follow these steps:

1. From the AdWords gateway page (adwords.google.com), click the Start
   Now button.

2. When the next page appears, as shown in Figure 12.2, specify whether you
   have an existing Google or AdSense account or want to create a new one.

3. If you already have a Google/AdSense account, opt to use that account for
   AdWords, enter your email address and password, and then click Continue.

4. If you don't already have a Google/AdSense account, enter your email
   address, select a password, and then click the Create Account button.

5. You're now prompted to select your time zone and currency. Do so and then
   click Continue.

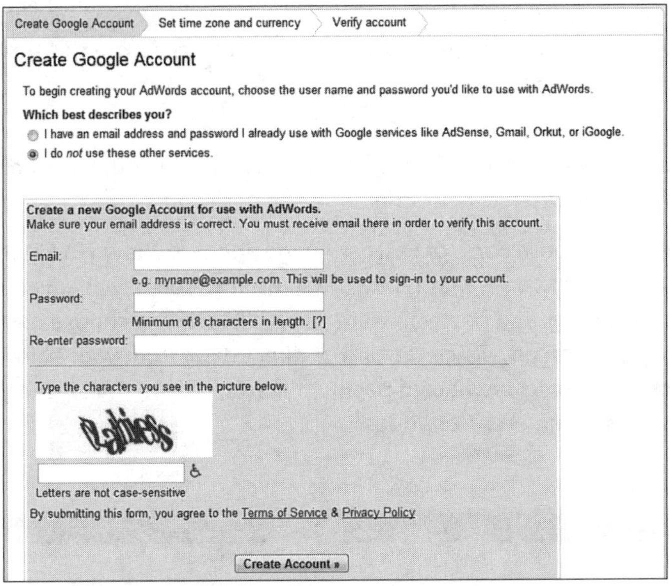

Create Google Account ⟩ Set time zone and currency ⟩ Verify account ⟩

Create Google Account

To begin creating your AdWords account, choose the user name and password you'd like to use with AdWords.

Which best describes you?

○ I have an email address and password I already use with Google services like AdSense, Gmail, Orkut, or iGoogle.

◉ I do *not* use these other services.

Create a new Google Account for use with AdWords.
Make sure your email address is correct. You must receive email there in order to verify this account.

Email: [   ]
e.g. myname@example.com. This will be used to sign-in to your account.

Password: [   ]
Minimum of 8 characters in length. [?]

Re-enter password: [   ]

Type the characters you see in the picture below.

[   ] ♿

Letters are not case-sensitive
By submitting this form, you agree to the Terms of Service & Privacy Policy

[**Create Account »**]

Figure 12.2 *Signing up for the AdWords program.*

SHOW ME Media 12.2—A video about how to sign up for AdWords

Access this video file through your registered Web Edition at my.safaribooksonline.com/9780131388666/media.

LET ME TRY IT

Entering Billing Information

That's it—you're now signed up for the AdWords program. But you're not quite done yet. You still need to enter your billing information, so Google will know how to bill you for the ads you run. Follow these steps:

1. Go to adwords.google.com and sign into your AdWords account.

2. You now see the AdWords home page. Click the Billing tab and select Billing Preferences.

Chances are you'll also see a red box at the top of the home page, asking you to submit your payment information. You can also click the link in this box to go to the Account Setup page.

3. When the Account Setup page appears, select your country from the pull-down list and then click Continue.

4. When the Choose Form of Payment page appears, shown in Figure 12.3, select whether you want prepay billing (that is, you pay in advance) or postpay billing, and how you want to be billed. If you choose postpay billing, you can pay via credit card or direct debit from your bank account; for prepay billing, credit card payment is your only option. Make your choice and then click Continue.

| Home | Campaigns | Opportunities | Reporting ▾ | Billing ▾ | My account ▾ |

Account Setup

Choose form of payment > Agree to terms > Provide billing details

Tell us how you would like to pay for your ads.
Select a single payment method from the list below. Please choose carefully. If you later decide to change your <u>payment options</u>, and you've already started your ads, you may have to set up a new account.

Note that you'll have a chance later in the sign-up process to enter any promotional code you may have received, but you'll still have to enter your billing information to complete setup. ⑦

Postpay Billing - After you receive clicks, we automatically charge your card or account.

   ○ Direct Debit   Bank account payments (US bank accounts only)
                         Payments directly debited from your bank account without credit card limits or late fees.

                         Important notes:
                         - By selecting this option you are confirming that you are an AdWords business customer. ⑦
                         - You *must* have an active bank account to process a payment.

   ○ Credit Card   American Express, JCB, MasterCard, Visa, and debit cards with a MasterCard or Visa logo

Prepay Billing - As you receive clicks, the cost is deducted from a prepaid balance.

   ○ Credit Card   American Express, JCB, MasterCard, Visa, and debit cards with a MasterCard or Visa logo

Note: You will pay Google AdWords for the ads you run. For details, read '<u>Understanding AdWords.</u>'

[« Back] [Continue »]

Figure 12.3 *Choosing the way you'll pay.*

5. When the next page appears, read the terms of service, check that you've agreed to them, and then click Continue.

6. On the Provide Billing Details page, enter the requested information about your credit card or bank account, and then click Save and Activate.

Your AdWords account is now ready to use—and you're ready to start your first campaign!

Exploring the AdWords Site

When you log onto the AdWords site, you see the AdWords home page. This page consists of a series of tabs; click each tab to access the related tasks and services.

Here's what you'll find on each tab:

- **Home.** This is the tab you see by default when you access the AdWords site. This tab displays your Account Snapshot, shown in Figure 12.4, a summary of key account information.

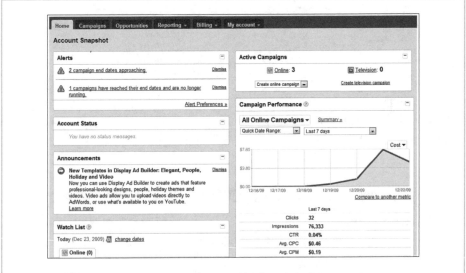

Figure 12.4   *Viewing your Account Snapshot on the AdWords Home tab.*

- **Campaigns.** This tab, shown in Figure 12.5, is where you create your AdWords ads and manage your ongoing campaigns.

- **Opportunities.** As you can see in Figure 12.6, this tab includes advice and ideas for how to improve your AdWords performance, as well as tools to help you manage your account.

- **Reporting.** This is actually a series of tabs; when you click the Reporting tab, you see a menu of available reporting options.

- **Billing.** Click this tab to access either your Billing Summary or Billing Preferences.

- **My Account.** Click this tab to view your Account Preferences or edit Account Access—that is, to invite others to co-manage your AdWords account.

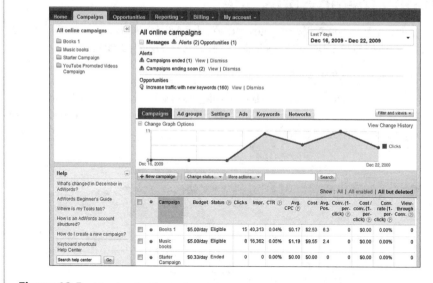

Figure 12.5 *Viewing the Campaigns tab.*

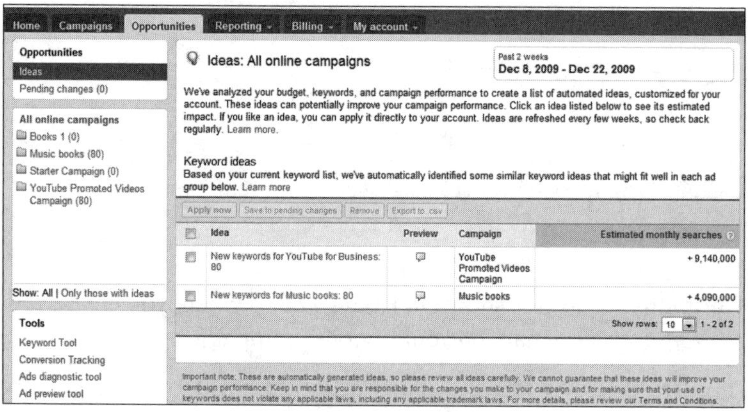

Figure 12.6 *Viewing ideas and tools on the Opportunities tab.*

SHOW ME Media 12.3—A video about the AdWords site
Access this video file through your registered Web Edition at
my.safaribooksonline.com/9780131388666/media.

When you want to get started creating your first ad, you go to the Campaigns tab. Here you get to define a new campaign, the ad groups within the campaign, and the individual ads in each ad group. If these terms sound a bit confusing, don't despair; we'll discuss exactly what they mean—and what you need to do to get started—in Chapter 13, "Creating Your First AdWords Campaign."

13

Creating Your First AdWords Campaign

An AdWords ad doesn't exist unto itself. No, each ad you create is part of a larger ad group, which in itself is part of a larger ad campaign. Your AdWords account can consist of multiple campaigns, each campaign can consist of multiple ad groups, and each ad group can consist of multiple ads.

As such, before you create any individual ads, you need to develop your AdWords account structure—which campaigns you want to run, and which ad groups should exist within those campaigns. Then you can create your first campaign, and then the individual ads for that campaign.

Understanding Campaigns and Ad Groups

Chances are, when you think of your AdWords account, you think of things like your login information, contact info, and billing info—the stuff we discussed in Chapter 12, "Creating Your AdWords Account." But to Google, your AdWords account is more than that—it consists not only of your key information, but also the various ads and campaigns you create.

To that end, your AdWords account is structured like a pyramid with three levels. From top to bottom, these levels include the following:

- **Account.** Your account is at the very top of the pyramid, and is associated with a unique email address, password, and billing information.

- **Campaign.** An ad campaign consists of multiple ads related to a specific topic or category. Each campaign has its own budget and targeting options, including start and end dates, a daily budget, cost-per-click payments, placement preferences, target locations, and the like. A single account can, and is likely to, contain multiple campaigns.

- **Ad group.** An ad group is where your ads are located; it's a combination of one or more ads and the keywords or placement lists that trigger the display of those ads. A single campaign can include multiple ad groups.

Figure 13.1 shows all these components all fit together.

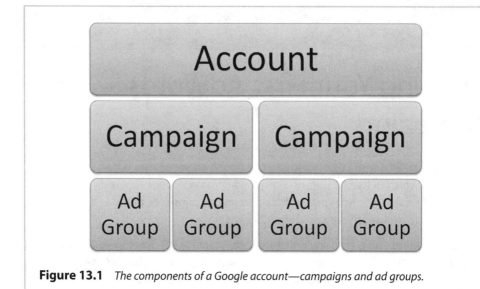

Figure 13.1   *The components of a Google account—campaigns and ad groups.*

An AdWords account can contain up to 25 campaigns. Each campaign can have up to 2,000 ad groups. Each ad group can contain up to 2,000 placements, 2,000 keywords, and 50 ads that show when those keywords are searched.

SHOW ME   **Media 13.1—A video about AdWords account structure**
Access this video file through your registered Web Edition at
my.safaribooksonline.com/9780131388666/media.

Before you create your first AdWords ad, you first have to create a campaign and an ad group in which that ad will reside. You can then create additional campaigns or ad groups to house additional ads you might create.

Each item or website you advertise should have its own unique ad group.

Structuring Your Account

You need to think through AdWords' account structure before you start creating ads and campaigns. The better structured your account, the easier it will be to determine which ads are working and which aren't—and thus fine-tune your advertising for maximum performance.

When you first create a campaign, you should determine what you want to achieve—that is, set goals for that campaign. Your goals might be stated in terms of revenue or unit sales, sales leads or subscribers, site traffic, or something similar. Whatever your goals, they should be quantifiable, in either precise numbers (25 new subscribers, $1,000 in sales, and so on) or percentage increases (25% more site traffic, a 50% sales increase, and the like).

There are many ways to structure campaigns and ad groups:

- By product line or category
- By brand
- By location or geography
- By language
- By time period

You can also structure your account along the same lines of your website. In this kind of structure, you might have different campaigns or ad groups for each major page or directory on your site.

Let's look at an example focusing on an online retailer that sells two types of consumer electronic products—computers and MP3 players. This advertiser creates two campaigns, one for each type of product. Then he creates separate ad groups for notebook and desktop computers, and for iPod and Zune MP3 players. The resulting account structure is shown in Figure 13.2.

In this example, the two campaigns (for computers and MP3 players) have their own daily budgets, target locations, and start and end dates. For example, you might budget $100 a day for your MP3 player campaign and have it last 30 days; you might budget $500 a day for your computer campaign and have it last 45 days. You would also specify unique cost-per-click ranges for each campaign.

Within each of the two campaigns, the individual ad groups have their own unique ads, triggered by their own sets of keywords. So, you'd create one ad group for notebook PCs and another ad group for desktop PCs, and have them triggered by unique sets of keywords.

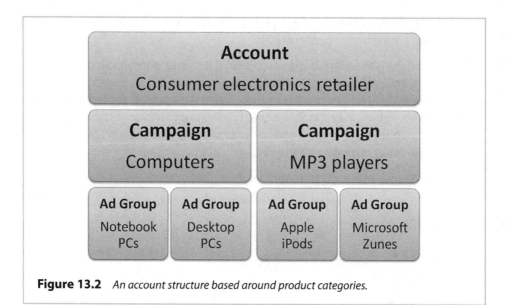

Figure 13.2   *An account structure based around product categories.*

What you don't want to do is include ads for different products or categories within the same ad group. This is because all the ads within an ad group share the same keywords. If you're advertising both perfume and flowers in the same ad group, for example, someone searching for "perfume" might see an ad for flowers—not a good match.

However you structure the account, you then create the ads and select the key-words that best match your chosen structure. At this point, it's really a matter of filling in the blanks. Structuring in this fashion is also useful when evaluating results; it's easy to compare the performance of multiple campaigns or ad groups, and thus determine which combinations are working best for you.

Understanding Campaign Parameters

Before you create your first campaign, you have to specify a number of different parameters. Once specified, these parameters apply to all the ad groups and ads within that campaign.

You need to work out your strategy for each of these options before you create the campaign. Of course, you can always change these settings at a later date, after your campaign has returned some useful results. And it's always good to fine-tune your campaign based on real-world performance.

What types of parameters are we talking about? There are a bunch, and we'll look at each separately.

Name

Every campaign needs a name. You should specify a name that is somewhat descriptive of what the campaign does or what you hope to accomplish.

Locations

Here we're talking geographic locations—those areas of the country or world you want to target. You can opt to display your ads in all languages and regions, or just to users in specific geographic locations. For example, you might choose to display your ad to users in the U.S. only, or just to users who live in a specific state, or just to users who live in a particular city or ZIP code.

Choosing a specific location is the best approach for local businesses, where you don't want to attract customers from a continent away.

Demographics

AdWords lets you filter your ad by gender and age range. That is, you can choose to display to either males or females, or to people within one or more specific age group. For example, you might want to display your ad only to females between the ages of 25 to 34—Google lets you do this.

Demographic filtering is useful if you have a product or service that appeals only to one gender, or to users of a specific age group.

TELL ME MORE   Media 13.2—A discussion about demographics
Access this audio recording through your registered Web Edition at
my.safaribooksonline.com/9780131388666/media.

Networks

When most people think of AdWords, they think of text ads displayed on Google's search results pages. But Google's search pages are just part of the AdWords network; you can display your ads in any or all of the following places:

- Google's search pages
- Google's search partners
- Google's affiliate sites (third-party websites that are part of the AdSense program)

You can opt to display on all these parts of the network, on some of them, or just on selected affiliated websites of your choosing. For example, you might choose to display on Google's search pages and search partners only, forgoing display on third-party sites. Or, you might skip Google's search pages and display only on third-party content pages. It's your choice.

> You'll pay a lower CPC on affiliated sites in the network, as compared to ads on the Google search site itself—although, you'll likely experience a lower click-through rate as well.

Devices

If you're like me, you're a little computer-centric; when you think of web-based ads, you envision them viewed in a web browser on a personal computer of some sort. But more and more Internet access is happening on iPhones and other mobile devices, and Google recognizes this.

For that reason, Google lets you specify on which types of devices you want your ads to appear. You can display your ads on computers only or on mobile devices (such as the iPhone) only, or on all devices.

> You might want to choose the mobile devices-only option if you offer a service designed for travelers or people on the go.

Bidding

This is a very important part of the campaign setup process—what price you want to pay for your ads. Google lets you bid for clicks either manually or automatically; the automatic option attempts to maximize the number of clicks you get for your target budget.

> For most advertisers, the Automatic option is the better way to go, as it lets Google bid the appropriate amount for each click, up to but never exceeding the bid limit you enter. With this approach, you're ensured not to overspend on any keywords, as you could if you bid a single manual amount.

You can also choose to focus your bidding on conversions or impressions, rather than clicks. Conversion bidding is good if you're trying to sell specific items directly from your ads, while impression bidding is best for image or brand-oriented ads. Click bidding remains the most common, as it's good for all types of promotion that drive traffic to your site.

If you focus on conversions, you pay on a cost-per-acquisition (CPA) basis. If you focus on impressions, you pay on a cost-per-thousand impressions (CPM) basis.

You can only use CPM (impressions) for ads on the Google content network, not on ads that display on Google search results pages.

☉ *Learn more about bidding strategies in Chapter 15, "Bidding the Right Price."*

Budget

You set a daily budget for your campaign. This is the maximum amount of money you want to spend per day for all the ads in this campaign. There is no minimum or maximum you can specify; spend enough to display a reasonable number of ads, but within the bounds of what you can afford.

Position Preference

By default, your ads can appear anywhere on the displaying pages. If you opt for manual bidding, however, you can have AdWords automatically manage your bids to target a preferred position.

Delivery Method

By default, your ads are evenly spaced over time; they'll appear over the course of a 24-hour period. If you opt for manual bidding, however, you can accelerate the ad display, so that your ads appear faster and earlier during the day.

Schedule

Naturally, you have to tell AdWords how long you want your campaign to run. To that end, you must specify the start and stop dates for your campaign.

Ad Rotation

Without an optimized rotation, all your ads are rotated more or less evenly. That is, your low performing ads appear just as often as your high performing ones do.

If you'd rather give heavier preference to your higher-performing ads, you can choose to optimize ad rotation. With this option, AdWords displays those ads with a higher click-through rate more frequently than your lower-CTR ads. (Optimized ad rotation is the default setting.)

Frequency Capping

For ads on Google's content network, a given user can see a specific ad as often as it appears. If you'd rather not overly inundate an individual user, you can employ frequency capping—that is, limit the number of times a unique user sees your ads.

> Frequency capping will expose your ad to more individual users without overexposing the ad to any given user. That said, disabling frequency capping will serve more impressions to your highest-potential customers—which theoretically could help boost the CTR and resulting sales.

 **LET ME TRY IT**

Creating a New Campaign

Creating an AdWords ad is part of a relatively drawn-out process. You first have to create a campaign, then an ad group within that campaign, and then finally you get to create the ad. This is just one reason why it's important to understand the whole campaign/ad group structure, of course—so figure out your structure before you get started.

With all that in mind, let's start by working through the steps to create a new campaign. Remember, you can have up to 25 individual campaigns running at any given time.

1. From the main AdWords page (adwords.google.com), select the Campaigns tab, shown in Figure 13.3.

2. Select the Campaigns sub-tab.

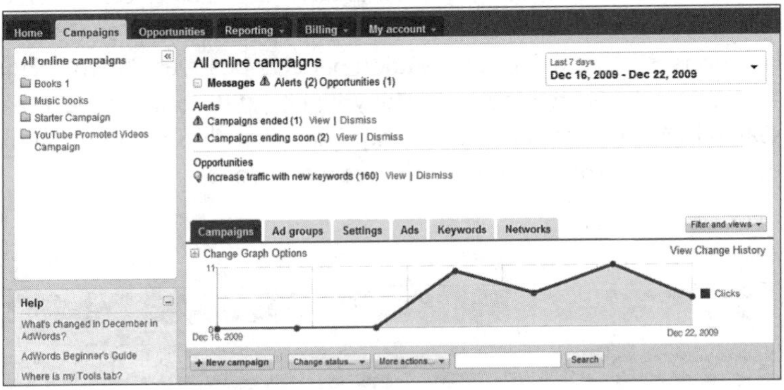

Figure 13.3   *The Campaigns tab on the AdWords site.*

3. Click the New Campaign button.

4. When the Select Campaign Settings page appears, as shown in figure 13.4, enter a name for the campaign into the Campaign Name box.

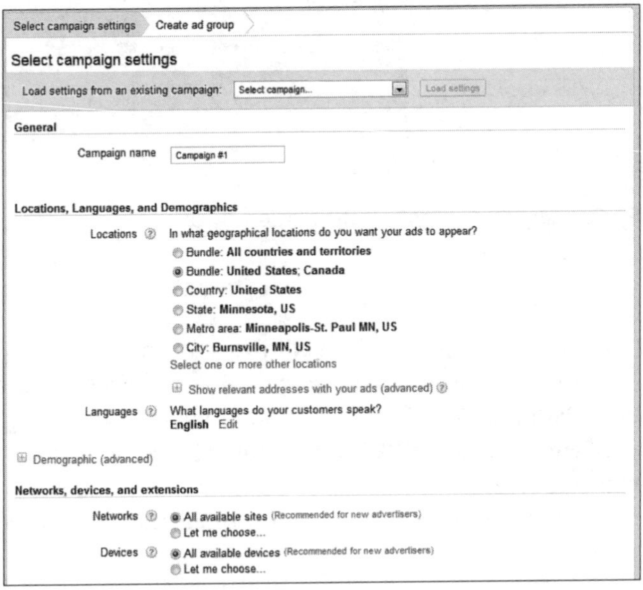

Figure 13.4   *Selecting campaign settings.*

5. In the Locations section, if you want to advertise to a more targeted area than the entire United States and Canada, click Select One or More Other Locations. When the Select a Location panel appears, as shown in Figure 13.5, select the Search tab and enter your city, state, or ZIP code into the search box. Click the Find button and then check those results that match the location you're targeting; click Save when done.

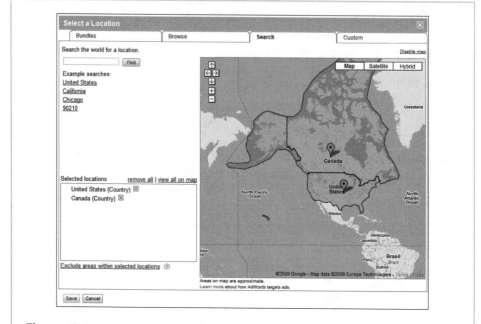

Figure 13.5 *Selecting a geographic location to display your ads.*

6. If you want to include your address with your ad and map it on Google Maps (a good idea if you're advertising locally), click Show Relevant Addresses With Your Ads. If you're a business owner with a Google Local Business Center account, click Edit to enter your proper address. To manually enter an address, click Add an Address; when the Add Business Location Information box appears, enter the appropriate information and then click Save.

7. Click the Demographic link, and then click the Edit link. When the Demographic Bidding panel appears, as shown in Figure 13.6, put a check mark next to any gender or age group you want to *exclude* from viewing your ad. Click Save when done.

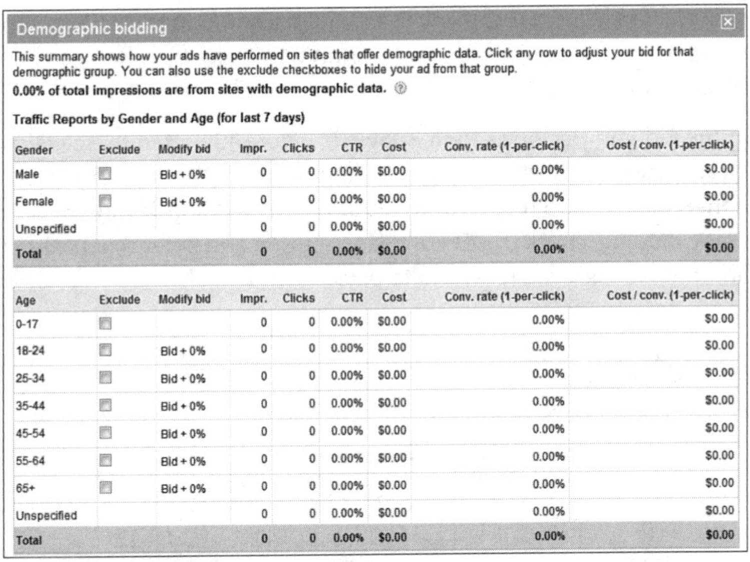

Figure 13.6   *Selecting demographic groups to display your ad to.*

8. In the Networks section, opt to advertise on All Available Sites, or click Let Me Choose. If you select this second option, the page expands as shown in Figure 13.7; from here you can opt to display your ads on Google Search, Google's Search Partners, or the Google Content Network. If you select Content Network, you can then choose to display on Relevant Pages Across the Entire Network (that is, to advertise across the full network) or on Relevant Pages Only On the Placements I Manage. If you choose this final option, use the Networks tab to select those sites where you want your ad to appear.

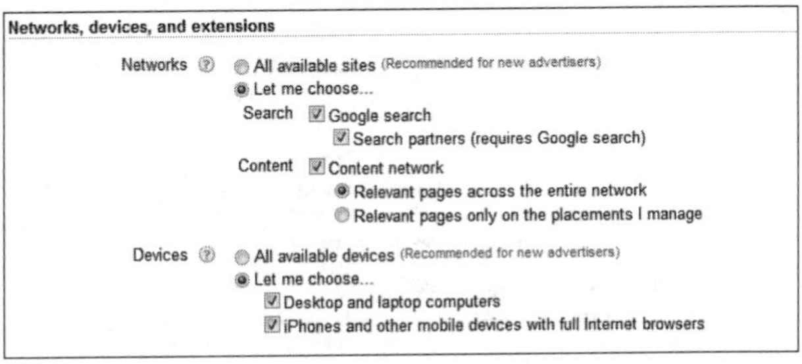

Figure 13.7   *Selecting networks and devices for your ads.*

9. In the Devices section, opt to display on All Available Devices (the default), or select Let Me Choose. If you select this second option, you can choose to display on either Desktop and Laptop Computers or iPhone and Other Mobile Devices.

10. In the Bidding Option section, shown in Figure 13.8, start by selecting Basic Options; this focuses your bidding on clicks. You can now select either Manual Bidding for Clicks or Automatic Bidding. If you select Automatic Bidding, check the CPC Bid Limit option and enter the maximum amount per click you're willing to pay.

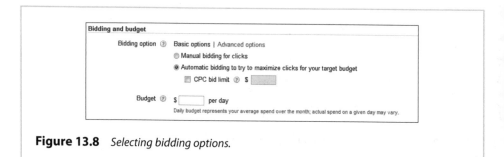

Figure 13.8   *Selecting bidding options.*

11. If you prefer to focus your bidding on either conversions (best for direct sales) or impressions (best for brand or image advertising), click the Advanced Options link in the Bidding Option then select the focus you want, as shown in Figure 13.9. Note that you can only select Focus on Impressions if your ad is *not* running on Google search or the search network. Also note that to focus on conversions, you must first set up conversion tracking, which we'll discuss later in this chapter.

12. In the Budget section, enter your daily budget—that is, the maximum amount you're willing to pay per day.

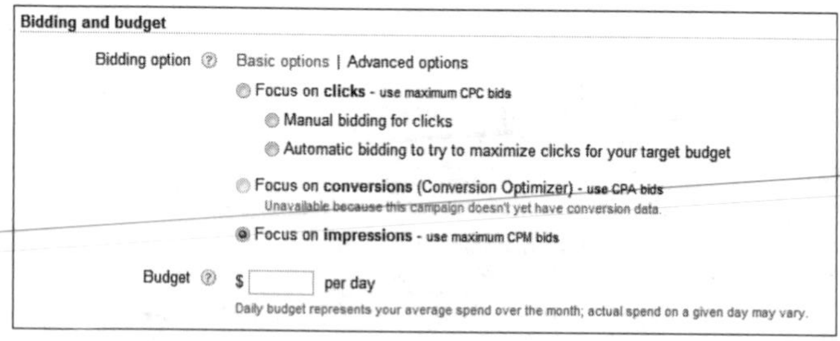

Figure 13.9   *Selecting advanced bidding options.*

13. If you selected manual bidding, you can expand the Position Preference, Delivery Method section, as shown in Figure 13.10. By default, position preference is turned off, and ads are displayed in any position on the page; turn on position preference to get a better bang for your buck, automatically managing your CPC bids to target a preferred position range. In addition, you can opt for an accelerated delivery method, where your ads are displayed earlier in the day; the default standard delivery method spreads the display of your ads over the course of the day.

> ☐ Position preference, delivery method (advanced)
>
> Position preference   ⦿ On: Automatically manage maximum CPC bids to target a preferred position range
>   ◯ Off: Show ads in any position
>
> Delivery method   ◯ Standard: Show ads evenly over time
>   ⦿ Accelerated: Show ads as quickly as possible
>
> > 💡 You may miss traffic later in the day if you choose accelerated delivery. Standard delivery is recommended for most advertisers. Learn more

Figure 13.10   *Selecting position preference and delivery method.*

> Position preference and delivery method options are not available if you selected automatic bidding.

14. In the Advanced Settings section, click the Schedule: Start Date, End Date, Ad Scheduling link. When the section expands, enter a start date and end date for your Campaign.

15. Click the Ad Delivery: Ad Rotation, Frequency Capping link. When the section expands, go to the Frequency Capping section and select either No Cap on Impressions (any given user can view an ad an unlimited number of times) or check the second option; if you check this option, enter how many impressions you want per period and per ad or ad group you want to display.

16. Click the Save and Continue button.

 SHOW ME   Media 13.3—A video about how to launch a campaign
Access this video file through your registered Web Edition at
my.safaribooksonline.com/9780131388666/media.

You've now created your first campaign. We'll stop these instructions at this point to give you a breather. The next part of the process is where you create an ad group and ad—which we discuss in Chapter 14, "Creating Effective Ads."

LET ME TRY IT

Setting Up Conversion Tracking

If you choose to focus on conversions instead of clicks when you're setting up bidding options for your campaign, you first need to set up something called
conversion tracking. This is a means of tracking the conversion of clicks to actual
sales, which is useful if the goal of your advertising is direct sales—that is, if you're
selling products or services directly from the landing page linked to from your ads.
Here's how you do it:

1. From the main AdWords page, click the Reporting tab and then select
    Conversions from the pull-down menu.

2. Select the Conversions sub-tab.

3. Click the New Conversion button.

4. This expands the Conversions sub-tab, as shown in Figure 13.11. Enter a
    name for this tracking into the Action Name box.

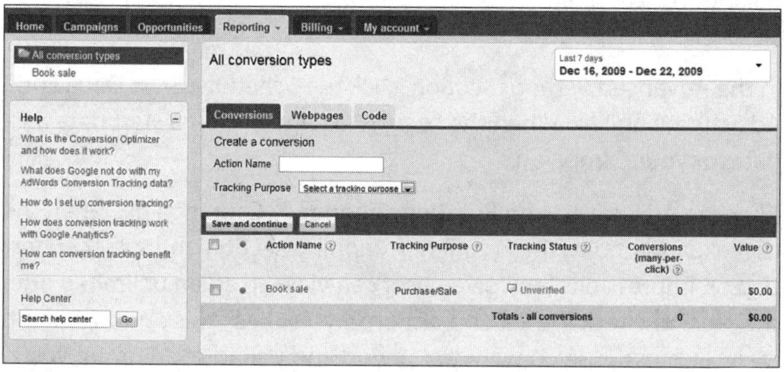

Figure 13.11 *Getting ready to set up conversion tracking, from the Reporting >
Conversions tab.*

5. Pull down the Tracking Purpose list and select what you're tracking: Pur-
    chase/Sale, Signup, Lead, View of a Key Page, or Other. For example, if
    you're tracking the sale of a specific item, select Purchase Sale; if you're
    tracking sales leads, select Lead.

6. Click the Save and Continue button.

7. AdWords now displays the page shown in Figure 13.12. Pull down the Page Security Level list and select the level of security for the landing page—either HTTP or HTTPS.

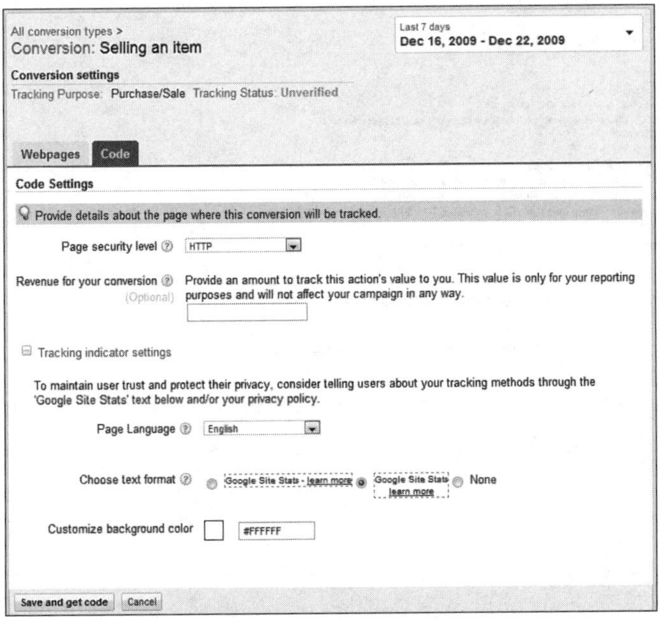

Figure 13.12 *Configuring AdWords conversion tracking.*

8. In the Revenue for Your Conversion box, enter the average value of the conversion. (If you're selling a product, use the sales price of that product.)

9. Google will display a small block on your landing page telling users about its tracking methods. In the Tracking Indicator Settings section, select the language of the landing page, as well as the text format and background color for the information block.

10. Click the Save and Get Code button.

11. Google now expands the current page to display a block of HTML code, like the one shown in Figure 13.13. Copy this Conversion Tracking Code and paste it into the source code of the landing page, anywhere between the <BODY> and </BODY> codes.

```
Code

♀ For your changes to take effect, copy and paste the code into the source of the page you would like to track.
Step 1 Copy the conversion tracking code.
<!-- Google Code for Selling an item Conversion Page -->
<script type="text/javascript">
<!--
var google_conversion_id = 1067780351;
var google_conversion_language = "en";
var google_conversion_format = "2";
var google_conversion_color = "ffffff";
var google_conversion_label = "ojvpCLn_nwEQ_5GU_QM";
var google_conversion_value = 0;
if ($10) {
  google_conversion_value = $10;
}
//-->
</script>
<script type="text/javascript"
src="http://www.googleadservices.com/pagead/conversion.js">
</script>
<noscript>
<div style="display:inline;">
<img height="1" width="1" style="border-style:none;" alt=""
src="http://www.googleadservices.com/pagead/conversion/1067780351/?
value=$10&amp;label=ojvpCLn_nwEQ_5GU_QM&amp;guid=ON&amp;script=0"/>
</div>
</noscript>

Step 2 Paste the conversion tracking code into the source of your action page.
<body>

  Paste the code between the body tags of your conversion pages.

</body>
```

Figure 13.13 *Copy the conversion tracking code into the source code of your landing page.*

This is nondisplaying code, so its position within the body of your page doesn't really matter.

 SHOW ME   **Media 13.4—A video about how to set up conversion tracking**
Access this video file through your registered Web Edition at
my.safaribooksonline.com/9780131388666/media.

After this code has been inserted into your landing page, you can then choose the conversion bidding option when you set up a new campaign.

Managing Your Campaigns

You can manage your campaigns, ad groups, and individual ads from the Campaigns tab of the main AdWords page.

All your existing campaigns are listed in the All Online Campaigns box on the left side of the page. Select a campaign and you see information about that campaign in the main part of the page. This section includes five sub-tabs, as detailed in the following sections.

SHOW ME   Media 13.5—A video about how to navigate the tabs of the AdWords site

Access this video file through your registered Web Edition at my.safaribooksonline.com/9780131388666/media.

If you want to view information for a specific ad group, simply select the ad group under the campaign in the All Online Campaigns box, or on the Ad Groups sub-tab for that campaign. AdWords now displays similar Settings, Ads, Keywords, and Networks sub-tabs for that specific ad group.

Ad Groups

The Ad Groups sub-tab, shown in Figure 13.14, tracks all the activity within the ad groups of the selected campaign.

	Ad group	Campaign	Status ⑦	Search Max. CPC	Content Managed Max. CPC	Content Auto Max. CPC ⑦	Clicks	Impr.	CTR	Avg. CPC ⑦	Cost	Avg. Pos.	Conv. (1-per-click)	Cost / conv. (1-per-click)	Conv. rate (1-per-click)	View-through Conv.
☑ ●	December	Books 1	Eligible	auto: $0.50	--	auto	15	40,313	0.04%	$0.17	$2.53	6.3	0	$0.00	0.00%	0
☑ ●	YouTube for Business	YouTube Promoted Videos Campaign	Eligible	$0.50	--	auto	9	19,658	0.05%	$0.29	$2.58	2.6	0	$0.00	0.00%	0
☑ ●	Music books	Music books	Eligible	$2.60	$1.50	$1.50	8	16,362	0.05%	$1.19	$9.55	2.4	0	$0.00	0.00%	0
☑ ●	Starter Ad Group	Starter Campaign	Campaign ended	auto: $0.33	--	auto	0	0	0.00%	$0.00	$0.00	0	0	$0.00	0.00%	0
	Total - all but deleted ad groups (in all but deleted campaigns)						32	76,333	0.04%	$0.46	$14.66	4.5	0	$0.00	0.00%	0
	Total - search ⑦						32	75,253	0.04%	$0.46	$14.66	4.5	0	$0.00	0.00%	0
	Total - content ⑦						0	1,080	0.00%	$0.00	$0.00	6.8	0	$0.00	0.00%	0
	Total - all ad groups						32	76,333	0.04%	$0.46	$14.66	4.5	0	$0.00	0.00%	0

Figure 13.14   *The Campaigns > Ad Groups sub-tab.*

At the top of this sub-tab you see a graph of clicks per day for the current campaign. Below the graph is a listing of all the ad groups within the campaign; for each group, AdWords displays the status, maximum CPC for both search and content sites, total number of clicks and impressions to date, the click-through rate (CTR), average CPC, total cost, and average position.

You can select any ad group and then use the Edit and Change Status buttons to edit, pause, enable, or delete that group. Use the More Actions button to create and manage alerts for this group, as well as download group data. In addition, you can create new ad groups within the selected campaign by clicking the New Ad Group button.

Settings

The Settings sub-tab, shown in Figure 13.15, displays key settings for the current campaign. Click the Edit link next to any option to make changes.

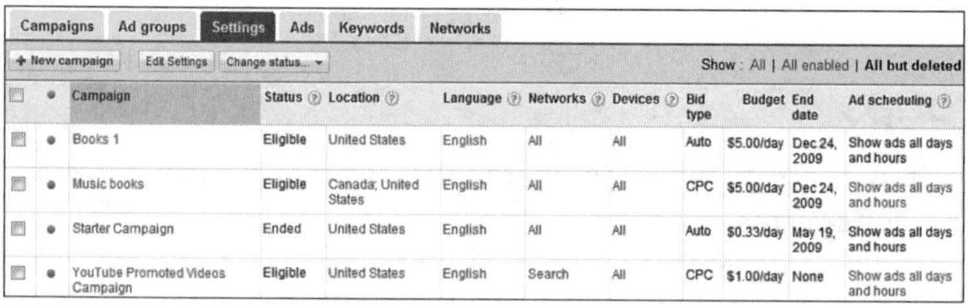

		Campaign	Status ⑦	Location ⑦	Language ⑦	Networks ⑦	Devices ⑦	Bid type	Budget	End date	Ad scheduling ⑦
☐	●	Books 1	Eligible	United States	English	All	All	Auto	$5.00/day	Dec 24, 2009	Show ads all days and hours
☐	●	Music books	Eligible	Canada; United States	English	All	All	CPC	$5.00/day	Dec 24, 2009	Show ads all days and hours
☐	●	Starter Campaign	Ended	United States	English	All	All	Auto	$0.33/day	May 19, 2009	Show ads all days and hours
☐	●	YouTube Promoted Videos Campaign	Eligible	United States	English	Search	All	CPC	$1.00/day	None	Show ads all days and hours

Figure 13.15   *The Campaigns > Settings sub-tab.*

Ads

The Ads sub-tab, shown in Figure 13.16, tracks the individual ads within the selected campaign.

At the top of this sub-tab you see a graph of clicks per day for the ads in the current campaign. Below the graph is a listing of all the ads in the campaign; for each ad, AdWords displays the ad group, status, percent served, number of clicks and impressions, CTR, and total cost for each ad.

You can select any ad and then use the Change Status button to pause, enable, or delete the ad. Use the More Actions button to create and manage alerts for this ad, as well as copy the ad or download ad data. In addition, you can create new ads by clicking the New Ad button.

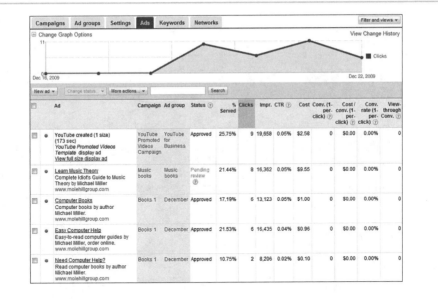

Figure 13.16   *The Campaigns > Ads sub-tab.*

Keywords

The Keywords sub-tab, shown in Figure 13.17, tracks performance of the keywords used in the current campaign.

At the top of this sub-tab you see a graph of clicks per day for these keywords. Below the graph is a listing of all the keywords in the campaign; for each keyword, AdWords displays the ad group, status, maximum CPC, number of clicks and impressions, CTR, average CPC, total cost, and average position for each keyword.

You can select any keyword and then use the Edit and Change Status buttons to edit, pause, enable, or delete the keyword. Use the More Actions button to create and manage alerts for selected keywords, as well as copy the keyword or download data. In addition, you can add new keywords to your campaign by clicking the Add Keywords button.

Networks

Use the Networks sub-tab, shown in Figure 13.18, to view and evaluate performance per channel. There are separate sections for search and content sites. For each channel, AdWords displays the number of clicks and impressions, CTR, average CPC, total cost, and average position.

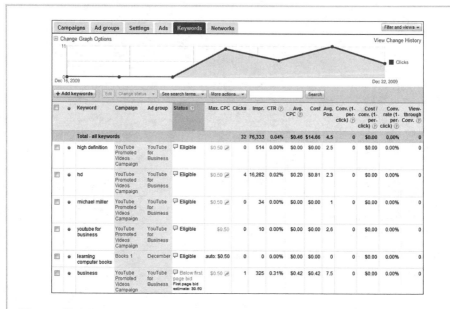

Figure 13.17   *The Campaigns > Keywords sub-tab.*

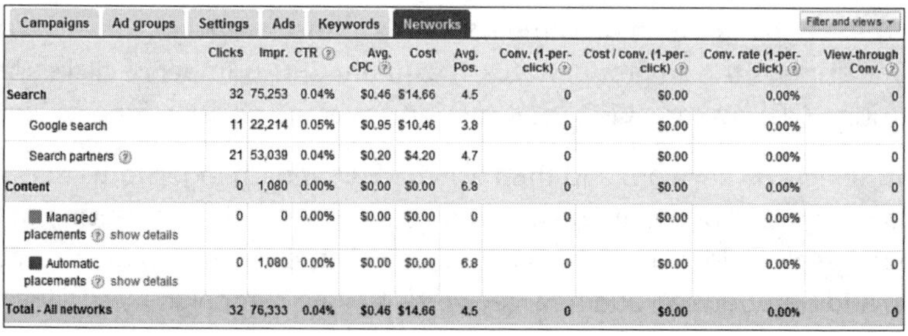

	Clicks	Impr.	CTR ⑦	Avg. CPC ⑦	Cost	Avg. Pos.	Conv. (1-per-click) ⑦	Cost / conv. (1-per-click) ⑦	Conv. rate (1-per-click) ⑦	View-through Conv. ⑦
Search	32	75,253	0.04%	$0.46	$14.66	4.5	0	$0.00	0.00%	0
Google search	11	22,214	0.05%	$0.95	$10.46	3.8	0	$0.00	0.00%	0
Search partners ⑦	21	53,039	0.04%	$0.20	$4.20	4.7	0	$0.00	0.00%	0
Content	0	1,080	0.00%	$0.00	$0.00	6.8	0	$0.00	0.00%	0
■ Managed placements ⑦ show details	0	0	0.00%	$0.00	$0.00	0	0	$0.00	0.00%	0
■ Automatic placements ⑦ show details	0	1,080	0.00%	$0.00	$0.00	6.8	0	$0.00	0.00%	0
Total - All networks	32	76,333	0.04%	$0.46	$14.66	4.5	0	$0.00	0.00%	0

Figure 13.18   *The Campaigns > Networks sub-tab.*

14

Creating Effective Ads

Every AdWords campaign you create can contain one or more ad groups, focused on a particular topic or product. Then, for each ad group, you create one or more ad(s), each designed to promote or sell whatever it is that your ad group is about.

You learned how to create a campaign in Chapter 13, "Creating Your First AdWords Campaign." With that campaign created, you can now create an ad group and get right to the process of creating your AdWords ads.

 **LET ME TRY IT**

Creating an Ad Group and Ads

After you've created your campaign, you can create an ad group and the ads within that group. The ad group/ad creation process is one and the same: You create an ad group, select the keywords for that ad group, and then create the ads that belong to that ad group.

This process flows seamlessly from the instructions presented in the previous chapter. Alternately, you can at any time go to your main AdWords page (adwords. google.com), select the Campaigns tab, select a campaign in the All Online Campaigns box, and then click the New Ad Group button.

To create an ad group and your first ad, go to your main AdWords page as described previously. Here's what happens next:

1. On the Create Ad Group page, shown in Figure 14.1, enter a name for this ad group in the Ad Group Name field.

2. In the Create an Ad section, determine whether you want to create a text ad, an image ad, or a mobile ad. (You can also opt to create an image ad using Google's Display Ad Builder.)

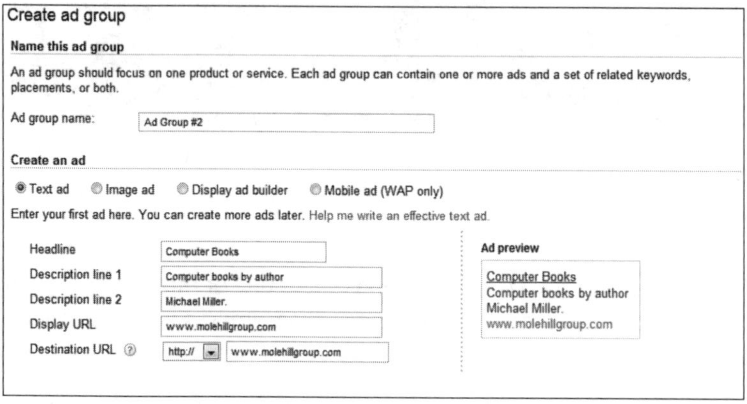

Create ad group

Name this ad group

An ad group should focus on one product or service. Each ad group can contain one or more ads and a set of related keywords, placements, or both.

Ad group name: Ad Group #2

Create an ad

● Text ad   ○ Image ad   ○ Display ad builder   ○ Mobile ad (WAP only)

Enter your first ad here. You can create more ads later. Help me write an effective text ad.

Headline	Computer Books	Ad preview
Description line 1	Computer books by author	Computer Books
Description line 2	Michael Miller.	Computer books by author
Display URL	www.molehillgroup.com	Michael Miller.
Destination URL ⑦	http:// [▼] www.molehillgroup.com	www.molehillgroup.com

Figure 14.1   *Creating a new ad group and ad.*

3. Assuming you want to create a text ad, enter the headline for your ad into the Headline field.

4. Enter two lines of text for your ad into the Description Line 1 and Description Line 2 fields.

5. Enter the URL you want displayed in the ad into the Display URL field.

6. Enter the actual destination URL into the Destination URL field.

The display URL can and probably should be different from the destination URL. It's best to display your site's simple home page URL, while having users click to a more targeted landing page.

🅖 *Learn more about landing pages in Chapter 17, "Maximizing Conversion with a Custom Landing Page."*

7. Scroll down to the Keywords section, shown in Figure 14.2, and enter the keywords you want to associate with this ad into the Keywords box. Enter one keyword (or key phrase, consisting of multiple words) per line; Google recommends using 10 to 20 keywords, at least initially.

You can estimate the search traffic (clicks per day) for your combination of maximum CPC and keywords by clicking the Estimate Search Traffic button.

🅖 *Learn more about keywords in Chapter 16, "Choosing the Right Keywords."*

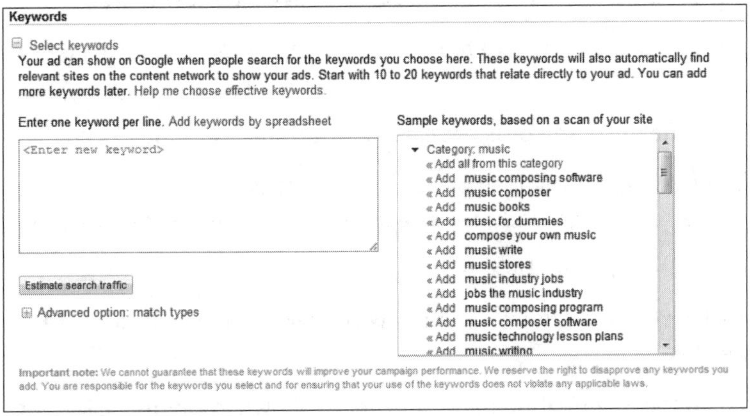

Keywords

⊟ Select keywords
Your ad can show on Google when people search for the keywords you choose here. These keywords will also automatically find relevant sites on the content network to show your ads. Start with 10 to 20 keywords that relate directly to your ad. You can add more keywords later. Help me choose effective keywords.

Enter one keyword per line. Add keywords by spreadsheet   Sample keywords, based on a scan of your site

<Enter new keyword>

▼ Category: music
« Add all from this category
« Add music composing software
« Add music composer
« Add music books
« Add music for dummies
« Add compose your own music
« Add music write
« Add music stores
« Add music industry jobs
« Add jobs the music industry
« Add music composing program
« Add music composer software
« Add music technology lesson plans
« Add music writing

[Estimate search traffic]

⊞ Advanced option: match types

Important note: We cannot guarantee that these keywords will improve your campaign performance. We reserve the right to disapprove any keywords you add. You are responsible for the keywords you select and for ensuring that your use of the keywords does not violate any applicable laws.

Figure 14.2 *Entering keywords for your new ad group.*

8. If you want to select specific sites or pages within the Google content network on which you want your ad to appear, click Select Managed Placements. Enter the URLs for each site or page within a site where you want your ad to appear, one URL per line.

You can also use the Select Managed Placements section to *exclude* sites and pages from display. If you have a specific site or page on which you don't want your ad to appear, enter it into the text box with a minus sign in front of it, like this: **-www.example.com.**

9. Click the Save Group button.

SHOW ME   Media 14.1—A video about how to create an ad group and ads
Access this video file through your registered Web Edition at
my.safaribooksonline.com/9780131388666/media.

And that's that. You've created a new ad group within your campaign, and created your first ad within the ad group. From here, you can either stick with that single ad or create additional ads for the ad group.

LET ME TRY IT

Adding More than One Ad to an Ad Group

An ad group can contain more than one ad. To add more ads to an ad group, follow these steps:

1. From the main AdWords page, select the Campaigns tab.

2. In the All Online Campaigns box, on the left side of the page, select the desired campaign, and then select the ad group under that campaign.

3. Click the Ads sub-tab.

4. Click the New Ad button and then select Text Ad (or another desired ad type).

5. When the New Text Ad pane appears, as shown in Figure 14.3, enter the ad's Headline, Description Line 1, Description Line 2, Display URL, and Destination URL.

Figure 14.3   *Adding a new ad to an ad group.*

6. Click the Save Ad button.

This new ad will run using the same parameters as other ads in this campaign, using the same keywords you specified when you created the ad group.

Creating Other Types of Ads

So far in this chapter we've focused on creating text ads. AdWords also lets you create image and mobile ads. We'll look at each additional type of ad next.

TELL ME MORE   Media 14.2—A discussion about what type of ad should you create?

Access this audio recording through your registered Web Edition at my.safaribooksonline.com/9780131388666/media.

Creating Image Ads

AdWords doesn't limit you to simple text ads. You can also choose to promote your website or product via an image or display ad—essentially a clickable image that fits into one of the common AdSense ad formats.

☞ *View the available image ad formats in Chapter 3, "Adding AdSense for Content to Your Website."*

Before you create a new image ad, you first have to create the ad's image. You do this offline; you can create it yourself using an image editing program, such as Adobe Photoshop, or you can contract with a graphic designer or ad agency to do the work for you.

What you have to do is create an image that fits in one of the available ad formats. Table 14.1 details the image sizes you can work with.

Table 14.1   Image Ad Sizes

Ad Type	Dimensions (Width × Height, in Pixels)
Leaderboard	728 × 90
Banner	468 × 60
Large rectangle	336 × 280
Inline rectangle	300 × 250
Square	250 × 250
Small square	200 × 200
Wide skyscraper	160 × 600
Skyscraper	120 × 600
Mobile leaderboard (for mobile devices only)	300 × 50

Create your image files to one of these dimensions, in one of the following file formats:

- JPG
- GIF
- PNG

You can also create Flash-based animation files (in the SWF format) in any of these dimensions, thus effectively placing a video ad via the image ad program.

 **LET ME TRY IT**

Launch an Image for Your AdWords Campaign

After you have created your image, follow these steps to launch an image ad for your AdWords campaign:

1. From the main AdWords page, select the Campaigns tab.

2. In the All Online Campaigns box, select the desired campaign and then select the ad group under that campaign.

3. Click the Ads sub-tab.

4. Click the New Ad button and then select Image Ad.

5. The page now expands, as shown in Figure 14.4. Click the Choose File button.

Figure 14.4 *Creating an image ad.*

6. Navigate to and select the image file you've previously created and then click Open.

7. Enter a name for this image in the Name Image box.

8. Enter the URL you want displayed with this ad into the Display URL box. (This is typically your website's home page URL.)

9. Into the Destination URL box, enter the URL of the landing page you want people to see when they click the ad.

10. Click the Save Ad button.

 SHOW ME   Media 14.3—A video about how to create an image ad
Access this video file through your registered Web Edition at
my.safaribooksonline.com/9780131388666/media.

Know that an image ad will probably result in fewer clicks than a similar text ad, because not all websites participating in the AdSense program choose to display image ads. That is, you'll have a smaller base of sites in the content network to work with.

It's also common for image ads to generate fewer clicks than text ads in general. This is because many users immediately view image ads as advertisements and thus avoid clicking them; text ads sometimes are confused for content or navigation on the host website, and thus receive more "accidental" clicks.

 **LET ME TRY IT**

Building Animated Image Ads with the Display Ad Builder

If you don't have the ability to create your own image ads, you can use Google's Display Ad Builder to do the work for you. This is a web-based utility that builds animated image ads from your text elements and pre-designed images.

Most of these ads consist of an animated image, initially accompanied by a piece of "teaser" text. When the initial animation completes, the main ad displays—the text you provide displayed against a pre-designed graphic supplied by Google. It has the look of a Flash animation ad, but it's really nothing more than a gussied-up version of a standard text ad.

To create one of these image ads using the Display Ad Builder, follow these steps:

Each display ad template is different, and contains different combinations of elements. The instructions here are for a typical template; the one you choose may have different options.

1. From the main AdWords page, select the Campaigns tab.

2. In the All Online Campaigns box, select the desired campaign and then select the ad group under that campaign.

3. Click the Ads sub-tab.

4. Click the New Ad button and then select Display Ad Builder.

5. The page now expands to display a series of image ad templates, as shown in Figure 14.5. Before you select a template, select a category for your ad from the list on the left.

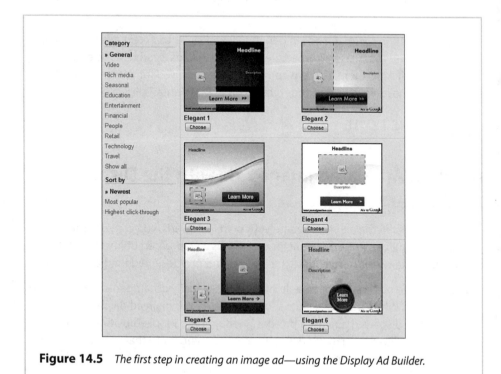

Figure 14.5   *The first step in creating an image ad—using the Display Ad Builder.*

6. Google now displays templates related to the category you selected. Click the Choose button for the template you want to use.

7. When the next page appears, as shown in Figure 14.6, enter a name for the ad into the Name field.

For any text in the ad, you can also specify the font and text color, if you desire.

8. Enter the headline for this ad into the Headline box.

9. Enter the ad copy into the Description box(es).

10. If the template you chose includes a space for your company or brand logo, click the Choose File button in the Logo section and then navigate to and select the appropriate image file. (The logo file should be sized to 100 × 60 pixels, in either GIF, JPG, or PNG format.)

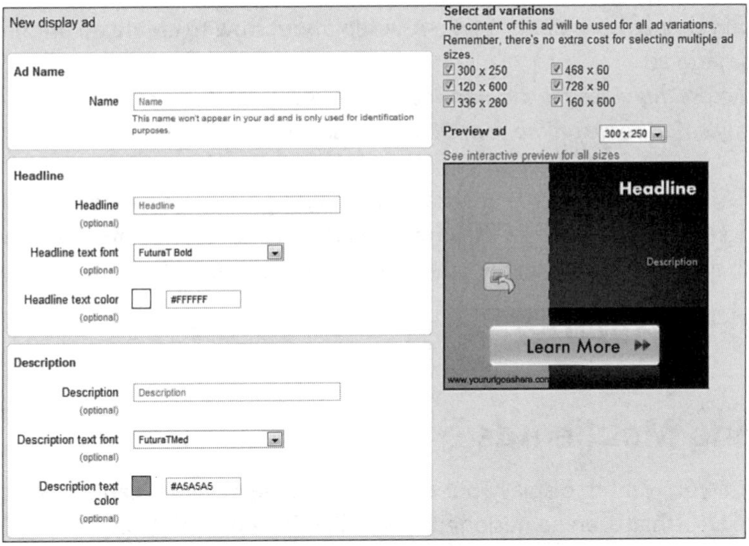

Figure 14.6 *Building an animated image ad.*

11. Enter the text you want displayed on the ad's button into the Click Text box. You can also specify the background color for the button, as well as the button text color and font.

12. If the template you chose lets you change the background color, do so now.

13. Enter the URL you want displayed in the ad (typically your home page URL) into the Display URL box. If you want, you can select the color for this URL.

14. Into the Destination URL box, enter the URL for the landing page displayed when someone clicks on the ad.

15. Move to the right side of this page and check all those sizes you want the ad displayed as. The available ad sizes differ slightly by template.

16. Click the Save Ad button.

View your in-progress ad on the right side of the page. You can preview the ad at various sizes; click the reload button at the top right of the ad to view the complete animation, including teaser text.

SHOW ME   Media 14.4—A video about how to create an animated image ad
Access this video file through your registered Web Edition at
my.safaribooksonline.com/9780131388666/media.

Google's Display Builder ads are great for smaller advertisers who don't have the graphics expertise to design their own image ads. You get a professional-looking ad with a lot of eye appeal; the opening animation really catches a lot of attention.

 LET ME TRY IT

Creating Mobile Ads

Finally, if you want to display your ads on mobile devices, you can opt to create a mobile ad—that is, an ad designed specifically for the smaller displays of iPhones and similar devices.

To create a mobile ad, follow these steps:

1. From the main AdWords page, select the Campaigns tab.

2. In the All Online Campaigns box, select the desired campaign and then select the ad group under that campaign.

3. Click the Ads sub-tab.

4. Click the New Ad button and then select Mobile Ad.

5. The page now expands, as shown in Figure 14.7. Select whether you want to create a WAP Text Ad or WAP Image Ad.

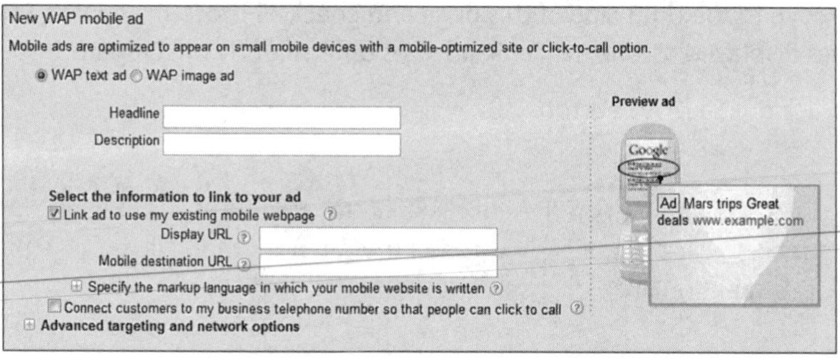

Figure 14.7 *Building a mobile text ad.*

6. If you choose to create a text ad, enter the headline and description for the ad.

If you create a text ad, you have the option of linking to a mobile web page or connecting customers to your business telephone number, which is a great way to get immediate business. If you choose this option, enter your business name and phone number as prompted.

7. If you choose to create an image ad, click the Choose File button and then navigate to and select the image file you want to use for the ad. The image can be in either JPG, GIF, or PNG formats, in any of the following sizes: 300 × 50, 216 × 36, 168 × 28, 300 × 75, 216 × 54, 168 × 42, or 192 × 53.

As there is no standard display size for mobile devices, creating mobile image ads is a bit problematic; it's tough to know which image size to use when every device is different.

8. Enter the URL you want displayed in the ad (typically your mobile home page URL) into the Display URL box.

9. Enter the actual destination URL into the Mobile Destination URL box.

10. If you want to limit display of this ad to particular cell carrier networks, click the Advanced Targeting and Network Options and then check the desired carrier(s).

11. Click the Save Ad button.

To test the effectiveness of different cell phone networks, create separate image ads for each carrier and then track the performance of each ad/carrier individually.

 SHOW ME   Media 14.5—A video about how to create mobile ads
Access this video file through your registered Web Edition at
my.safaribooksonline.com/9780131388666/media.

A good strategy is to create a separate campaign just for mobile devices. This way, you can select to display on mobile devices only (when you create the campaign), and then create mobile image ads specific to this campaign.

Writing More Effective Text Ads

When it comes to creating an effective text ad, the text you write is of utmost importance. It takes a lot of talent to drive sales from a simple three- or four-line text ad.

SHOW ME   Media 14.6—A video about how to write effective text ads

Access this video file through your registered Web Edition at my.safaribooksonline.com/9780131388666/media.

In the AdWords program, a text ad consists of four lines of text. The first line is the headline or title, with a relatively short character count. The next two lines contain the body of the ad, often a product description, which can hold more characters, but still not a lot. The final line is the URL of the site where you're driving traffic. (All of this is detailed in Table 14.2.)

Table 14.2   Text Ad Character Limitations

Ad Component	Maximum Characters
Headline	25
Description 1	35
Description 2	35
URL	35 (includes spaces and slashes)

The most important part of any text ad is the title. This is because some ad formats on some pages display *only* the title and URL, skipping the two description lines. So, your title has to do the heavy lifting; it has to grab potential customers at a literal glance. You can then fill in more details in the next two lines, but the title pretty much has to stand alone, if necessary.

Figure 14.8 shows a typical AdWords text ad. The title, "Books by Michael Miller," is the short and sweet grabber that gets the customer's attention. The second and third lines in this example, "How-to books by popular author; Computers, music, eBay, and more!" describe the products being sold. The final line, "www. molehillgroup.com," is the URL for the product page.

An effective text ad includes many of the same keywords you use to trigger the display of the ad. In this example, note how keywords are placed in both the title and the description. The keyword "books" appears twice, while other keywords ("computers," "music," and "eBay") also make their appearances. It's tight and punchy, not at all wordy, and keyword-dense. That's all you have room for.

Books by Michael Miller
How-to books by popular author
Computers, music, eBay, and more!
www.molehillgroup.com

Figure 14.8   *A four-line AdWords text ad.*

Don't even think about putting puff words ("lowest" or "best") or punctuation (! or *) in your text ads. There simply isn't space to waste on these unnecessary words and characters.

It's important to remember the character limitations, and to work within those limitations. You definitely don't have room for puff words or excessive verbiage; you might not even have room for proper grammar and complete sentences. Your writing has to be short and to the point. You have to get your message across in the minimum amount of space.

If you're not comfortable writing this sort of super-tight ad copy, it's worth hiring a copywriter. This is the toughest kind of copywriting out there, and well worth using a pro to implement effectively.

For your ad to be successful, this message needs to entice users to click your ad for more information. This means informing them about what you have to offer, as well as presenting a strong call to action. That is, your ad text needs to encourage users to do something—in most instances, click for more information or to buy a product or service.

And that means clicking *your* ad, not somebody else's. This requires that your ad—both the information presented and the call to action—be unique. Users have to know why to click your ad instead of someone else's.

With all this in mind, you should experiment with different copy blocks—that is, presenting your message in different ways. Write several different variations of your main copy and then run them as competing ads in the same ad group. (This way, they'll be triggered by the same keywords.) From this exercise you can determine which ad copy pulls the best, and use that information to inform future ads.

You also have to present your URL in just 35 characters—including dots and slashes. That effectively rules out displaying individual pages or directories; you pretty much have room to display your home page URL and nothing more. (In fact, if you have an overly long domain name, 35 characters might not be enough—you might need to establish an alternate, shorter domain.) Of course, you can have the ad link to a more specific landing page with a longer URL—it's just that you can display only your shorter home page URL.

15

Bidding the Right Price

Whether you're new to AdWords or an old hand, one question inevitably emerges: How much should you pay for each click?

It's an important question. If you bid too low, you won't win enough keywords, your ad won't appear as high or as often, and you won't generate much traffic. If, on the other hand, you bid too high, you'll end up overpaying for your ads—and generate too low a return on your investment.

Although there's no single right price to bid for all possible keywords, there are some proven strategies that will help you optimize your bid—and get the most bang for your buck. Read on to learn more.

Understanding CPC Bidding

When you create a pay-per-click ad on the AdWords network, you have to bid on one or more keywords that will trigger the display of that ad. You tell AdWords how much you're willing to pay for each click on that ad; that's your bid, on a cost-per-click (CPC) basis. If your bid is higher than other advertisers bidding on the same keyword, your ad will appear more often (in both Google search results and on Google's affiliated network sites) and higher on those pages. If your bid is lower than other advertisers, your ad will appear lower on those pages and less frequently—and might, over time, no longer appear at all.

Put another way, although your daily budget determines how often an ad displays each day (assuming it appears at all, that is), your CPC bid determines the position on the displaying page each time the ad appears. To improve your ad position, increase your CPC bid.

Manual Versus Automatic Bidding

If all the CPC bidding strategies presented in this chapter make your head spin, consider letting AdWords do your bidding for you—up to a limit, of course. When you create a new campaign, you have the option of using manual bidding or automatic bidding. If you select manual bidding, you can specify exact CPC rates for each keyword or keyword group you create. The other option is to use automatic bidding, for which you don't have to make an exact CPC bid.

When you use AdWords' manual bidding feature, you can set your bids for individual keywords, or for all the keywords in an ad group. Automatic bidding doesn't let you set different rates for different keywords.

When you choose automatic bidding, the only choice you have to make is the maximum amount you want to pay per click. AdWords will then make the best bid below that level to maximize the number of potential clicks for your daily budget.

You don't even have to set a maximum click level when using automated bidding, although I recommend it. If you don't set a maximum click level, AdWords will bid as high as necessary—which could eat up your daily budget pretty fast in some circumstances.

The good thing about automated bidding is that it's less work—and guesswork—for you. You set a maximum bid and AdWords does all the bidding, never exceeding your maximum amount per click. For that reason, automatic bidding is the recommended approach for new or inexperienced AdWords advertisers.

The bad thing is that automated bidding applies to all the keywords in an ad group. You can't set different CPC rates for different keywords or keyword groups, which is required for some of the more sophisticated bidding strategies; you give up a lot of control. For that reason, manual bidding is the recommended approach for many advanced AdWords advertisers.

 SHOW ME   Media 15.1—A video about the difference between manual and automatic bidding

Access this video file through your registered Web Edition at my.safaribooksonline.com/9780131388666/media.

Bid Rates Versus ROI

Of course, different keywords sell for different rates. It's logical, really. Those keywords that more advertisers want to use get bid higher and have higher CPC rates; those keywords that aren't as popular have lower CPC rates. So it's just as easy to bid high on a low-priced keyword as it is to bid low on a high-priced one.

If you bid way too low, your ad simply won't appear for a given keyword. You can see whether you've bid too low by examining the Campaigns > Keywords sub-tab. As you can see in Figure 15.1, this sub-tab includes a list of all keywords you're bidding on for a given campaign. If you've bid too low on a given keyword, the Status column for that keyword will display a "Below first page bid" message, along with the level of that first bid. You can then compare that actual bid with your own maximum bid, in the Max CPC column to the immediate right. This will show you how much you've underbid that particular keyword.

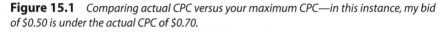

Figure 15.1   *Comparing actual CPC versus your maximum CPC—in this instance, my bid of $0.50 is under the actual CPC of $0.70.*

If you consistently bid too low on keywords, you won't generate enough traffic to make your campaign profitable—and thus reduce your campaign's return on investment (ROI). On the other hand, if you consistently bid too high on keywords, you'll spend more advertising funds than you need to—and also reduce your ROI. That's why you need to figure out how to bid the right amount—neither too high or too low—to strike the right balance between traffic and cost; this will maximize your ROI for a given campaign.

Ad position is determined by both the CPC rate you bid and the Quality Score for the keywords you select.

🄶 *Learn more about this Quality Score in Chapter 16, "Choosing the Right Keywords."*

Using the Bid Simulator Tool

AdWords offers two tools to help you determine the right bid range for any given keyword. Although these tools don't provide perfect advice, they are good guides you can use within the specific bidding strategy you adopt.

The first such tool is the Bid Simulator, which lets you see probable advertising results for different CPC bids. It works with ads for Google search and the search network only, not for ads on the content network.

The Bid Simulator uses historical data to estimate the clicks, costs, and impressions that an ad would have received over the last seven days at different bid levels. It doesn't actually predict the future—or guarantee that these past rates will hold going forward.

To use the Bid Simulator, go to the Campaigns > Keywords tab and click the Bid Simulator icon in the Max CPC column for any given keyword, as shown in Figure 15.2. The Bid Simulator now displays a range of CPCs, as shown in Figure 15.3, with estimated clicks, estimated cost, and estimated impressions for each CPC level; you can also enter any bid level into the Set Bid To box. Select any bid level to see a corresponding cost-versus-clicks graph to the right.

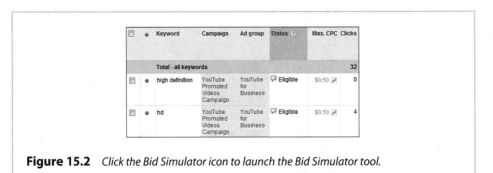

Figure 15.2   *Click the Bid Simulator icon to launch the Bid Simulator tool.*

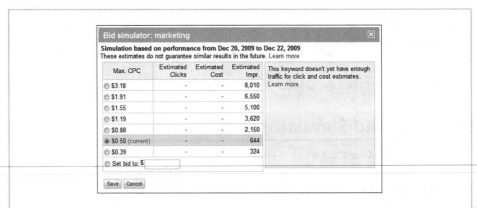

Figure 15.3   *Comparing clicks and impressions for different CPCs with the Bid Simulator tool.*

From this information, you can make the determination whether the increased costs associated with a higher bid level are worth it, in terms of increased clicks and impressions. You might even determine that it's better to go with a lower click rate—that is, you can accept fewer clicks and impressions for the associated lower cost.

Using the Traffic Estimator Tool

The other useful tool is the Traffic Estimator. As you can see in Figure 15.4, this tool looks at the keywords you enter and estimates the traffic you're likely to generate in terms of clicks per day; the average CPC rate for those keywords; and the cost per day you're likely to incur.

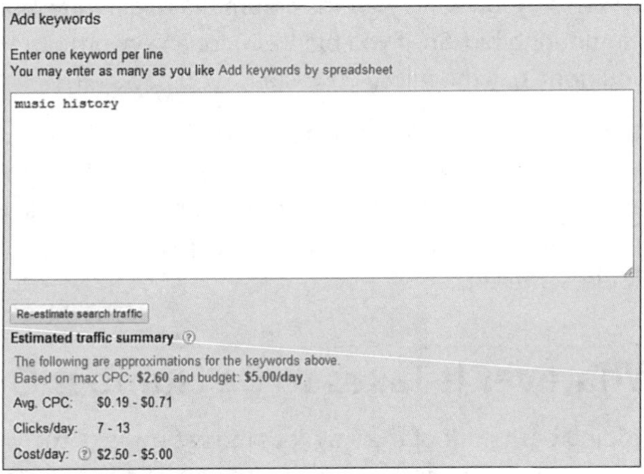

Figure 15.4 *Estimating a CPC range for a group of keywords, using the Traffic Estimator tool.*

For our immediate purposes, the average CPC is the number to look at. The Traffic Estimator tool will provide a CPC range; you should place your bid somewhere in this range. Bid in the low end of the range to minimize your expenses (and also minimize your ad placement); bid in the high end of the range to ensure higher placement (but with fewer overall impressions).

To use the Traffic Estimator tool, go to the Campaigns > Keywords sub-tab and click the Add Keywords button. Enter one or more keywords into the Add Keywords box and then click the Estimate Search Traffic button.

SHOW ME   Media 15.2—A video about how to use the Traffic Simulator tool
Access this video file through your registered Web Edition at
my.safaribooksonline.com/9780131388666/media.

Ways to Reduce Your Maximum Bid

Whether you use manual or automatic bidding, you still enter a maximum CPC bid. This is the maximum you're willing to pay; in reality, you might end up paying less, thanks to two different Google technologies.

Google's AdWords Discounter technology is the one that will probably save you the most money, as it manages your CPC bids so that you don't have to pay more than you have to. It works by lowering your maximum bid to a penny more than the next-highest competing bid. So, if you bid $2.00 for a keyword but the next highest bid is $1.50, you don't pay the full $2.00; instead, you pay $1.51.

In addition, AdWords' Smart Pricing will often lower the maximum CPC bid for ads appearing on Google Network sites. Even though you set a single maximum bid, if Google's data shows that a click from a given site or page is less likely to result in a sale, Smart Pricing will reduce the bid level for that particular site. In other words, you pay less for lesser results.

Bidding Whatever It Takes to Be Number One

With those bidding basics out of the way, let's look at some of the various bidding strategies you can employ for an AdWords campaign. The first strategy is one aimed at always winning the keywords you choose—no matter what the price.

 SHOW ME   Media 15.3—A video about bidding strategies
Access this video file through your registered Web Edition at
my.safaribooksonline.com/9780131388666/media.

The thinking behind this strategy is simple. When your ad ranks in the number one (or number-two) position for a given keyword, it appears *above* Google's organic search results for that keyword, as shown in Figure 15.5. That's the best position possible, as it results in more clicks and traffic than lower positions—sometimes a lot more.

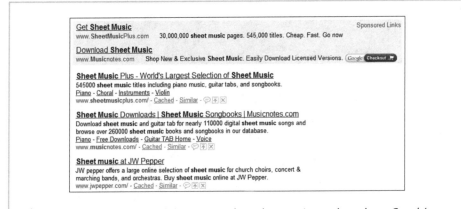

Figure 15.5 *The top two ad slots appear above the organic search results on Google's search results pages.*

Of course, you have to pay top dollar to get that top slot, so this can be a costly strategy. This is especially true if you get into a bidding war with another advertiser following the same strategy; when two advertisers are both intent on being number one, the price for a given keyword can skyrocket.

You can only bid *so* high—Google has a $50 per-click maximum bid.

This strategy also has its limits. Remember, your bid price is only part of what determines your final ad position; you also have to figure in your site's Quality Score. So, you can't guarantee top position by bidding only, as it's possible to be outbid by a competitor with a higher Quality Score.

That said, the key to this strategy is to use manual bidding and to always bid at the upper end of the recommended bid range. When you create your campaign and enter a new keyword, click the Estimate Search Traffic button. The Traffic Estimator tool will now display an average CPC range; enter your bid at the upper end of this range—or above.

After your campaign is underway, keep a watch on the ad position for this keyword. Go to the Campaign > Keywords sub-tab and look in the Avg. Pos. column; this displays the average position you're getting for this keyword. If you're not in the number-one or number-two position, you need to increase your bid. Just go to the Campaign · > Keywords sub-tab, click the keyword in question, and enter a new bid amount, as shown in Figure 15.6.

	Keyword	Campaign	Ad group	Status ⑦	Max. CPC	Clicks	Impr.	CTR ⑦	Avg. CPC ⑦	Cost	Avg. Pos.
	Total - all keywords					35	80,737	0.04%	$0.45	$15.71	4.4
	high definition	YouTube Promoted Videos Campaign	YouTube for Business	Eligible	$0.50	0	714	0.00%	$0.00	$0.00	2.6
	hd	YouTube Promoted Videos Campaign	YouTube for Business	Eligible	$0.50	7	19,397	0.04%	$0.27	$1.86	2.4
	michael miller	YouTube Promoted Videos Campaign	YouTube for Business	Eligible	$0.50	0	60	0.00%	$0.00	$0.00	1
	youtube for business	YouTube Promoted Videos Campaign	YouTube for Business	Eligible	$0.50	0	18	0.00%	$0.00	$0.00	2.7

Figure 15.6   *Changing your bid amount for a specific keyword.*

You can only change your bid amount if you selected manual bidding; if you selected automatic bidding, there's nothing you can change.

Key to this strategy is constant monitoring of your ad's position, at least daily. If your position starts to slip, that means someone else is outbidding you—and you'll need to increase your bid.

Bidding for a Specific Position

The problem with bidding for the number-one or number-two position is that it's costly—and apt to get more costly over time, as other advertisers also bid for those keywords. For many advertisers, a better approach is to bid for a lower position—something in the 3–6 range, for example. These positions will cost you a lot less than the number-one position, but still land you on the first page of Google's search results—which typically results in a good CTR for a much lower CPC.

The key to this strategy is to fine-tune your bid after your campaign is running to find the sweet spot you want. Go to the Campaign > Keywords sub-tab and keep an eye on the Avg. Pos. column. If your average position is below your target range, increase your CPC bid for that keyword; if your average position is above your target range, decrease your bid. Like I said, it's a fine-tuning process, but one that guarantees a decent ROI over time.

Bidding High—Then Lowering Your Bids

Here's a quirk in the AdWords system that can work to your benefit. As you know, Google uses the Quality Score to help determine your ad's position, and one component of the Quality Score is your ad's click-through rate (CTR). Get a higher CTR, and your Quality Score goes up. Your Quality Score goes up and you get a better position—which improves your CTR. And a higher CTR makes your Quality Score go up again... and on and on, in this fashion.

The key here is to realize that if your ad is working and your CTR is going up, thus improving your Quality Score, you can maintain the same ad position at a lower cost. That's right, when your CTR rises, you decrease your bid level and maintain the same ad position; the improved Quality Score works in your favor in this regard. You end up at the same (or higher) position at a lower cost.

This strategy works best if you start with a higher bid level. That is, you go in strong to establish your position, and after your position has been established, you can then lower your bid. Naturally, you'll want to monitor your average position and Quality Score from the Campaigns > Keywords sub-tab, and then use your best judgment on when to change your bid.

Bidding the Bare Minimum

The first strategy we presented was to always bid high to capture the top display position for a keyword. The flip side to that strategy is to always bid low—to contain your costs and work within a budget.

The thinking here is that you can waste a lot of money trying to get the top positions, and your budget might be better spent bidding low for your traffic, especially if you have a high Quality Score that can pull up your position compared to lower-performing competitors. Now, you'll probably never rise to the top spot, but you might end up on the first page of search results—which isn't bad.

This cost containment strategy works if you believe users browse all the AdWords listings on a page, not just those at the top. That's not always the case, of course; if it were, the top position wouldn't pull as highly as it typically does. Still, some users *do* consider more than just the first listing, at least on the first page of search results, so there's some merit to this strategy. It's certainly a strategy that's worth considering if your budget is limited.

If you decide to go this route, use manual bidding and always bid at the lower end of the range suggested by Google's Traffic Estimator tool. You should also consider *not* bidding on keywords that are estimated to have a high CPC; you might get better results bidding on less popular keywords.

Bidding What It's Worth

All the previous bidding strategies were externally focused—that is, you have goals related to ad position. But you can also bid with an internal focus—in particular, how much a given keyword is worth to you.

If you do a little research beforehand and performance tracking after your campaign starts, you can determine the *optimal* cost per click for any keyword. Here's how to do it.

Start by determining how much profit you make off a sale from your website. As an example, let's say you sell an item for $100 retail that costs you $60 to purchase or manufacture; you generate $40 profit on each sale.

Next, determine your conversion rate for a given keyword. You can find this on the Campaigns > Keywords sub-tab, in the Conv. Rate column. For most sites, expect your conversion rate to be in the low single digits. For our example, let's say that your conversion rate is 1%, meaning that 1 out of every 100 people who click your ad end up buying your product.

Now it's math time. Each sale you make is worth $40 to you, and it takes 100 clicks to make one sale. Divide $40 by 100, and you discover that each visitor you attract costs you $0.40. This means you can afford to spend a maximum of $0.40 per click before you start losing money on each click. So, in this example, you'd set your maximum price per click to $0.40.

This calculation works only when you're selling products or services directly from your website, and it requires a little post-launch calculation. (That is, you won't know your conversion rate until you get some experience under your belt.) If, on the other hand, you're using PPC advertising to generate non-sales leads or build your brand image, the value of each click is much more difficult to determine—so difficult, in fact, that each company must determine this on its own.

 TELL ME MORE   Media 15.4—A discussion about what's the best bidding strategy?
Access this audio recording through your registered Web Edition at my.safaribooksonline.com/9780131388666/media.

16

Choosing the Right Keywords

One of the most important factors in creating a successful AdWords ad and campaign is the set of keywords you choose. Select the right keywords and everyone searching for a given topic will see your ad; select the wrong keywords and nobody will be searching for them.

How do you know what keywords to choose? It's as much an art as it is a science, as you'll soon discover.

What Is a Keyword—and Why Is It Important?

A *keyword* is a word that someone includes in a search query. Similarly, a keyword phrase (sometimes called a *key phrase)* is a group of words that someone includes in a query. In other words, keywords and phrases are what people search for. And, as you know, Google uses these search queries to match PPC ads to what people are searching for.

This is why you must specify one or more keywords to trigger the AdWords ads you create. The keywords you select are matched against the keywords that Google's users search for, and when someone searches for one of your keywords, your ad is placed in the running to be displayed. (Whether it's actually displayed depends on how much you bid per click, your site's Quality Score, and what other advertisers are bidding on that same keyword.)

So, for example, if someone is searching for the word *golf,* only advertisers who bid on the word *golf* will have their ads considered for display. If you haven't specified *golf* as one of your keywords, your ad won't be displayed on this person's search results page. So, if you want to target golfers for your advertising, you want to specify the word *golf* as one of the keywords for your campaign—and also include that keyword on the landing page linked to from your ad.

Similarly, if someone is searching for the phrase *golf club,* only advertisers that specify that phrase will register as a match. If your campaign includes the word *golf* but not the phrase *golf club,* it won't be a match for that particular query. You need to specify the entire key phrase as part of your campaign.

In short, keywords are important because they're what people are searching for. If your campaign includes the keywords that people are searching for, your ads will display more often and in higher positions than ads from competing advertisers that aren't targeted by those keywords. And if you don't include the keywords people are searching for, you might as well not be advertising at all.

TELL ME MORE   Media 16.1—A discussion about keywords
Access this audio recording through your registered Web Edition at
my.safaribooksonline.com/9780131388666/media.

Compiling Your Keyword List

How, then, do you determine which keywords people are searching for? It's really a matter of learning how to *think like the customer*. In other words, you need to get inside searchers' heads to determine which words they're using in their queries—and then specify those keywords for your campaign.

Performing Keyword Research

The art of determining which keywords to use is called *keyword research*. When you know which keywords and phrases your target customers are likely to use, you can optimize your site for those words and phrases; if you don't know how they're searching, you don't know what to optimize.

Some advertisers go all out, conducting extensive (and expensive) market research to determine how their target audience is searching. Other advertisers play it totally by ear, just guessing what the top searches are. But there are simpler and more effective ways to get smart about this, in the form of keyword research tools.

These tools are software utilities or web-based services that compile and analyze keyword search statistics from Google and (sometimes) the other major search engines. You can use the results from these keyword research tools to determine which are the most powerful keywords to include on your site.

It's never a good idea to guess what keywords searchers are using, or assume that the way you search is the way everyone else searches. Instead, use keyword research tools or traditional market research to determine the real keywords used.

How Keyword Research Tools Work

Most keyword research tools work by matching the thrust or content of your website with keywords relevant to your content; they've already searched through hundreds of thousands of possible keywords and phrases on the most popular search engines and mapped the results to their own database. You enter a word or phrase that describes what your site has to offer, and the research tool returns a list of words or phrases related to that description, in descending order of search popularity.

For example, if you have a website that's selling travel guides, you might describe your site with the phrase *travel guides*. The keyword research tool, then, would return a list of keywords and phrases. Those words and phrases at the top of the list are the ones that show up most often in search results, and thus will best improve the ranking of your site on those search engines.

Choosing a Keyword Research Tool

When it comes to choosing a keyword research tool, the most popular among SEO professionals is Trellian's KeywordDiscovery (www.keyworddiscovery.com). KeywordDiscovery is available on a subscription basis; a standard subscription costs $69.95 per month.

Also popular with professionals is Wordtracker (www.wordtracker.com). Like KeywordDiscovery, Wordtracker is available on a subscription basis, with a $59.00 per month cost.

Finally, WordZe (www.wordze.com) is an up-and-coming keyword research tool. It's priced a little lower than KeywordDiscovery or Wordtracker, at just $38.98 per month.

The best of these tools provide more than just raw keyword research data. They may also include features such as industry keyword tracking (the top keywords that drive traffic to sites in specific industries), spelling mistake research (common misspellings in user queries), related keywords, seasonal trends, and the like.

You can pick up a lot of keywords—and potential customers—on the cheap by bidding on misspellings of common keywords. For example, if you're selling golf clubs, you might want to bid on *gulf clubs*, *golf culbs*, and *golf blubs* and other similar typos that fumble-fingered users might enter by mistake into the Google search box.

Using Google's Keyword Tool

These keyword research tools are all good, but they're somewhat pricy. Fortunately, there's another research tool available that's completely free to use—and it's available from Google.

Google's Keyword Tool is a free web-based utility you can use to find new keywords for your AdWords campaigns. To access this tool, go to the Opportunities tab on the AdWords site and click Keyword Tool in the Tools section.

 SHOW ME   Media 16.2—A video about how to use Google's Keyword Tool
Access this video file through your registered Web Edition at
my.safaribooksonline.com/9780131388666/media.

There are two ways to use Google's Keyword Tool. You can enter one or more words or phrases to describe your site, or you can just enter the URL for your ad's landing page—or, to generate a list of truly focused keywords, you can enter both phrases and your website URL. Click the Search button and the tool displays a list of possible keywords, like the one in Figure 16.1.

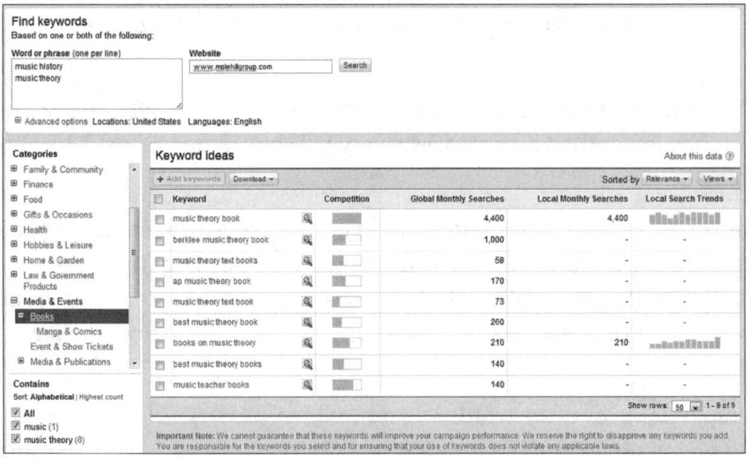

Figure 16.1   *Using Google's free Keyword Tool to search for the best keywords for your ad campaigns.*

For each keyword or keyword phrase identified, the tool displays the following information:

- **Competition.** This small bar graph indicates how popular this keyword is among competing advertisers; a fuller bar indicates a more popular keyword.

- **Global monthly searches.** The average number of searches made each month for that keyword on the Google search site and related search sites.

The global monthly searches number is a good indication of the maximum number of clicks an ad tied to this keyword is likely to generate. In fact, you probably won't generate anywhere near this number, as not all people searching will see or click on your ad.

- **Local monthly searches.** If you specified a country or language for your search, this is the total number of Google searches for this keyword within the specified country or in the specified language.

- **Local search trends.** This chart shows the fluctuation in traffic for this keyword over the past twelve months.

You can make this tool even more useful by clicking the Advanced Options link near the top of the page and then selecting a country or language; opting to display statistics for mobile search only; estimating traffic by a specific maximum CPC and daily budget; or filtering keywords by a number of factors, such as estimated impressions or estimated CTR.

I find it particularly useful to enter the maximum CPC I'm thinking of bidding, along with my estimated daily budget. When you do this and then click the Search button, the Keyword Tool more precisely estimates the performance of the selected keywords.

You can also view search trends over time by clicking the little magnifying glass next to a given keyword. This displays a Google Insights page for that keyword, as shown in Figure 16.2. Google Insights offers more detailed search tracking, including search interest by location, time, and type of search (web search, image search, and the like). It's a more sophisticated tool for more sophisticated advertisers.

Using the Search-Based Keyword Tool

If you want even more keyword ideas, try Google's other free utility, the Search-Based Keyword Tool. You can access this tool at www.google.com/sktool/. This tool provides more detailed data for each keyword, including category information, AdWords share, and the suggested bid that might place the ad in the top three positions—always a good thing to know.

Figure 16.2   *Viewing search trends for a keyword with Google Insights.*

    SHOW ME   **Media 16.3—A video about how to use the Search-Based Keyword Tool**
Access this video file through your registered Web Edition at
my.safaribooksonline.com/9780131388666/media.

As you can see in Figure 16.3, you enter your website URL (for your site's top domain or home page), along with any descriptive words or phrases, and then click the Find Keywords button. You now see a page of suggested keywords, like the one shown in Figure 16.4. For each keyword, the Search-Based Keyword Tool displays the following information:

- **Monthly searches.** The average amount of monthly traffic the keyword receives from the Google search site.

- **Competition.** A small bar graph that indicates how popular this keyword is with competing advertisers; the more full the bar, the more advertisers who are targeting this keyword.

- **Sugg. bid.** This is the amount that Google suggests you bid for this keyword to place in the top three display positions.

- **Ad/Search share.** The ad share is the percentage of time that an ad for your website appeared for the given query. The search share is the percentage of time your website (not your ad) appeared in the first page of search results for this query.

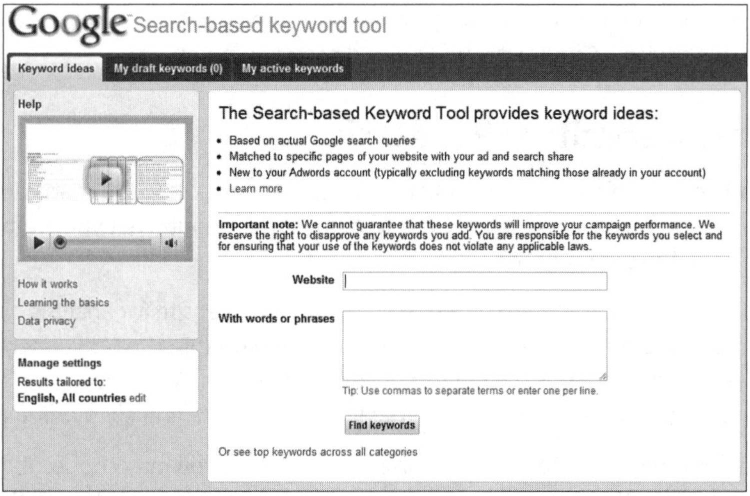

Figure 16.3 *Using the Search-Based Keyword Tool.*

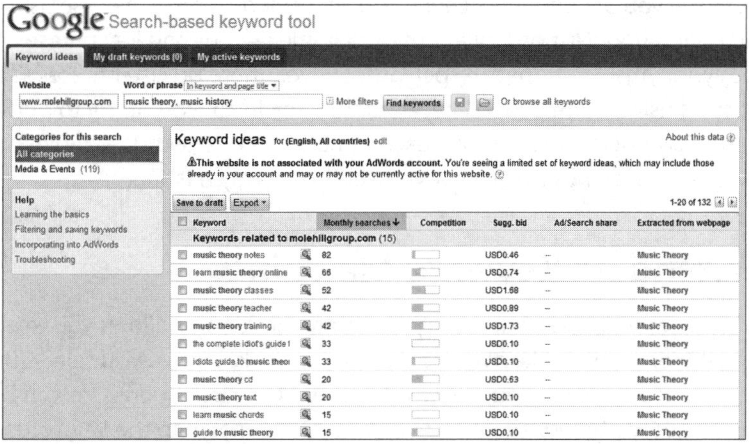

Figure 16.4 *Keyword suggestions from the Search-Based Keyword Tool.*

You must have already advertised to have an ad share. Any site can have a search share.

- **Extracted from webpage.** The specific page on your site that best matched the keyword suggestion.

I particularly like the suggested bids generated by this tool. It's good to know what Google thinks you need to bid to garner a high display position; you can choose to follow this advice or ignore it, but it's a good starting point.

Doing Competitive Research

You can use any of these search tools to generate keywords for your ad campaigns, of course. You can also use these tools to get smarter about what your competitors might be doing with AdWords.

You see, you're not limited to entering just your own website for analysis. You can also enter the URL for a competitor's site. When you do this, the tool generates the list of keywords that your competitor is likely bidding on. And, depending on the tool, you might also see the amount that your competitor is likely bidding per click.

You can use this knowledge in a number of ways. First, you may choose to go head-to-head with a successful competitor. In this instance, you'd bid on the same keywords, but at a higher level. This way, you'll steal position away from that competitor—at least until he catches on to what you're doing.

Another approach is to use this information to develop an alternative strategy. In this instance, you deliberately *avoid* the exact keywords this advertiser is using, instead generating a list of similar but different keywords and key phrases. These may be synonyms or alternative spellings, or even more precise phrases (if the advertiser is using more general keywords). In any instance, you try to outflank the competitor by not going head-to-head with the same keywords—and generate page views for searches that this advertiser is currently missing.

Understanding Keyword Matching

When you're entering keywords for your campaign, Google allows you to employ several different types of keyword matching for the keywords you select. That is, you can choose to match your keywords exactly to search queries, match keyword phrases to query phrases, or perform a more broad match to the keywords you select. You can even enter *negative keywords*—those keywords you do not want your ad associated with under any circumstance.

SHOW ME   Media 16.4—A video about keyword matching
Access this video file through your registered Web Edition at
my.safaribooksonline.com/9780131388666/media.

Table 16.1 describes each of these approaches and details how to enter each type of keyword when you're creating your ad or ad group. We'll examine all these types of keyword matching in more detail in the following sections.

Table 16.1 AdWords Keyword Matching

Keyword Matching	Notation (Enter This)	Description
Broad match	*keyword phrase*	This is the default matching type when you select a keyword or keyword phrase. Broad matching displays your ad when someone searches for any keyword in your selected keyword phrase, in any order, or when used with any other search words. This approach ensures that your ad will show up as often as possible.
Phrase match	*"keyword phrase"*	Phrase matching displays your ad if someone searches for the exact phrase you've selected, with or without additional words appended. With phrase matching, your ad can also be displayed if someone searches for the exact phrase plus additional keywords.
Exact match	[*keyword phrase*]	Exact matching displays your ad if someone searches for *only* the exact phrase you've selected—with no other keywords appended.
Negative match	*-keyword*	Using a negative keyword prevents AdWords from displaying your ad when the selected word is entered as part of a search.

Getting More Results with Broad Matching

The default type of keyword matching is *broad matching*. With broad matching, your ad is displayed when any keyword from your search phrase is entered in any order, or is accompanied by any additional search words. As you can no doubt see for yourself, this results in the broadest possible exposure for your ad—but also displays your ad to a lot of people who really aren't looking for what you're offering.

For example, if you bid on the phrase *monty python*, broad matching will display your ad whenever someone searches for *monty python*, which is fine, but it will also display if someone searches for *monty hall*, *python programming*, *python*, *monty*, and so forth. If you're selling Monty Python merchandise, you probably don't want your ad displayed to someone searching for old episodes of *Let's Make a Deal*—thus the problem with this approach.

So, broad matching will greatly increase the number of times your advertisement is displayed—but will also result in a somewhat unfocused audience for your ad. This might be okay if your site or product is rather broad in its appeal, but not so good if you want to generate highly targeted clicks.

Some AdWords experts recommend that you never use broad keywords, as they waste too much of your budget. I think it's more a matter of what you're selling, and how broad your potential audience is.

For example, if you're selling vacuum cleaners, which have a broad appeal, you might be already doing broad matching for the term *vacuum*. But if you're selling hard-to-find vacuum tubes, broad-matching the word *vacuum* will deliver too many people uninterested in what you're selling.

Matching Requests with Phrase Matching

If you're bidding on a keyword phrase, you probably don't want to use broad matching. That's because Google will match your ad against any of the words included in the phrase, which often results in too many unwanted or inappropriate displays of your ad.

You can narrow down the display by using *phrase matching*. With phrase matching, a searcher has to include your exact phrase in her search for your ad to be displayed; searching for a single word or even the phrase words in a different order will not trigger your ad.

Take the keyword phrase *brake pad lining*. With broad matching, someone could search for *lining*, *cotton pad*, or *brake light* and see your ad displayed. Use phrase matching instead, and none of these partial or non-exact searches will trigger your ad; the user will have to search for *brake pad lining* to see your ad.

You activate phrase matching by surrounding your keyword phrase with quotation marks. Using the current example, you'd enter **"brake pad lining"** as your keyword phrase, and AdWords will apply phrase matching.

Producing Exact Results with Exact Matching

The only problem with phrase matching is that it will also display your ad if someone searches for the exact phrase *plus* one or more other keywords. For example, if you bid on the phrase *brake light*, someone searching for a "brake light repair" will see your ad. This might not be a bad thing, if you do brake light repair, but if you only sell brake lights and not repair them, you'll generate some ad placements that don't directly relate to your business at hand.

If you want your ad displayed only when someone *exclusively* searches for your keyword phrase, use AdWords' exact matching feature. When you surround your keyword phrase with brackets, only people searching for your exact phrase—and nothing more—will see your ad.

In our current example, you'd enter **[brake light]** as your keyword phrase. With phrase matching, your ad will be displayed only to people searching for *brake light*—not for *brake light repair, ford brake light,* or *broken brake light.*

Filtering Out Bad Prospects with Negative Keywords

There's another way to make sure your ad doesn't display to people who aren't interested in what you're offering. You can use *negative keywords* to keep your ad from displaying when someone searches for a given word.

Using our brake light example, you could simply append the negative keyword *repair* to your list of normal keywords and phrases. This way, if someone searches for *brake light repair*, the negative keyword *repair* will cause AdWords not to display your ad to the person doing that search.

You enter negative keywords by placing a minus sign (-) in front of the given word. In our example, you'd enter **-repair** in your keyword list, and that's that. (Similarly, you can enter a negative keyword phrase, like this: **-keyword phrase.**)

Many advertisers routinely use the negative keyword *-free,* thus ensuring that their ads won't be displayed for anyone looking for free goods—who are unlikely to pay for anything you're selling.

Diagnosing Keyword Performance

Want to see how specific keywords you've selected are performing? It's easy enough to do without running any special reports. Just open your AdWords page and select Campaigns > Keywords. This page displays a table with all your keywords listed, and key information about each keyword. As you can see in Figure 16.5, this table includes the following data:

 SHOW ME   Media 16.5—A video about how to diagnose keyword problems
Access this video file through your registered Web Edition at my.safaribooksonline.com/9780131388666/media.

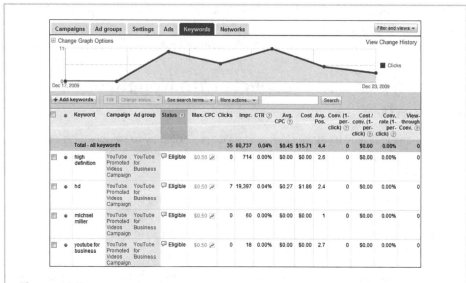

Figure 16.5 *Viewing data for your keywords on the Campaigns > Keywords sub-tab.*

- **Enabled/paused.** A green dot before the keyword indicates that it is enabled for use. Two vertical lines indicate that the keyword is "paused," or not currently in use.

- **Keyword.** This is the keyword you're bidding on. To edit this keyword, simply click it.

- **Campaign.** This is the campaign that the selected keyword is part of.

- **Ad group.** This is the ad group that the selected keyword is part of.

- **Status.** This column indicates the current disposition of the selected keyword; a keyword can be eligible, paused, or deleted. In addition, any special messages can be displayed in this column, such as if a keyword is "rarely shown due to low quality score."

- **Max. CPC.** This is the keyword's maximum cost per click—the maximum amount you're bidding for this keyword.

- **Clicks.** This column displays the total number of clicks this keyword has received during the selected time period.

- **Impr.** This is the total number of impressions garnered by the current keyword—that is, the number of times the keyword has been viewed.

- **CTR.** This column displays the click-through rate for the current keyword—clicks divided by impressions.

- **Avg. CPC.** This is the average cost-per-click for the keyword—the actual CPC paid, in contrast to the max CPC you're willing to pay. This number can be lower than your max CPC, in which case you're bidding on the high end; it can also be higher than your max CPC, in which case you're probably not getting ads displayed for this keyword. (You're bidding too low, in other words.)

- **Cost.** This is the total amount of money you've spent on this keyword for the selected time period.

- **Avg. Pos.** This is the average position your ad is generating for this keyword on Google's search results pages.

- **Conv. (1-per-click).** If you're using conversion tracking, this measures how many conversions (that is, actual sales) result from each click on this keyword's ad.

☛ *Learn more about conversion tracking in Chapter 13, "Creating Your First AdWords Campaign."*

- **Cost/conv. (1-per-click).** This metric calculates the cost of each conversion (conversion tracking must be activated).

- **Conv. Rate (1-per-click).** This calculates your conversion rate—the percentage of clicks that result in actual conversions (conversion tracking must be activated).

- **View-through Conv.** This column measures how many conversions happened within 30 days of a user seeing, but not immediately clicking through, your ad (conversion tracking must be activated).

When tracking conversions, 1-per-click counts only the first conversion resulting from an ad click. Many-per-click tracking counts multiple conversions from a single click, if they occur. So, if someone buys two items after clicking your ad, 1-per-click tracking counts only one conversion, while many-per-click tracking counts two conversions.

Understanding Your Quality Score

In addition, if you hover your cursor over the icon in the Status column for any keyword on the Campaigns > Keywords sub-tab, you see an information box like the one in Figure 16.6. This box tells you whether the keyword is currently triggering any ads, and also displays your ad's Quality Score.

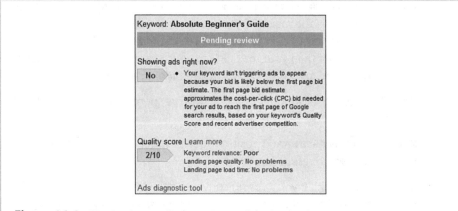

Figure 16.6 *Viewing keyword information and the Quality Score.*

What is this mysterious Quality Score? It has to do with the relevance of your landing page to the keywords you select. If you select keywords that have nothing to do with the content of the page you link to in your ad, you get a low Quality Score; if you select targeted keywords, you get a high Quality Score. That's it in a nutshell.

It's important to know that the CPC rate you bid for a keyword isn't the only factor determining your ads' visibility. Ad position is based on a combination of the cost you pay and the quality of your ad, as measured by something called the Quality Score. More specifically, your position is your maximum CPC bid multiplied by this Quality Score. You can improve your ad position by either increasing your bid rate or by improving your Quality Score.

> You can reduce the price you pay per-click for a given keyword by improving the Quality Score.

Google uses the Quality Score to ensure that consumers see only the most relevant ads. It does Google no good for people to see ads totally unrelated to their searches or to a page's content; more clicks (and more AdSense revenues) result when people see highly targeted ads online.

How can you improve your keywords' Quality Scores? The best approach is to optimize your account—make sure your ads are descriptive of what your linked-to page is actually about, and that your keywords reflect the content of the linked-to page. That means you can't choose keywords willy nilly; you must carefully target your keywords to your site's content.

As noted previously, you can view your Quality Score for any given keyword by going to the Campaigns > Keywords sub-tab and clicking the icon in the Status column for that keyword. The resulting information box displays not only the Quality Score but also the keyword relevance, landing page quality, and landing page load time; problems with any of these variables will lower your Quality Score.

17

Maximizing Conversion with a Custom Landing Page

Running an AdWords advertisement is just the first part of a process. When someone clicks on your ad, they're transferred to your web page, where you can then provide more information or attempt to conclude a sales transaction.

So, the page potential customers land on—dubbed, quite logically, the *landing page*—is just as important as your AdWords ad. The right landing page can convert a click into a sale and generate good revenue; the wrong landing page can cause users to click away seconds after landing, with no transaction being made.

Where Should Customers Land?

A landing page is the page that appears when a potential customer clicks your AdWords advertisement. The landing page could be your site's home page, a product page for whatever it is you're advertising, or a page specially designed to accompany the specific advertisement.

Research and history have shown that most users don't travel farther than the first page when they click an ad to the advertiser's website. If they don't like what they find, or if the landing page doesn't contain the information they want, they leave immediately.

For this reason, you need to set up a well-structured landing page to greet those users who click on your ad. The more effective your landing page, the more clicks you will convert to sales.

The best landing pages display content that is a logical extension of the advertisement or link. Depending on the nature and intent of the page, it should provide additional information, ask for information from the customer, or ask for the sale.

As I said, you could link to your site's home page, but that generally isn't a great idea. That's because most home pages are rather general in nature; they advertise your company or brand, not necessarily the specific product or service mentioned in your ad. That is, they don't follow directly from your ad—which could be confusing to potential customers.

Likewise, linking to any existing page on your site might not be the best approach. Remember, if you're looking for conversions rather than raw clicks, your landing page has to close the sale. That means you shouldn't point to a generic brand or product page; customers need to see a page that displays the product or service you talked about in the ad. Going to any nonspecific page requires unnecessary work on the part of the customer to learn more about what's advertised and to place an order.

The best approach, then, is to link to a page on your site custom-designed for readers of your AdWords advertisement. This page should display information only about the product promoted in your advertising—and include an ordering mechanism, the better to convert that click into a sale.

 TELL ME MORE   Media 17.1—A discussion about landing pages
Access this audio recording through your registered Web Edition at
my.safaribooksonline.com/9780131388666/media.

Why design a special landing page for each ad you create? It's simple: You want to make it as easy as possible for people to give you their money. If you just dump potential customers on your site's home page, they could get lost, or they might have trouble finding the product they want and give up. In any instance, you don't want them randomly browsing your site; you want them immediately responding to your specific offer.

As far as AdWords is concerned, linking to a nonspecific landing page costs the same as linking to one custom-designed for your ad; you pay the same rate per click, no matter what page you link to. Because nonspecific landing pages result in fewer sales, you end up paying more per conversion than you do with a more effective custom-designed page.

Creating an Effective Landing Page

I hope I've convinced you of the necessity of creating a custom landing page. You might want to create a different landing page for each ad you place. Depending on how you've organized your account, you might be able to get by with a single landing page for all the ads in an ad group, or all the ads in a campaign. In any instance, some custom page design is in order.

When it comes to designing a landing page for an image ad, it should convey the same look and feel of the ad itself. Obviously, this is less important if you're running a text ad, which really doesn't have a visual design.

The connection between your ad and the landing page is of utmost importance. Your landing page *must* discuss or display the product or service promoted in the ad, and it probably shouldn't display any other products or services; you don't want to confuse the customer. Remember, a potential customer clicks your ad to find out more about what the ad talked about. He expects to click to a page that follows seamlessly from what was discussed in the ad.

For this reason, your landing page needs to be consistent with your advertisement, both in terms of content and presentation. This means using the same terminology employed in your ad; talk about the same product in the same way. Don't change things up or get greedy about presenting other products. There will be time enough for that later, if the customer decides to buy what you're advertising.

Remember that customers see your ad because they're interested in particular keywords. Make sure to include those keywords, not only in your ad, but also on your landing page.

Naturally, the landing page can and should include more information than you had space to present in the ad. After all, you have a lot more than three lines to work with now. The landing page should include detailed information about the featured product, as well as more detailed product photos. It should be a real sell page.

Some experts recommend a more stripped-down landing page, with links to additional information if the customer needs it. The thinking is that anyone clicking to your landing page has already been convinced to buy; you don't want to introduce any element that might make her rethink her decision. Although I don't necessarily adhere to this advice, I understand the impetus of striking while the iron is hot and getting right to the ordering process.

That said, you don't want to hit the customer over the head with too much information. Displaying a landing page that contains paragraph after paragraph of boring details or useless marketing drivel will kill the interest of even the most dedicated potential customers. The information you present has to be both relevant and valuable, or it doesn't belong on the page.

SHOW ME   Media 17.2—A video about how to create an effective landing page

Access this video file through your registered Web Edition at my.safaribooksonline.com/9780131388666/media.

Creating a Great-Looking Landing Page

It goes without saying that your landing page should have a professional look and feel. A landing page shouldn't look quick and dirty, but rather have a quality design, just like the big sites. Your page needs to look trustworthy; users are never sure what's on the other side of a click, and are quickly turned off by sites that don't make them feel safe.

Your landing page should also be visually clean and easy to read. Customers who can't find what they're looking for will quickly click away; make it easy to find the information that people want.

Remember, first impressions count, and your landing page is the first exposure customers have to your site after they click your ad. Wow them visually, impress them with your content, and then ask for the order. That's the way landing pages are supposed to work.

Asking for the Order

Useful information and professional design aside, the most important element on the product landing page is the click-to-order button. You want customers to buy your product, and presumably they clicked on your ad because they're thinking of buying. Don't make the customer do a lot of work; make it easy to click one button to initiate the order process.

When the customer clicks the order button, she can move to your site's normal shopping cart or checkout section. You can even present add-on items that the customer might also be interested in buying. But don't get in the customer's way when they're in the purchasing mood; make sure the order button is big and obvious and easy to use.

Another good reason to create a different landing page for each of your AdWords ads is because that makes it easier to track sales for each ad. You should be able to track each page separately, and thus analyze your sales on a per-ad basis.

Of course, not all advertisers are in the direct sales business. If you have a different goal for your AdWords ad, your landing page should reflect that goal. For example, if you want to collect sales leads, your landing page should contain a form to collect customer information. Just make sure that your landing page is the natural next step after clicking your ad, and that it asks the customer to take a specific action.

Don't clutter your landing page with unnecessary elements that confuse or obscure your call to action.

Improving Your Quality Score with a Quality Landing page

One more thing that bears mentioning is the relationship between your landing page and your Quality Score. A poorly focused landing page can result in a low Quality Score, while a high-value landing page can improve your Quality Score immensely. And as I'm sure you remember, a high Quality Score can help improve your ad placement and lower your per-click costs.

⊙ *Learn more about AdWord's Quality Score in Chapter 16, "Choosing the Right Keywords."*

Probably the most important influence on your Quality Score is the relevance of your landing page to the content of your AdWords ad. Your landing page should address the same topic or product presented in the ad. It should also include all the keywords you use to trigger the ad display.

Here's the deal: A landing page that isn't directly related to an ad or its triggering keywords will receive a low Quality Score. And if your Quality Score is too low, your ad might never be displayed for the keywords you select. Everything has to work in concert—your keywords, your ads, and your landing pages have to be part of a whole.

So, how can you improve your landing page to affect a higher Quality Score? Here are a few quick tips to consider:

- Make sure the content of your landing page is relevant to your ad and to the triggering keywords. Original content is also helpful; copying content from another page will trigger a low Quality Score.

- Include all the keywords for your campaign on the related landing page. Make sure these keywords are included in the body of the page, in the page title, and in the page's <KEYWORDS> HTML tag.

- Make sure your landing page isn't too large. Believe it or not, Google factors the load time of your landing page into the page's Quality Score; pages that take too long to load get a lower score than do faster pages.

- If your landing page includes a form of any type, make sure it also includes a link to your site's privacy policy.

- Be transparent about your business, the products you offer, and how you interact with consumers. That includes informing users how you might use any personal information they might enter. (That's the privacy policy thing.) You should never create a misleading landing page or AdWords campaign; Google does not look kindly on you suckering users in with one message and then trying to sell them something completely different on your landing page.

- Don't include any elements that alter users' browser behavior or settings. In addition, your landing page shouldn't surreptitiously install any software on users' computers.

Landing Page Versus Display Page

It's probably worth reminding you that the landing page you create can be a different page than the one you display in your PPC text ad. What customers see and what they click to can—and probably should—be two different things.

As Figure 17.1 should remind you, Google always displays a URL in your ads. This URL needs to be short (35 characters or less) and is typically the address of your site's home page.

Figure 17.1   *A typical AdWords text ad—the URL displayed doesn't have to be the URL for your landing page.*

As you've learned, however, you seldom want to use your site's home page as an ad's landing page. You want customers to link to a different, more specific page when they click to your ad.

You accomplish this when you first create your ad. When you're creating a new ad, AdWords asks for both a display URL and a destination URL, as shown in Figure 17.2. The display URL is the address that users see in your ad; the destination URL is your landing page. Enter your site's home page address into the Display URL box and then enter your landing page's address into the Destination URL box. Customers will never see the often long and complex landing page URL, but will be taken to that page when they click on your ad.

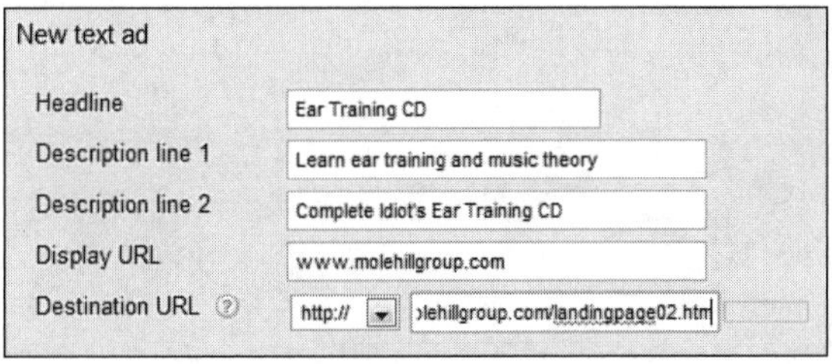

New text ad

Headline	Ear Training CD
Description line 1	Learn ear training and music theory
Description line 2	Complete Idiot's Ear Training CD
Display URL	www.molehillgroup.com
Destination URL ⓘ	http:// ▼)lehillgroup.com/landingpage02.htm

Figure 17.2   *Creating a text ad with different display and destination URLs.*

 SHOW ME   Media 17.3—A video about how landing and display pages differ
Access this video file through your registered Web Edition at
my.safaribooksonline.com/9780131388666/media.

18

Combining PPC Advertising with Search Engine Marketing

For most websites, PPC advertising is just part of a larger, more involved online marketing effort. This online marketing most often includes search engine marketing—the act of promoting your website by seeking higher placement on search engine results pages.

That's higher placement for your web pages, not for your ads. Search engine marketing is not advertising; there are no ads or clicks to buy. Instead, search engine marketing concerns itself with organic search results—which you can improve by optimizing your site for search.

Understanding Search Engine Marketing

Search engine marketing is different from most types of marketing you're probably familiar with. It's all about increasing your site's ranking with Google and the other search engines; the higher your ranking, the more traffic the search engines will drive to your site.

    ☞ *Learn more about all the various components of an online marketing plan in Chapter 11, "Creating an Online Advertising Plan and Determining Your AdWords Budget."*

What Search Engine Marketing Is—and What It Isn't

Technically, search engine marketing involves any and all activities that drive traffic from the major search engines to your website. Looking at it this way, then, search engine marketing includes both PPC advertising and organic search results; both these activities can result in users clicking their way from a search results page to your site.

That said, I tend to separate organic search results from PPC advertising, and refer to the former as search engine marketing. That's because I (and many others) find it useful to separate advertising from organic activities.

You see, advertising—including PPC advertising—is all about purchasing results. In contrast, organic search engine marketing doesn't have anything to purchase. You don't (in fact, you *can't*) pay the search engines to get listed, nor for a specific ranking within that engine's search results. There's no way to pay for clicks.

You see, Google doesn't sell its search results; placement on a search results page—those *organic results* I've been talking about—are determined by Google solely on the merits of the pages themselves. If you have a page that is relevant to a query and contains unique, high quality information, that page will rank high in the search results. And, as you might imagine, appearing high up in the search results page results in more people seeing your listing and clicking to your site. That increased traffic can then be converted into more customers and sales.

> Search engine marketing is both effective and efficient because it's relatively simple to translate a search query into the ultimate intentions and desires of the customer. They essentially state, in their queries, what they're interested in—nothing is hidden.

This, of course, is why it's important to optimize your site for search—what we call *search engine optimization*, or SEO. You need to optimize your site so that it appears as high as possible in the search engine rankings when someone searches for a relevant keyword. Because you can't directly buy your way to the top of the results, you have to improve your rankings organically, by making your site as authoritative and relevant as possible. With search engine marketing, success really is a result of hard work—not how much money you have in your budget.

 TELL ME MORE   Media 18.1—A discussion about search engine marketing
Access this audio recording through your registered Web Edition at
my.safaribooksonline.com/9780131388666/media.

Why Search Engine Marketing Is Important

How important is search engine marketing? For most websites, it's extremely important. That's because the majority of traffic for most sites doesn't come from PPC advertising, as important as that might be; instead, most new traffic comes from users linking from Google's search results pages. Check your own website logs if you don't believe me—it's probably true of your own traffic as well.

If half or more of your site traffic comes from the search engines, you need to increase your site's search ranking for those keywords that drive the most traffic to your site. You do this by employing tried and true SEO techniques.

Search engine marketing is also important because it's a relatively low-cost way to increase traffic and generate revenues. Because you can't buy placement in search engine results, your primary cost is the SEO effort itself. And because SEO isn't that expensive, whether you do it yourself or hire someone to get it done, search engine marketing provides a huge bang for your marketing buck.

For most online marketers, search engine marketing and the attending SEO represent a major component of their online marketing mix. It's at least as important as PPC advertising—if not more so.

PPC Advertising and Search Engine Marketing: Working Together

For online marketers, it's really a short step from PPC advertising to search engine marketing and optimization. Because they both target search engine users, search engine marketing and PPC advertising have a lot in common. (And are, in fact, treated as a larger whole by many marketers.)

First, both PPC and search engine marketing revolve around keywords. A key component of search engine optimization is identifying a list of keywords for your website. When you do your keyword research for SEO, you now have a list of keywords you can purchase for your PPC ads. There's no difference between which keywords work for search engine marketing and which work best for PPC advertising. An effective keyword for one is an effective keyword for the other.

Second, both organic page listings and PPC ads appear on the same search engine results pages. When someone is searching for a keyword, he will see both the pages that best match the query and the paid ads for that purchased keyword. If you have both an organic listing and a paid listing on the same page, that reinforces the quality of your site in the mind of the user, making it more likely that he will click on one of them. And, it goes without saying, two placements on the same page is always better than one; you're twice as likely to be noticed.

PPC advertising is also a good contingency in case you don't do a good job with SEO. If your page doesn't make it onto the first page of organic search results, you at least have the paid ad as a backup.

Beyond the commonalities, PPC advertising supplements your organic search results. When you use Google AdWords, your ad appears on more than just search results pages; it also appears on content pages throughout the ad network's affiliate sites. This adds countless impressions to what you receive organically and helps to drive additional traffic to your website.

In this aspect, PPC advertising is a good supplement to traditional search engine marketing. PPC advertising can't replace organic search results in your marketing plan, but it can work in addition to your normal search engine marketing. This is why most larger websites engage in both search engine marketing and PPC advertising; they work together to maximize your visibility online.

Improving Your Search Results with SEO

As you now know, achieving a high ranking in the search results at Google and other search sites is the primary means of attracting new visitors and increasing traffic; PPC advertising is subsidiary to the traffic driven by the search engines. This is why you need to optimize your site for search, using various search engine optimization techniques.

What exactly does SEO entail? It's really a series of techniques, each designed to push your site higher on Google's search results pages.

⊙ *Learn more about SEO techniques in my companion book, The Complete Idiot's Guide to Search Engine Optimization (Alpha Books, 2009).*

 SHOW ME   Media 18.2—A video about search engine optimization
Access this video file through your registered Web Edition at
my.safaribooksonline.com/9780131388666/media.

Better Content = Better Search Results

Why do people visit a given website? It's all about what's on the site; the more unique and useful the content, the more visitors the site attracts.

That's why of all the SEO techniques available to you, the one that has the biggest impact is improving your website's content. It's simple: The better your site is, content-wise, the higher it will rank.

You see, when it comes to search rank, content is king. Ultimately, Google and the other search engines find some way to figure out what your site is all about; the higher the quality and more relevant your site's content is to a particular search, the more likely it is that a search engine will rank your site higher in its results.

The key, then, is to focus on what it is your site does and says. If your site is about model airplanes, work to make it the most content-rich site about model airplanes you can; if it's about lawn mower repair, make it the highest-quality lawn mower repair site possible. Don't skimp on the content—the more and better content you have, the better.

The most effective thing you can do to improve your site's search rank is to make it more useful to visitors—and that means providing the best possible content you can. Everything else follows from this.

Organization and Hierarchy Are Important

How does Google determine the search rank for a given page? It all starts with a web crawler—a piece of software that crawls the pages on the web, looking for and indexing important content. These web crawlers can find more content on a web page and more web pages on a website if that content and those pages are in a clear hierarchical organization.

Let's look at page organization first. You want to think of each web page as a mini-outline. The most important information should be in major headings, with lesser information in subheadings beneath the major headings. One way to do this is via standard HTML heading tags, with the most important information in <H1> tags, the next most-important in <H2> tags, and less-important information in <H3> tags.

This approach is also appropriate for your entire site layout. Your home page should contain the most important information, with subsidiary pages branching out from that containing less important information—and even more sub-pages branching out from those. The most important info should be visible when a site is first accessed via the home page; additional info should be no more than a click or two away.

Keywords Count

Just as important as a page's layout is the page's content, in terms of keywords—those words and phrases that users search for. In calculating search ranking, the major search engines try to determine how important a keyword or phrase is on your page.

When they examine your page, Google's web crawlers look for the most important words—those words used in the site's title or headings, those words that appear in the opening paragraph, and those words that are repeated throughout the page. The more and more prominently you include a word on your page, the more important a search engine will think it is to your site.

A site with a keyword buried near the bottom of a page will rank lower than one with the keyword placed near the top, or used repeatedly in the page's text. It's not a foolproof way of determining importance and appropriateness, but it's a good first stab at it.

For this reason, you want to make sure that each and every page on your site contains the keywords that users might use to search for your pages. If your site is all about drums, make sure your pages include words like *drums, percussion, sticks, heads, cymbals, snare*, and the like. If your site is about dogs, include words like *dog, puppy, canine, beagle, collie, dachshund*, and such. Try to think through how *you* would search for this information, and work those keywords into your content.

It's just like when you choose the keywords that trigger your PPC advertising. The better you are at identifying what people are searching for—and the more effectively you incorporate those keywords into your pages—the higher your ranking will be.

🔄 *Learn more about keywords in Chapter 16, "Choosing the Right Keywords."*

<META> Tags Matter

Google looks not just to the text that visitors see when trying to determine the content of your site. Also important is the presence of keywords in your site's HTML code—specifically within the <META> tag.

The <META> tag includes metadata about your site, such as your site's name and keyword content. This tag appears in the head of your HTML document, before the <BODY> tag and its contents.

It's easy enough for Google and the other search engines to locate the <META> tag and read the data contained within. If a site's metadata is properly indicated, this gives the search engine a good first idea as to what content is included on this page.

You can insert multiple <META> tags into the head of your document, and each tag can contain a number of different attributes. For example, you can assign attributes for your page's name, description, and keywords to the <META> tag.

You use separate <META> tags to define different attributes, using the following format:

```
<META NAME="attribute" CONTENT="items">
```

Replace *attribute* with the name of the particular attribute, and *items* with the keywords or description of that attribute.

For example, to include a description of your web page, you'd enter this line of code:

```
<META NAME="DESCRIPTION" CONTENT="All about stamp collecting">
```

To include a list of keywords, use the following code:

```
<META NAME="KEYWORDS" CONTENT="keyword1, keyword2, keyword3">
```

Inbound Links Affect PageRank

Google got to be Google by recognizing that web rankings could be somewhat of a popularity contest—that is, if a site got a lot of traffic, there was probably a good reason for that. A useless site wouldn't attract a lot of visitors (at least not in the long term), nor would it inspire other sites to link to it.

If a site has a lot of other sites linking back to it, it's probably because that site offers useful information relevant to the site doing the linking. The more links to a given site, the more useful that probably is.

Google took this to heart and developed its own algorithm, dubbed PageRank, which is based first and foremost on the number and quality of sites that link to a particular page. If your site has a hundred sites linking to it, for example, it should rank higher in Google's search results than a similar site with only 10 sites linking to it. Yes, it's a popularity contest, but one that has proven uncannily accurate in providing relevant results to Google's users.

The quality of your inbound links matters just as much as their quantity. That is, a link from a site that includes content related to your page is more important than a link from some random site. For example, if you have a site about Barbie dolls, you'll get more oomph with a link from another Barbie-related site than you would with a link from a site about snow blower repair. Relevance matters.

When it comes to increasing your Google search ranking, you can get a big impact by getting more higher-quality sites to link back to your site. There are a number of ways to do this, from just waiting for the links to roll in to actively soliciting links from other sites. You can even pay other sites to link back to your site; when it comes to increasing your site's search ranking, little is out of bounds. However you do it, increasing the number and quality of inbound links is essential.

Submitting Your Site Makes Sense

Although you could wait for each search engine's crawler to find your site on the web, a more proactive approach is to manually submit your site for inclusion in each engine's web index. It's an easy process—and one that every webmaster should master.

Fortunately, submitting your site to a search engine is an easy process. In fact, it's probably the easiest part of the SEO process. All you have to do is go to the submission page for each search engine, as noted here:

- Google: www.google.com/addurl/
- Yahoo!: siteexplorer.search.yahoo.com/submit/
- Bing (Microsoft): http://www.bing.com/docs/submit.aspx

As easy as this site submittal process is, some webmasters prefer to offload the task to a site submittal service. These services let you enter your URL once and then submit it to multiple search engines and directories; they handle all the details required by each search engine. Some of the more popular site submittal services include 1 2 3 Submit Pro (websitesubmit.hypermart.net), AddMe! (www.addme.com), AddPro.com (www.addpro.com), and SubmitExpress (www. submitexpress.com).

Sitemaps Help

Something else you can submit to increase your site's ranking is a *sitemap*. A sitemap is a map of all the URLs in your entire website, listed in hierarchical order. Search engines can use this sitemap to determine what's where on your site, find otherwise hidden URLs on deeply buried pages, and speed up their indexing process. In addition, whenever you update the pages on your website, submitting an updated sitemap helps keep the search engines up to date.

The big three search engines (Google, Yahoo!, and Bing), along with Ask.com, all support a single sitemap standard. This means you can create just one sitemap that all the search engines can use; you don't have to worry about different formats for different engines.

Your sitemap is created in a separate XML file. This file contains the distinct URLs of all the pages on your website. When a searchbot reads the sitemap file, it learns about all the pages on your website—and can then crawl all those pages for submittal to the search engine's index.

The new unified sitemap format allows for autodiscovery of your site's sitemap file. Previously, you had to notify each search engine separately of where on your site the file was located. Now you do this universally by specifying the file's location in your site's robots.txt file.

Although you could create a sitemap file by hand, it's far easier to generate that sitemap automatically. To that end, many third-party sitemap generator tools exist for just that purpose. For most of these tools, generating a sitemap is as simple as entering your home page URL and then pressing a button. The tool now crawls your website and automatically generates a sitemap file. After the sitemap file is generated, you can then upload it to the root directory of your website, reference it in your robots.txt file, and, if you like, submit it directly to each of the major search engines.

Some of these tools are web-based, some are software programs, and most are free. The most popular of these tools include the following:

- AutoMapIt (www.automapit.com)
- AutoSitemap (www.autositemap.com)
- G-Mapper (www.dbnetsolutions.co.uk/gmapper/)
- GSiteCrawler (www.gsitecrawler.com)
- Gsitemap (www.vigos.com/products/gsitemap/)
- SitemapDoc (www.sitemapdoc.com)
- XML-Sitemaps.com (www.xml-sitemaps.com)

Images Don't Count

It's important to know that today's generation of search engines, Google included, parse only text content. They can't figure out what a picture, video, or Flash animation is about, unless you describe it in the text. If you use graphic buttons or banners (instead of plain text) to convey important information, the search engines simply won't see it. You need to put every piece of important information somewhere in the *text* of the page—even if it's duplicated in a banner or graphic.

If you want to use images on your site, which you probably do, make sure you employ the <ALT> tag for each image—and assign meaningful keywords to the image via this tag. A searchbot will read the <ALT> tag text; it can't figure out what an image is without it.

Similarly, don't hide important information in Flash animations, JavaScript applets, video files, and the like. Remember, searchbots can only find text on your page—all those non-text elements are invisible to a search engine.

Fresh Content Is Best

It pays to constantly update your site. Because most search engines crawl the web with some frequency, looking for pages that have changed or updated content, your ranking can be affected if your site hasn't changed in a while. You'll want to make sure you change your content on a regular basis; in particular, changing the content of your heading tags can have a big impact on how "fresh" the search engine thinks your site is.

It Pays to Know Your Customer

This final SEO technique is a piece of business advice I've been hawking for the past two decades, in various forums. Everything you do in business—or on your website—should come in service to your customers. You don't develop a new product just because you have the capability; you do it because it's something your customers want.

To that end, knowing what your customers want is the most important part of your business. If you know your customer, you can develop a website that they will want to visit—and that search engines will want to rank highly. Know what your customers want and you'll know what kind of content to create, and how to present that content. And, because SEO starts with your optimizing site's content, the better and more relevant that content, the higher your site will rank with Google, Yahoo!, and the other search engines.

Know your customer, and everything else follows.

Making PPC Advertising and Search Engine Marketing Work Together

So what do search engine marketing and SEO have to do with PPC advertising? Well, if you've been reading carefully, you've seen several similarities in approach, and many things that are important to both search ranking and PPC ad placement.

Content Is King...

The most important thing about any web page is its content. Without the right content, users who visit your site will quickly click away—whether they got there by clicking on an organic search result or an AdWords ad.

Your site's content not only has to match what you're promoting in your ads, it also has to be unique and useful. That's important both in attracting and retaining users, and in achieving high rankings with the search engines. Remember, Google and the other search engines place a high premium on relevant content when assigning search rankings for a given keyword; the higher the quality of your content, the higher your search rankings will be. If you have low-quality or irrelevant content, you won't rank high at all—which means you won't drive much traffic from the search engines.

This is why you need to work hard to develop your site's content. Pick a topic and then create the best content you can about that topic. Then you can write an ad that promotes that topic, and choose the best keywords to attract people searching for that topic. It all starts with the content; everything flows from there.

For best results, you need original content for your site. Stealing content from another site is not only unethical, it will decrease your search ranking.

...and So Are Keywords

The other key way in which PPC advertising and search engine marketing work together involves keywords. Think about it: Both your organic search ranking and your ad placement on search results placement are triggered by the keywords and phrases that people are searching for. Identify the most popular and relevant keywords—and use them properly on your pages—and both your ads and your site links will appear high on Google's search results pages.

For that reason, you need to pay utmost attention to the keyword selection process, both for your ads and for the pages on your site. This includes, of course, the landing pages you link to from your ads. In fact, you should probably use the same keyword list to populate both your site and your ads. The right keyword for one is most likely the right keyword for the other.

Use all the techniques discussed so far to pick the ultimate keyword list, and then use those keywords in your AdWords ads and on your web pages. The better the keywords, the better your ad placement and search results.

19

Advertising on YouTube

You're probably familiar with YouTube, the world's largest video sharing community. You probably know that it's a great place to view just about any kind of video, and you might even be aware that you can upload your own videos for others to view.

What you might not know is that YouTube is owned by Google. You might also not be aware that YouTube is a great channel for promoting your business and products—and that you can advertise on the YouTube site, via a program related to Google's AdWords.

Choosing the Type of Video to Produce

YouTube is the world's largest video sharing community, and one of the top ten sites on the web, period. As you can see in Figure 19.1, viewers can find just about any type of video on the YouTube site—including promotional videos from businesses of all types.

Promoting your business on YouTube involves shooting short videos, uploading those videos to the YouTube site, and then advertising those videos on YouTube. Viewers of your videos are then directed to a landing page on your own website to get more information or purchase your product or service.

The key, of course, is to offer a video that YouTube users actually want to watch. In most instances, this means a video that has some sort of entertainment, educational, or informational value. In other words, your video needs to entertain, educate, or inform—or no one will watch it.

 TELL ME MORE   Media 19.1—A discussion about promoting on YouTube

Access this audio recording through your registered Web Edition at my.safaribooksonline.com/9780131388666/media.

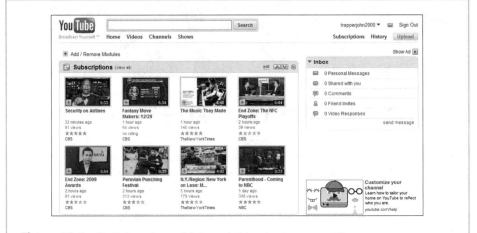

Figure 19.1   *YouTube—the world's largest video sharing community.*

Informative Videos

One way to do this is to create the YouTube equivalent of a newscast. You (or someone in your organization) sits behind the desk and talks about what's new in your company or your industry. Maybe it's all facts; maybe you use the opportunity to voice your opinion on a burning issue. In any case, you impart useful information in your video, and in the process establish yourself as an expert in your field—so that when the viewer wants to buy something, they'll think of you first.

And when they think of you, they need to know where to go. To that end, you need to display a title card or graphic with your website address and maybe even your company's toll-free phone number. You can display this info at the beginning and end of your video, or maybe even during the video, superimposed on the screen.

The key is to provide enough useful information to be of practical value to viewers, and then make it easy for those viewers to click through to your site for more information or to purchase what you have for sale. It can't be a straight advertisement; it has to be real information, presented in as straight a fashion as possible.

Educational Videos

Another approach is to create a "how to" video—that is, show the viewer how to do something useful. For example, if you sell appliance parts, you could create a video showing how to change the water filter in a refrigerator or the light bulb in a dryer. If you offer custom woodworking services, create a video showing how to build a bookcase or install wood trim. If you're a tire store, create a video showing how to check tire pressure or change a flat. You get the picture.

The key here is to offer truly useful content. Nothing theoretical or ethereal; down-to-earth practicality is what attracts YouTube viewers. Make the task common enough to draw a large audience, produce an easy to follow step-by-step tutorial, and then use the video to sell other goods and services.

Entertaining Videos

Informing and educating are important, and will draw a fair number of YouTube viewers if you do it right. But everybody likes to be entertained, which is why pure entertainment videos typically show up at the top of YouTube's lists of most viewed videos.

What's entertaining? Like art, entertainment is often in the eye of the beholder. For most videos, however, entertainment equals humor, so if you can make viewers laugh, you're onto a good thing. Of course, the video's entertainment needs to somehow relate to your company or what you're selling; that's a challenge you have to meet.

Learn more about using YouTube for business purposes in my companion book, *YouTube for Business: Online Video Marketing for Any Business* (Michael Miller, Que, 2008)

Producing a YouTube Video

This isn't a book about producing videos, so there isn't space to go into all the ins and outs of creating videos for YouTube. Know, however, that YouTube video production doesn't have to cost an arm and a leg; in fact, most YouTube videos—including those produced by businesses—are shot on low-cost consumer equipment, without costly production services.

Equipment Needed

What do you need to shoot a YouTube video? Here's the short list:

- **Video camcorder.** Any consumer-grade camcorder will do, but if you want to shoot high-definition videos, you'll need a high-def camcorder.
- **Tripod.** To hold your camcorder steady while recording.
- **Lights.** While you can shoot in existing light, you get much better results if you use some form of supplemental lighting. This can be one of those little lights that snap onto the top of your camcorder, or a set of multiple external floodlights like the ones you can buy at any camera store.

- **Video editing software.** You'll need to edit the videos you shoot, cutting out the scenes you don't want and splicing together the ones you do. Video editing software also lets you add transitions between scenes, onscreen graphics (to display your website URL, for example), and other special effects.

There are lots of good, low-priced video editing programs available, including Sony Vegas Movie Studio (www.sonycreativesoftware.com/moviestudiohd) and Adobe Premiere Elements (www.adobe.com/products/premiereel/), both priced under $100. You can also download Microsoft's Windows Live Movie Maker (download.live.com/moviemaker), an easy-to-use program that is available free of charge.

That's it, that's all you need. You probably have some of these items already; if not, you can get started for well under a total of $1,000.

Video Specifications

Your YouTube videos need to meet the following specifications:

- **File format.** AVI, Flash (FLV), MPEG-4 (MPEG), QuickTime (MOV), Windows Media Video (WMV), .MP4, .MKV, or .3GP
- **Resolution.** 640 × 480 pixels (HQ), 1280 × 720 (HD), or 1920 × 1080 (HD)
- **Length.** Up to 10 minutes long
- **File size.** No more than 2GB

These are fairly standard settings, although you do need to watch the length and file size to make sure you come in under the limits. With all this in mind, you can write your script, set up your equipment, and get ready to shoot. It's really that easy!

 **LET ME TRY IT**

Uploading Your Video

Uploading a finished video to YouTube is actually an easier process than shooting the video. Follow these steps:

1. Sign into your YouTube account then click the Upload button at the top of any YouTube page and select Upload Video File.

2. When the Video File Upload page appears, click the Upload Video button.

3. When the next dialog box appears, navigate to and select the file to upload, and click the Open button.

4. While the video uploads, you're prompted to enter information about the video, as shown in Figure 19.2. Start by entering a title for your video into the Title box.

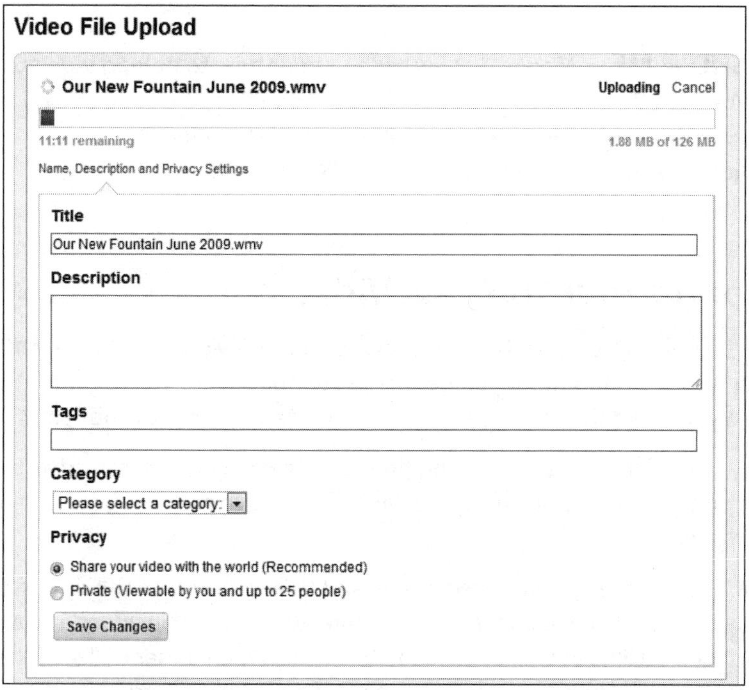

Video File Upload

○ **Our New Fountain June 2009.wmv**　　　　　　　Uploading　Cancel

11:11 remaining　　　　　　　　　　　　　　　　　　1.88 MB of 126 MB

Name, Description and Privacy Settings

Title

Our New Fountain June 2009.wmv

Description

Tags

Category

Please select a category: ▾

Privacy

◉ Share your video with the world (Recommended)
○ Private (Viewable by you and up to 25 people)

Save Changes

Figure 19.2　*Entering information about an uploaded video.*

5. Enter a brief description of your video into the Description box.

6. Enter one or more tags for the video into the Tags box, separating each tag by a space.

A *tag* is what YouTube calls a keyword—those words that viewers enter when searching for videos on the YouTube site.

7. Pull down the Category list and select the best category for your video.

8. If you want all YouTube users to be able to view your video, check the Share Your Video with the World option. If you prefer to keep your video private, check the Private option.

9. Click the Save Changes button.

That's it. After the video uploads, YouTube converts it to the proper viewing format and creates a viewing page for the video. To view your video, click the My Videos link on any YouTube page and then click the thumbnail for your new video.

SHOW ME   **Media 19.2—A video about how to upload video to YouTube**
Access this video file through your registered Web Edition at my.safaribooksonline.com/9780131388666/media.

Promoting Your YouTube Videos

Given the right strategy and execution, your YouTube videos can drive traffic back to your website. But how do you get people to notice your videos on YouTube? How do you stand out among the millions of videos on the YouTube site?

The key is YouTube's PPC advertising program. That's right, you can advertise your videos on the YouTube site, using similar techniques to the ones you employ with AdWords text ads.

YouTube calls these ads *promoted videos*, and they're found on the right side of most search results pages, as shown in Figure 19.3. Each ad includes a brief text description and link, as well as a video thumbnail. When a user clicks on the ad or thumbnail, they're taken to your video page—and you're charged for that click.

SHOW ME   **Media 19.3—A video about how to promote my videos on YouTube**
Access this video file through your registered Web Edition at my.safaribooksonline.com/9780131388666/media.

Not surprisingly, YouTube's promoted videos work just like Google's AdWords program—with the addition of a video thumbnail to accompany the ad's text. This is a pay-per-click program, just like AdWords; you're charged only when someone clicks on your ad. You bid on specific keywords and pay a certain price per click.

Figure 19.3 *Promoted videos on a YouTube search results page.*

To get started, you select a keyword or group of keywords that best describe your video. You bid on these keywords and select how much you're willing to pay for each click. When someone searches YouTube for a keyword that you've purchased, your ad will appear on that person's search results page, in the Promoted Videos section. At that point your account is charged for the click, at the previously agreed-upon rate.

Of course, you also set a total budget for your campaign. This budget is YouTube-specific, independent of your AdWords budget. When your PPC charges reach this amount, your ad is disabled. You determine how much you're willing to spend each month, and your advertising charges will never exceed this amount.

Sound familiar? That's because the Promoted Videos program is part of Google's AdWords PPC advertising service. To advertise using Promoted Videos, you must have a Google AdWords account—and a YouTube account, of course. Then you're ready to go.

Creating a Promoted Videos Campaign

You can set up advertising campaigns for any video you've uploaded to the YouTube site. In fact, you have to promote each video individually; you can set up separate campaigns for different videos, but you can't set up a generic campaign for all your videos.

LET ME TRY IT

Advertising a Video on YouTube

1. Go to the YouTube Promoted Videos Dashboard (ads.youtube.com).

2. If you're not yet a member of Google's AdWords program, you'll be prompted to sign up and enter your payment information. Follow the onscreen instructions to proceed.

3. After you've signed up, or if you're already an AdWords advertiser, click the Edit link in the Budget box at the top left side of the page.

4. Enter your daily budget into the Max. Daily (Average) box, shown in Figure 19.4, and click the Submit button.

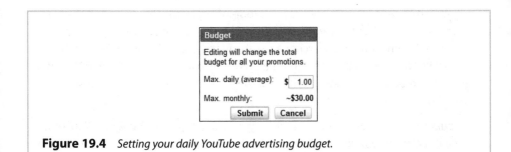

Figure 19.4   *Setting your daily YouTube advertising budget.*

5. Click the Create a New Promotion button.

6. When the Choose Video page appears, as shown in Figure 19.5, select the videos you want to promote and then click the Next, I Agree button.

7. When the Write Your Promotion page appears, as shown in Figure 19.6, enter a title for your ad in the first box, followed by two lines of text for your ad. The title must be 25 characters or less; each line of text must be 35 characters or less.

8. Select the thumbnail to use for the ad and then click Next.

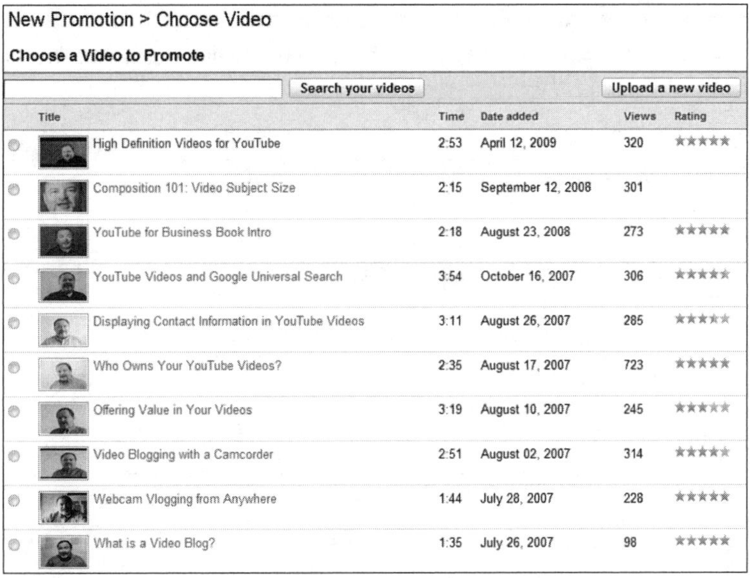

New Promotion > Choose Video

Choose a Video to Promote

| Search your videos | | | | Upload a new video |

	Title	Time	Date added	Views	Rating
◎	High Definition Videos for YouTube	2:53	April 12, 2009	320	★★★★★
◎	Composition 101: Video Subject Size	2:15	September 12, 2008	301	
◎	YouTube for Business Book Intro	2:18	August 23, 2008	273	★★★★★
◎	YouTube Videos and Google Universal Search	3:54	October 16, 2007	306	★★★★★
◎	Displaying Contact Information in YouTube Videos	3:11	August 26, 2007	285	★★★★★
◎	Who Owns Your YouTube Videos?	2:35	August 17, 2007	723	★★★★★
◎	Offering Value in Your Videos	3:19	August 10, 2007	245	★★★★★
◎	Video Blogging with a Camcorder	2:51	August 02, 2007	314	★★★★★
◎	Webcam Vlogging from Anywhere	1:44	July 28, 2007	228	★★★★★
◎	What is a Video Blog?	1:35	July 26, 2007	98	★★★★★

Figure 19.5   *Selecting videos to promote.*

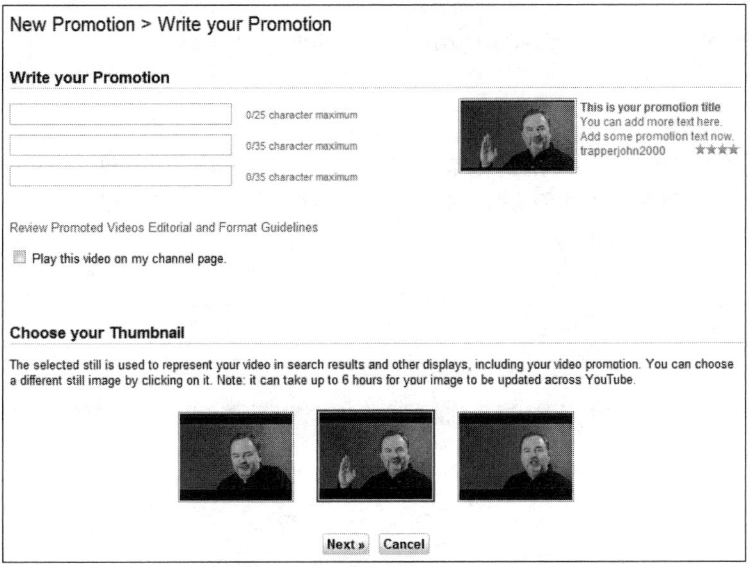

New Promotion > Write your Promotion

Write your Promotion

	0/25 character maximum
	0/35 character maximum
	0/35 character maximum

This is your promotion title
You can add more text here.
Add some promotion text now.
trapperjohn2000   ★★★★

Review Promoted Videos Editorial and Format Guidelines

☐ Play this video on my channel page.

Choose your Thumbnail

The selected still is used to represent your video in search results and other displays, including your video promotion. You can choose a different still image by clicking on it. Note: it can take up to 6 hours for your image to be updated across YouTube.

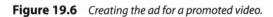

Next »   Cancel

Figure 19.6   *Creating the ad for a promoted video.*

9. You now see the Choose Keywords page, shown in Figure 19.7. Enter a group of keywords or phrases that best describes your video, with each keyword or phrase on a separate line, and then click the Next button.

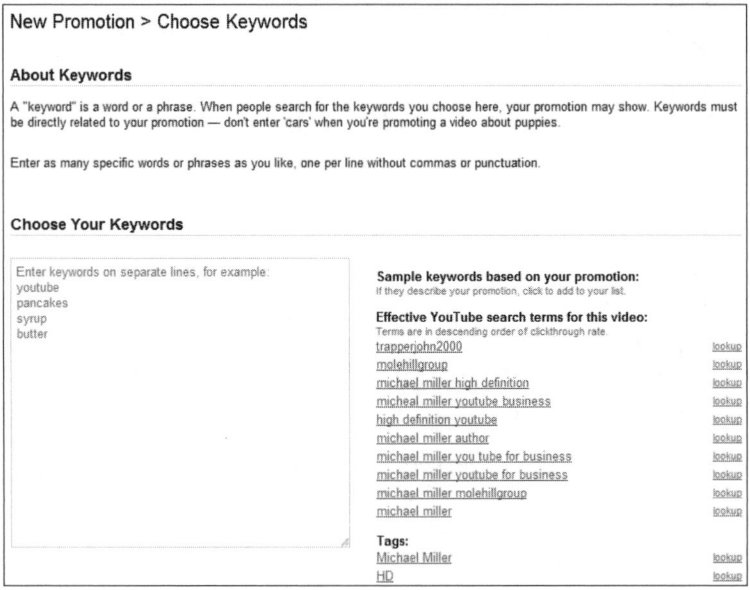

Figure 19.7 *Choosing the keywords for your YouTube campaign.*

10. When the Set CPC page appears, shown in Figure 19.8, enter the amount you're willing to pay per click and then click the Next button.

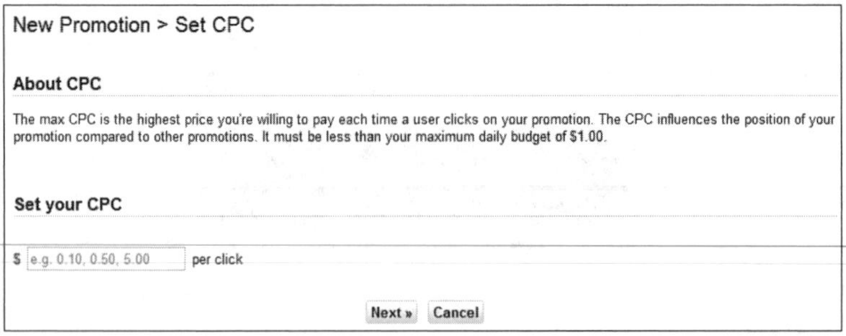

Figure 19.8 *Setting your CPC bid.*

As with AdWords advertising, the higher the CPC you set for your YouTube ad, the more likely your ad will place high on matching search results pages. That's because YouTube uses the same bidding system as used by AdWords, assigning placement based on bids by multiple advertisers. Set too low a CPC, and higher-bidding advertisers for a given keyword will have their ads appear higher and more often.

11. When the Confirm Promotion page appears, shown in Figure 19.9, you see the ad you've just created. Click the Okay, Run My Promotion! button to get things started.

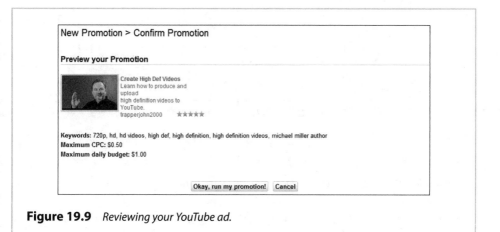

Figure 19.9 *Reviewing your YouTube ad.*

You can add an overlay to any promoted video that displays ad text and a link to a landing page on your website. (You can add only non-YouTube links to promoted videos.) Go to the YouTube page for this video and click the Edit Video button; when the next page appears, enter the appropriate information into the Call-to-Action Overlay section.

Your ad is now added to YouTube's promoted videos database. It will appear on search results pages when someone searches for one of the keywords you entered.

 SHOW ME   Media 19.4—A video about how to create a promoted videos campaign
Access this video file through your registered Web Edition at
my.safaribooksonline.com/9780131388666/media.

Tracking Performance from the Promoted Videos Dashboard

You track the performance of your promoted videos from the Promoted Videos Dashboard (ads.youtube.com). This Dashboard, shown in Figure 19.10, displays key information about your current campaigns:

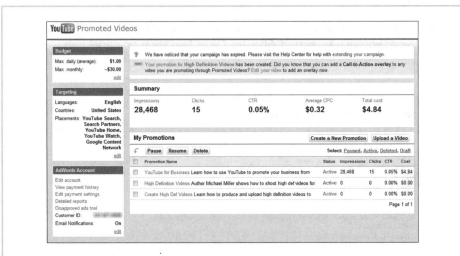

Figure 19.10   *Tracking performance from the Dashboard Summary page.*

You can also use the Promoted Videos Dashboard to pause, resume, and delete individual campaigns, as well as create new promotions.

- **Impressions.** The number of page views for your ads.

- **Clicks.** The number of times your ads have been clicked.

- **CTR.** The click-through rate for your ads, which is the number of impressions divided by the number of clicks.

- **Average CPC.** The average cost per click you're paying.

- **Total cost.** The total amount you've spent on your YouTube campaign.

SHOW ME   Media 19.5—A video about how to track the performance of promoted videos
Access this video file through your registered Web Edition at my.safaribooksonline.com/9780131388666/media.

To view information about a specific campaign, click that campaign on the main Dashboard. You now see detailed information about that campaign, as shown in Figure 19.11, including performance data for each of the keywords you selected. This keyword-specific data includes the following metrics:

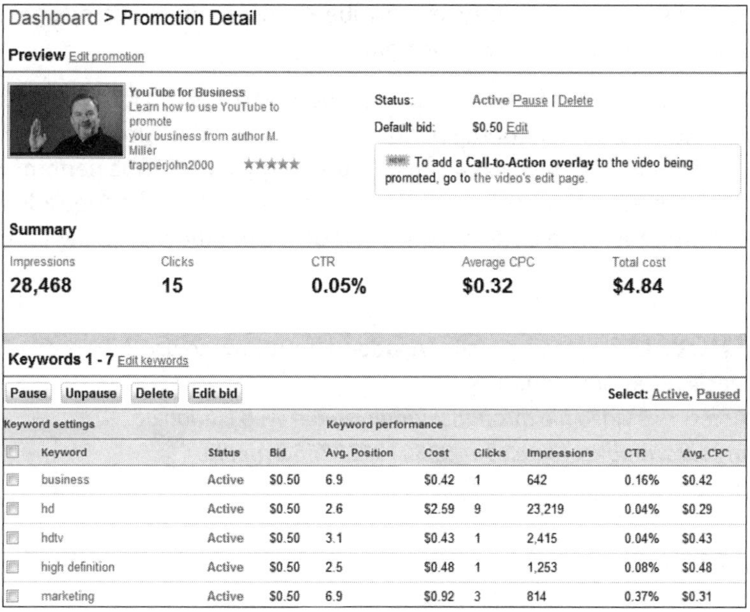

Figure 19.11 *Tracking performance about specific campaigns.*

- **Keyword.** The selected keyword or key phrase.

- **Status.** Active or paused.

- **Bid.** The amount you bid per click.

- **Avg. Position.** The average position on the YouTube search results page for the ad generated by this keyword.

- **Cost.** The total amount you've spent on this particular keyword.

- **Clicks.** The total number of clicks you've received for the generated ad.

- **Impressions.** The total number of times the ad associated with this keyword has been displayed.

- **CTR.** The click-through rate for this keyword's ads.

- **Avg. CPC.** The actual average cost per click for this keyword.

Tracking Performance from the AdWords Dashboard

Because your YouTube Promoted Videos account is tied to your Google AdWords account, you can also track your YouTube campaigns from the main AdWords page. Go to adwords.google.com, select the Campaigns tab, and select the Campaigns sub-tab. You should see an entry for YouTube Promoted Videos Campaign; this is, not surprisingly, your YouTube campaign.

From here you can view the individual ad groups and ads you've created for your YouTube videos, and monitor the performance of these the same way you would with a traditional AdWords text ad. In fact, tracking your YouTube performance in AdWords is a great way to compare the performance of your YouTube ads versus your AdWords ads—and determine which is delivering the most bang for the buck.

 SHOW ME   Media 19.6—A video about how to use AdWords to track video performance
Access this video file through your registered Web Edition at
my.safaribooksonline.com/9780131388666/media.

20

Monitoring Your Campaign's Performance

Once your AdWords campaign is started, it's time to start tracking its performance. That means looking at raw data, such as clicks, as well as analyzing that data in various ways.

Performance analysis is key to improving your AdWords campaigns. You can learn from both your successes and your failures, and use this information to create better-performing campaigns in the future.

Monitoring from the AdWords Dashboard

Much of the raw data regarding your AdWords campaigns can be found on your main AdWords page, what we'll call the dashboard. You can monitor performance at the campaign, ad group, or individual ad level; you can also monitor the performance of the individual keywords you select.

You access all this data from the Campaigns tab on the main AdWords page (adwords.google.com). From there you can select different sub-tabs for specific types of data.

 SHOW ME   Media 20.1—A video about how to monitor AdWords data
Access this video file through your registered Web Edition at
my.safaribooksonline.com/9780131388666/media.

Monitoring Campaign Performance

Let's start by tracking performance at the campaign level. Obviously, this looks at the performance of your entire campaign—all the ad groups and individual ads you've created.

From the Campaigns tab, select the Campaigns sub-tab. As you can see in Figure 20.1, all your campaigns—active and inactive—are listed, along with key data about each campaign:

- **Budget.** Your specified daily budget.

- **Status.** Whether your campaign is active ("eligible") or ended.

- **Clicks.** The total number of clicks received in this campaign.

- **Impr.** The total number of impressions—the times the ads in this campaign have been displayed.

- **CTR.** The click-through rate; the number of clicks divided by the number of impressions. (The higher the better, as with most of these numbers.)

- **Avg. CPC.** The average cost per click—what you're paying on average for the keywords in this campaign.

- **Cost.** The total cost for this campaign for the specified time period.

- **Avg. Pos.** The average position attained for the ads in this campaign.

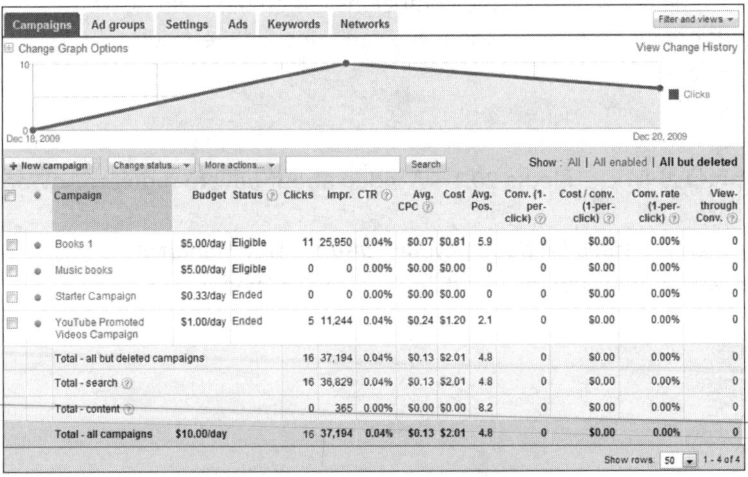

Figure 20.1 *Viewing campaign data in the AdWords dashboard.*

- **Conv. (1-per-click).** If you have conversion tracking enabled, the number of conversions for this campaign—the number of clicks that have resulted in sales.

- **Cost/conv. (1-per-click).** If you have conversion tracking enabled, the cost for each conversion attained.

- **Conv. rate (1-per-click).** If you have conversion tracking enabled, the conversion rate for this campaign.

- **View-through Conv.** If you have conversion tracking enabled, measures the number of conversions that occurred within 30 days of a user viewing your ad.

Below the main data table are a few "total" rows. You see a row for total performance of all campaigns except deleted ones, for total performance from Google search, and total performance from Google's content network. The final row sums up the performance from all your campaigns in total.

Monitoring Ad Group Performance

Select the Ad Groups sub-tab and you see a similar data table, this time tracking performance by ad group, as shown in Figure 20.2. The initial view of this data table displays all ad groups for all your campaigns. You can display ad groups for a single campaign by selecting that campaign from the All Online Campaigns box on the left side of the page.

The columns for this data table are similar but not identical to those on the Campaigns sub-tab. Here's what you'll find:

- **Ad group.** The selected ad group.

- **Campaign.** The campaign that this ad group is a part of.

- **Status.** Whether the selected ad group is active ("eligible") or ended.

- **Search Max. CPC.** The maximum cost per click specified for this ad group for display on Google search.

- **Content Managed Max. CPC.** The maximum cost per click specified for this ad group for display on Google content network websites.

- **Clicks.** The total number of clicks received for this ad group.

- **Impr.** The total number of impressions—the times the ads in this ad group have been displayed.

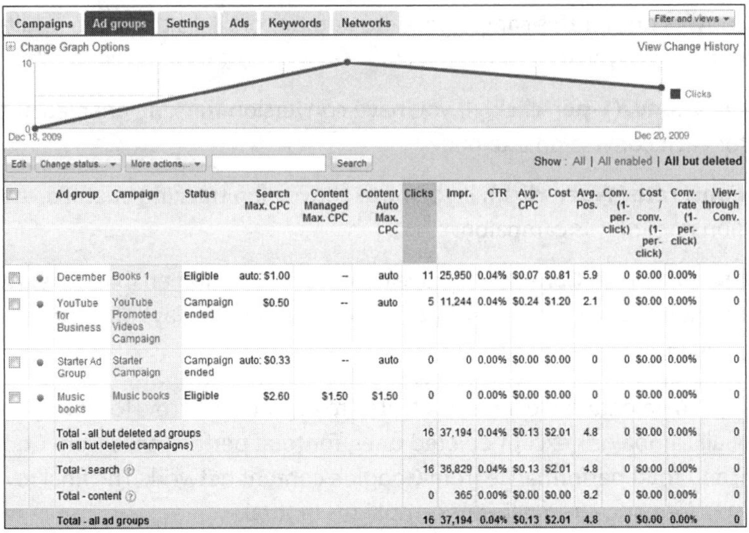

Figure 20.2   *Viewing ad group data in the AdWords dashboard.*

- **CTR.** The click-through rate; the number of clicks divided by the number of impressions.

- **Avg. CPC.** The average cost per click—what you're paying on average for the keywords in this ad group.

- **Cost.** The total cost for this ad group for the specified time period.

- **Avg. Pos.** The average position attained for the ads in this ad group.

- **Conv. (1-per-click).** If you have conversion tracking enabled, the number of clicks that have resulted in sales.

- **Cost/conv. (1-per-click).** If you have conversion tracking enabled, the cost for each conversion attained.

- **Conv. rate (1-per-click).** If you have conversion tracking enabled, the conversion rate for this ad group.

- **View-through Conv.** If you have conversion tracking enabled, measures the number of conversions that occurred within 30 days of a user viewing your ad.

Monitoring Ad Performance

Next up is the Ads sub-tab, where you track the performance of all the individual ads you've created. As you can see in Figure 20.3, this sub-tab displays each ad individually; you can filter the table to display ads for a specific campaign by selecting that campaign in the All Online Campaigns box on the left side of the page.

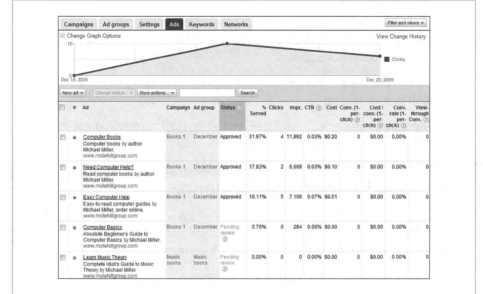

Figure 20.3   *Viewing data for individual ads in the AdWords dashboard.*

Here are the columns of data you see:

- **Ad.** The selected ad, as it appears on a page.

- **Campaign.** The campaign that this ad is a part of.

- **Ad group.** The ad group that this ad is a part of.

- **Status.** Whether the selected ad group is approved or pending review.

- **% Served.** The percentage of time that this ad has been shown, in relation to the rest of the active ads in this ad group. The higher this percentage, the more often the ad has been displayed.

- **Clicks.** The total number of clicks received for this ad.

- **Impr.** The total number of impressions—the times this ad has been displayed.

- **CTR.** The click-through rate; the number of clicks divided by the number of impressions.

- **Cost.** The total cost for this ad for the specified time period.

- **Conv. (1-per-click).** If you have conversion tracking enabled, the number of clicks that have resulted in sales.

- **Cost/conv. (1-per-click).** If you have conversion tracking enabled, the cost for each conversion attained.

- **Conv. rate (1-per-click).** If you have conversion tracking enabled, the conversion rate for this ad.

- **View-through Conv..** If you have conversion tracking enabled, measures the number of conversions that occurred within 30 days of a user viewing the ad.

Monitoring Keyword Performance

You can also track the performance of each keyword within a campaign or ad group. When you select the Keywords sub-tab, you see the data table shown in Figure 20.4. The columns in this data table include the following:

- **Keyword.** The selected keyword or key phrase.

- **Campaign.** The campaign that this keyword is associated with.

- **Ad group.** The ad group that this keyword is associated with.

- **Max. CPC.** The maximum cost-per-click you've elected to bid for this keyword.

- **Clicks.** The total number of clicks received for ads associated with this keyword.

- **Impr.** The total number of impressions—the times ads associated with this keyword have been displayed.

- **CTR.** The click-through rate; the number of clicks divided by the number of impressions.

- **Avg. CPC.** The average cost-per-click for this keyword.

- **Cost.** The total cost for ads associated with this keyword for the specified time period.

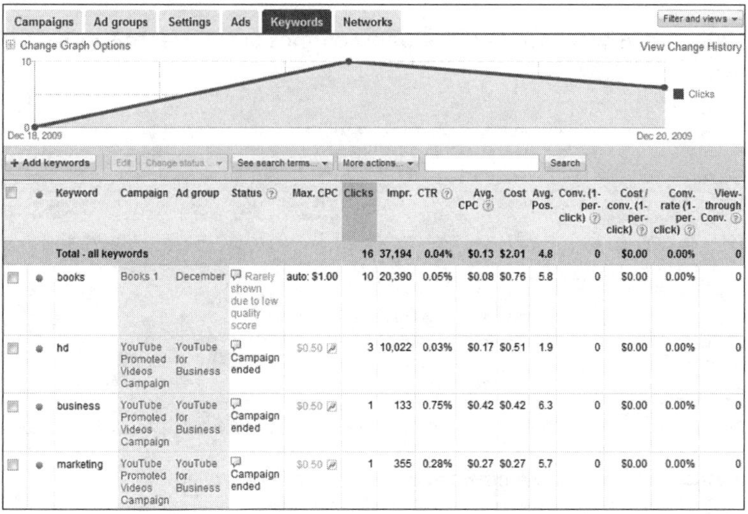

Figure 20.4 *Viewing data for individual keywords in the AdWords dashboard.*

- **Avg. Pos.** The average position attained for the ads associated with this keyword.

- **Conv. (1-per-click).** If you have conversion tracking enabled, the number of clicks that have resulted in sales.

- **Cost/conv. (1-per-click).** If you have conversion tracking enabled, the cost for each conversion attained.

- **Conv. rate (1-per-click).** If you have conversion tracking enabled, the conversion rate for this keyword.

- **View-through Conv.** If you have conversion tracking enabled, measures the number of conversions that occurred within 30 days of a user viewing the ads associated with this keyword.

Monitoring Network Performance

Finally, you can segment your campaigns' performance by channel, by selecting the Networks sub-tab. From here you can see how your campaigns perform on the following sites:

- Google search site
- Google's search partners

- Google content network—both managed and automatic placements

Figure 20.5 shows what you see; the data columns are similar to those on the other sub-tabs.

	Clicks	Impr.	CTR ⑦	Avg. CPC ⑦	Cost	Avg. Pos.	Conv. (1-per-click) ⑦	Cost / conv. (1-per-click) ⑦	Conv. rate (1-per-click) ⑦	View-through Conv. ⑦
Campaigns Ad groups Settings Ads Keywords **Networks**									Filter and views ▼	
Search	16	36,829	0.04%	$0.13	$2.01	4.8	0	$0.00	0.00%	0
Google search	1	973	0.10%	$0.05	$0.05	5	0	$0.00	0.00%	0
Search partners ⑦	15	35,856	0.04%	$0.13	$1.96	4.8	0	$0.00	0.00%	0
Content	0	365	0.00%	$0.00	$0.00	8.2	0	$0.00	0.00%	0
▦ Managed placements ⑦ show details	0	0	0.00%	$0.00	$0.00	0	0	$0.00	0.00%	0
▦ Automatic placements ⑦ show details	0	365	0.00%	$0.00	$0.00	8.2	0	$0.00	0.00%	0
Total - All networks	16	37,194	0.04%	$0.13	$2.01	4.8	0	$0.00	0.00%	0

Figure 20.5   *Viewing data segmented by search and content network.*

Creating Performance Reports

So far we've examined the raw data available for your AdWords campaigns, as displayed on the Campaigns tab. You can also generate a series of reports that slice and dice this data different ways. You access these reports by clicking the Reporting tab and clicking Reports from the drop-down menu.

This opens AdWords' Report Center, shown in Figure 20.6. Any report you've previously created is listed here; click a report to re-display it.

 **LET ME TRY IT**

Creating AdWords Reports

You can also, of course, create new reports. To do so, follow these steps:

1. From the Report Center page, click the Create a New Report link.

2. When the Create Report page appears, as shown in Figure 20.7, go to the Report Type section and select the type of report you want to create.

3. Go to the Settings section, shown in Figure 20.8, and select how you want your data summarized from the View list. You can select to display Summary, Daily, Day of Week, Weekly, Monthly, Quarterly, or Yearly data.

4. In the Date Range section, select a predefined range from the pull-down list or enter specific start and end dates.

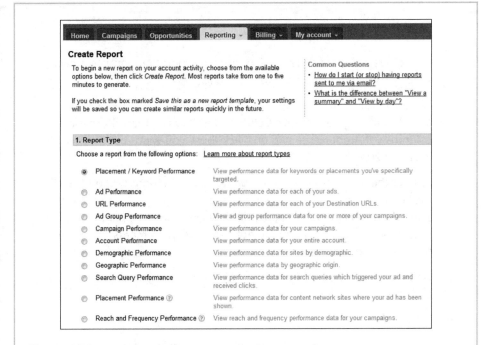

Figure 20.6 *Google's AdWords Report Center.*

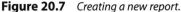

Figure 20.7 *Creating a new report.*

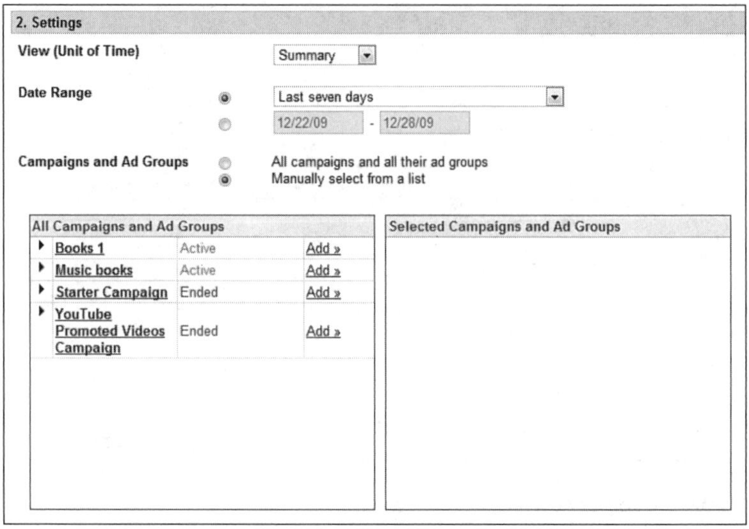

Figure 20.8   *Selecting report settings.*

5. Opt to display either all campaigns and ad groups, or manually select specific campaigns or ad groups from a list.

6. To customize the data displayed, go to the Advanced Settings section and click the Add or Remove Columns link. You can then check those columns you want to see and uncheck those you want to hide, as shown in Figure 20.9.

7. To filter the data displayed, go to the Advanced Settings section and click the Filter Your Results link. As you can see in Figure 20.10, you can then select a display criteria from the pull-down list and enter parameters in the accompanying box. You can also opt to include placements or keywords that have zero impressions.

8. Go to the Templates, Scheduling, and Email section, shown in Figure 20.11, and enter a name for your report.

9. To save this report as a new template, check that option.

10. To run this report on a given schedule, check the Scheduling option and select a schedule from the pull-down list.

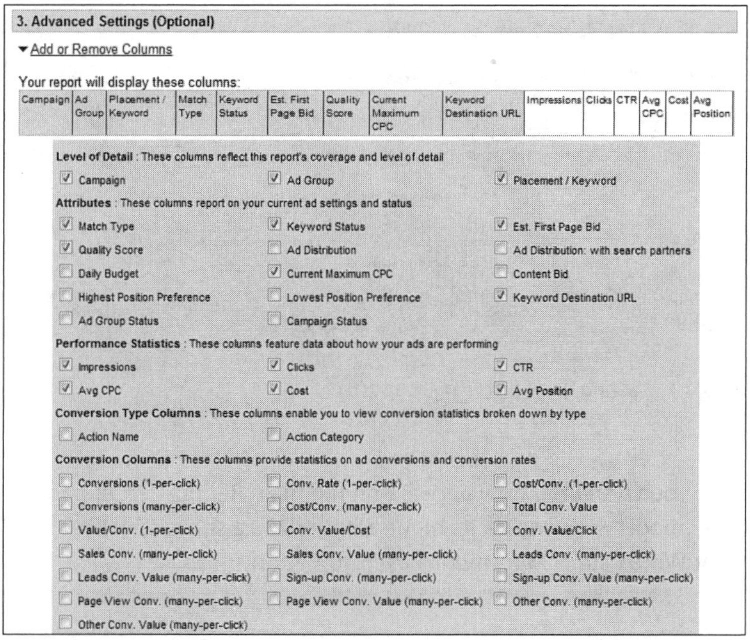

Figure 20.9   *Customizing the data display.*

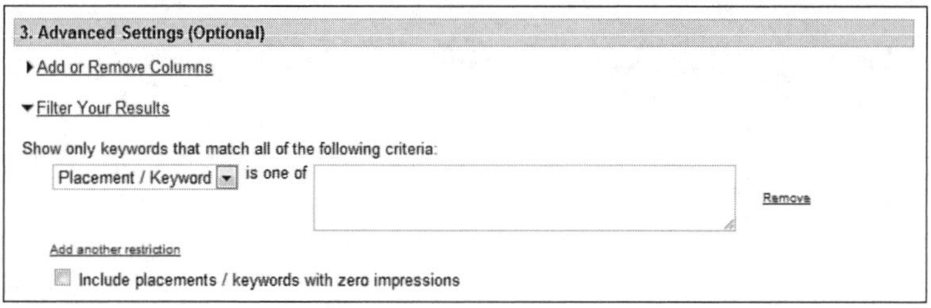

Figure 20.10   *Filtering the data.*

11. If you want to be notified (by email) whenever this report runs, check this option and enter your email address. You can also opt to include a copy of the report in this email; the report can be in .xml, .csv, .csv for Excel, .tsv, or .html file format.

12. Click the Create Report button to create the report according to the parameters you've specified.

4. Templates, Scheduling, and Email

Name Your Report	Placement / Keyword Report
Template	☐ Save this as a new report template
Scheduling	☐ Schedule this report to run automatically: every day ▾
Email	☐ Whenever the report runs, send email to:
	For multiple recipients, separate email addresses with commas.
	☐ with report attached as: .xml ▾

Create Report

Figure 20.11   *Saving and scheduling a report.*

The report you've created now appears on the main Report Center page. To display the report, simply click its name. (Figure 20.12 shows a typical report—AdWords' stock Placement/Keyword Report.)

Placement / Keyword Report

Report Generated: Dec 29, 2009 12:54:36 PM Show report detail

Export Report | Create Another Report Like This

Dec 22, 2009 - Dec 28, 2009

View: Summary

Impressions	Clicks	CTR	Avg CPC	Cost	Avg Position
87,743	**21**	**0.02%**	**$0.87**	**$18.34**	**4.30**

Campaign	Ad Group	Placement / Keyword	Match Type	Keyword Status	Est. First Page Bid	Quality Score	Current Maximum CPC	Keyword Destination URL	Impressions	Clicks	CTR	Avg CPC	Cost	Avg Position
Books 1	December	Computer Basics	Broad	Active	2		$1.00	default URL	22	0	0.00%	$0.00	$0.00	5.7
Books 1	December	PCs	Broad	Active	2		$1.00	default URL	18	0	0.00%	$0.00	$0.00	3.9
Books 1	December	Total - content targeting	Content						54,177	9	0.02%	$0.76	$6.83	5.0
Books 1	December	Windows 7	Broad	Active	2		$1.00	default URL	1,717	0	0.00%	$0.00	$0.00	8.2
Books 1	December	books	Broad	Active	2		$1.00	default URL	872	0	0.00%	$0.00	$0.00	6.4
Books 1	December	computer books	Broad	Active	2		$1.00	default URL	8	0	0.00%	$0.00	$0.00	5.4
Books 1	December	computers	Broad	Active	2		$1.00	default URL	108	0	0.00%	$0.00	$0.00	8.0
Books 1	December	learning computer books	Broad	Active	2		$1.00	default URL	4	0	0.00%	$0.00	$0.00	8.8

Figure 20.12   *Viewing the Placement/Keyword Report.*

SHOW ME   Media 20.2—A video about how to generate AdWords reports

Access this video file through your registered Web Edition at
my.safaribooksonline.com/9780131388666/media.

 **LET ME TRY IT**

Downloading Reports

You can download any report you create so you can manipulate it on your computer on your own time. To do so, follow these steps:

1. Generate and display the desired report.

2. Click the Export Report button at the top of the report page, as shown in Figure 20.13.

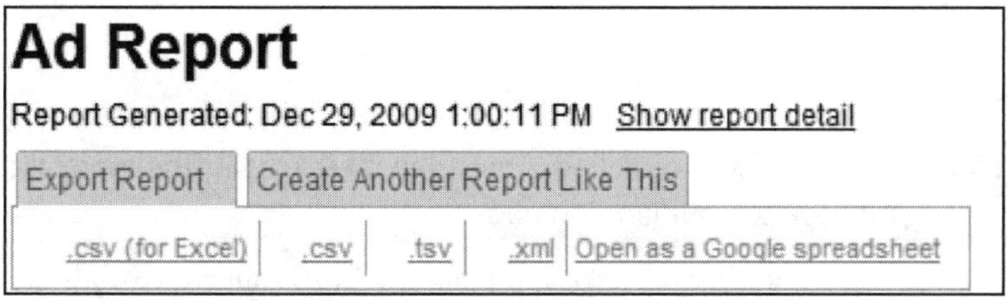

Ad Report

Report Generated: Dec 29, 2009 1:00:11 PM Show report detail

Export Report   Create Another Report Like This

.csv (for Excel)   .csv   .tsv   .xml Open as a Google spreadsheet

Figure 20.13 *Exporting a report to a specific file format.*

3. Select the file format you want—.csv for Excel, .csv, .tsv, or .xml.

You can also opt to display the report as a Google Spreadsheet.

4. When the Save As dialog box appears, select a name and location for the file, and then click the Save button.

The report file is now saved in the location you specified.

Understanding Key Metrics

However you get your data, there are some key metrics you want to pay particular attention to. We'll examine these next.

 SHOW ME   Media 20.3—A video about how to analyze AdWords data
*Access this video file through your registered Web Edition at
my.safaribooksonline.com/9780131388666/media.*

Impressions

How many times was your ad displayed? That's the *impressions* metric; the more impressions, the more people who were exposed to your ad.

Obviously, when it comes to impressions, more is better. If your ad or campaign is generating a low number of impressions, you can't generate a lot of clicks—even if you have a high click-through rate.

To improve your impressions, you need to improve the performance of your keywords. This might mean changing from broad (inexact) to exact matching, or even selecting a different set of keywords for a particular ad.

You can also work to improve the Quality Score of your landing page; a low Quality Score can result in your ad not being displayed as often.

Clicks

How many times was your ad clicked? That's the *clicks* metric; the more clicks, the more traffic you have to your landing page.

As with impressions, the more clicks you have the better. Of course, you can't get a lot of clicks if you don't start with a lot of impressions, so that's always job one. But a large number of impressions doesn't always result in a large number of clicks; if your ad isn't interesting or compelling, people won't be inspired to click it.

You can improve the number of clicks by improving the effectiveness of your ad. Use more powerful words, make sure you talk about your unique selling proposition, and include a compelling call to action. The more effective your ad, the more clicks you'll get.

Click-Through Rate (CTR)

The number of raw clicks is an important, but not necessarily the best, measurement of an ad's effectiveness. A highly effective ad, after all, can't generate a lot of clicks if you have minimal impressions.

A better measurement of ad effectiveness, then, is the click-through rate (CTR). This metric measures the number of clicks as a percentage of the number of impressions. A high CTR indicates that your ad is doing its job; a low CTR indicates that you need to retool your ad copy.

You can estimate the number of clicks you might generate if you increase the number of impressions by multiplying your current CTR by the higher impressions number.

Percent of Clicks Served

When looking at the performance of individual ads within an ad group, take a gander at the *% of clicks served* metric. This data point tells you which ads in your ad group are getting the most displays; it divides the number of impressions for a given ad by the total number of impressions for all the ads in this ad group.

An ad with a higher % of clicks served number is outperforming the other ads in the ad group; an ad with a lower number is underperforming the other ads. Of course, this isn't so much a measurement of the ad as it is the keywords chosen to display that ad, so consider this in your analysis.

Average Position

In what position was your ad displayed on Google's search results pages? That's the *average position* for an ad, and higher is always better. (Higher also costs more per click, so keep that in mind, as well.)

The higher an ad's position, the more clicks the ad will get and the more traffic that ad will drive to your landing page. Advertisers are always striving for higher positions—to a point. You don't want to outspend your campaign by bidding to achieve one of the top two positions. You might be better off aiming for a slightly lower position at a corresponding lower cost.

Sophisticated (or obsessed) PPC advertisers constantly monitor the position metric, tracking changes in position on a daily basis. You can fine-tune this number by adjusting your CPC bid; bid more to improve your position, or bid less to move down a bit—and spend less money.

Cost

How much have you paid in total for a given keyword, ad, ad group, or campaign? That's the *cost* metric—as in, this item cost you this much money over a specific time frame.

Note that your cost for a campaign will never exceed your daily budget. In fact, it most often will come in under your budget, as you won't always be the high bidder on all the keywords you choose. Consider your daily budget as a maximum spending amount; your actual spending is reflected in the cost metric.

Conversions

Finally, we come to the topic of conversions. A conversion occurs when someone clicks your ad and then proceeds to purchase what you're selling. To monitor conversions, you have to first enable conversion tracking; when you do so, you tell AdWords exactly what you want to track, whether that be sales, subscriptions, leads, or whatever.

When conversion tracking is activated, you can track four different metrics:

- **Conversions**, which is the total number of actions taken by people who clicked on your ad. Conversions can never exceed clicks.

- **Cost per conversion**, which is how much each conversion cost you.

- **Conversion rate**, which is the number of conversions divided by the number of clicks.

- **View-through conversions**, a somewhat controversial number that tracks the number of conversions that happen within 30 days of a customer clicking your ad. (Regular conversions measure actions that occur immediately after a click.)

Obviously, if you're trying to generate sales revenue from your advertising, tracking conversions is important. Although clicks matter, revenue matters more—and conversions directly related to revenue generated.

 TELL ME MORE   **Media 20.4—A discussion about key metrics**
Access this audio recording through your registered Web Edition at
my.safaribooksonline.com/9780131388666/media.

21

Dealing with Click Fraud

When it comes to placing PPC advertising, there's one important issue you need to be aware of: *Click fraud*. This type of fraud is a deliberate effort to defraud advertisers who pay for their ads by the click; it occurs when a link within an online ad is clicked for the sole purpose of generating a charge per click, with no actual interest in the ad itself or the site linked to within the ad. Click fraud drives up your ad costs without generating additional revenues.

Click fraud can be perpetrated by a person, automated script, or computer program. In fact, there are numerous different varieties of click fraud, using various methods to initiate the fraudulent clicks.

Who Benefits from Click Fraud?

Who reaps the profit from click fraud? It depends on who's doing the clicking and why.

Most instances of click fraud directly benefit the entity doing the clicking. Typically the clicked ad resides on the perpetrator's own website. Because host websites receive a portion of all PPC revenues via Google's AdSense program, every click on a site's ads results in money flowing into the pockets of the site's owner. By perpetrating click fraud, the site owner artificially inflates the revenues his site earns from the hosted ads.

Here's the way it often works. An individual obtains a web domain and creates a website, often nothing more than a *link farm*—a site without any real content of its own, just links to other sites and text designed to attract hits from popular keywords at the major search sites. The site owner signs up with AdSense or other ad programs and places a variety of PPC ads on the site. To generate revenue, the site owner—through manual or automated means—clicks multiple times on the ads on his own site. Each click generates PPC revenue, thus lining his own pockets.

Savvy readers will note that Google and the other PPC ad networks also indirectly benefit from click fraud, in that they also receive revenue from all fraudulent clicks.

Other instances of click fraud are designed more to harm the advertiser than to benefit the host website. In these instances, non-contracting parties (not part of any PPC agreement) use click fraud to harm their competitors in the marketplace. For example, a competitor of the advertiser might use click fraud to generate a bevy of irrelevant clicks, thus draining the competitor's advertising budget with nothing to show for it. Or, a competitor to the host website might use click fraud to make it look as if the owner of the website is clicking on his own ads, thus harming the website's relationship with the ad network.

Impression fraud is where fraudsters scheme to disable competitors' ads by creating an artificially low click-through rate on those ads. This is accomplished by making numerous searches for a keyword, but then never clicking on the competitors' ad. The result is a high number of impressions with an artificially low click-through rate; the competitor's ads thus get placed lower in the ad queue, while the fraudster's competing ads get a higher ranking.

Then there are those instances of click fraud that are out-and-out malicious. Online vandalism does occur, and unwarranted ad clicking is part of that pattern. An individual might use click fraud to perpetuate a personal vendetta against an advertiser or website, or might target a site just for kicks. It happens, often with no rhyme or reason.

 SHOW ME   Media 21.1—A video about click fraud
Access this video file through your registered Web Edition at my.safaribooksonline.com/9780131388666/media.

How Click Fraud Works

There are many ways to generate click fraud. We'll look at the most common.

Not only is click fraud a violation of most ad networks' participation agreements (you agree not to click on your own ads), it's also a crime. In many jurisdictions, use of a computer to commit this type of Internet fraud is a felony, and law enforcement has been eager and willing to go after alleged perpetrators.

Manual Click Fraud

The simplest form of click fraud comes when an interested individual manually clicks the link in an ad, over and over and over. This type of click fraud is fairly small potatoes, more often perpetrated by the host site's owner than outside parties. (The owner is trying to generate additional ad revenues by click-click-clicking away on his own.)

Because the number of clicks and their value is often quite small, this type of manual click fraud often goes undetected.

It's not surprising that manual click fraud is also the least effective method; one can only click so fast for so long. For that reason, the instances of manual click fraud today are rare and relatively insignificant, in terms of magnitude.

Script-Based Click Fraud

Manual click fraud is small potatoes. Fraud is perpetrated on a much larger scale when the fraudulent clicks are automated.

One of the easiest ways to automate click fraud is via the use of computer scripts—bits of programming code that simulate manual clicking on ad links. This is typically accomplished by running the script on one or a few computers owned by the website host and his friends; from these few computers come thousands of fraudulent clicks.

Automated clicking scripts or programs are called *clickbots*.

The problem with script-based click fraud is that it's relatively easy to catch. An ad network, noticing a suspiciously large number of clicks on an ad, can examine the IP addresses of the computers that generated those clicks. If the clicks are concentrated on one or a few computers in a small geographic area, it's a sure sign of script-based click fraud—and the perpetrator is easily tracked down and brought to justice.

Script-based click fraud is popular with organized crime groups, who can install click scripts on computers throughout their widespread organizations. Because the computers are dispersed geographically, the fraud is harder to identify.

Traffic-Based Click Fraud

Then there's traffic-based click fraud, where the fraudster uses a variety of technologies to make it look as if every page view is a click. Although the users don't in fact click on anything, their mere presence registers as a click in the ad network. Making traffic look like clicks is a tricky approach, but one that can avoid identification from a concentration of similar IP addresses.

Paid-to-Read Click Fraud

An even better approach for a click fraudster is to get someone else to click an ad for you. This is the goal of so-called *paid-to-read* (PTR) sites, where other individuals are paid to repeatedly click on a given ad on the fraudster's website.

The way this fraud works is simple: The website owner joins a click-fraud ring or advertises his site to users willing to participate in the scam. Site visitors are then paid small amounts of money (typically a fraction of a cent) to visit the site and click on ad links. The more the visitors click, the more money they earn for themselves—and the more revenue is generated by the ads on the fraudster's site. Obviously, the fraudster pays the clickers a subset of the revenue he earns from the PPC ads; some PTR sites have hundreds of thousands of users merrily clicking away in their free time.

Some participants in PTR rings (the people who do the clicking) claim to make hundreds of dollars a week for their efforts. This is particularly appealing to low-wage workers in some foreign countries—which explains why the incidence of click fraud is higher in those parts of the world.

Hijacked PC Click Fraud

Another way to use other computers to commit click fraud is to hijack those computers via a computer virus. As soon as the virus is installed on the PC, it is effectively hijacked; it can now be controlled remotely by a host computer. (A hijacked computer used in this fashion is called a *zombie computer*.)

The remote control operation, of course, is focused on using the computer to commit click fraud. The zombie computer is directed to connect to the website in question and repeatedly click the site's ad links, typically via a clickbot script installed on the machine without the user's knowledge. Thus click fraud is perpetrated without the computer's owner ever knowing about it.

TELL ME MORE   Media 21.2—A discussion about click fraud
Access this audio recording through your registered Web Edition at
my.safaribooksonline.com/9780131388666/media.

Combating Click Fraud

Google and the other PPC ad networks have various mechanisms in place to identify and block click fraud inside their ad networks. But they can't block all attempts;
Click Forensics estimates that in the third quarter of 2009, 14.1% of all ad clicks
were fraudulent. (For what it's worth, Google disputes this figure, claiming that
click fraud on its network is less than 2%).

Whatever the rate, click fraud does exist—and can affect your online advertising
campaign. What can you as an individual advertiser do to minimize losses from
fraudulent clicks?

Monitoring Ad Performance

First, you need to constantly monitor your click-through rates and your conversion
rates (measured by information requests, leads, merchandise sales, or whatever). If
you see a spike in PPC traffic that is not offset by a corresponding increase in conversion rates, you can suspect click fraud for that traffic increase.

For example, if you see your click-through traffic increase by 50%, you might think
your ad program is working quite well. But if, during the same period, your conversion rate increased by only 5%, you know that most of those new clicks aren't con-
verting to leads or sales—a common sign of fraudulent traffic.

Using Click Fraud Detection Tools

Second, you should consider using a click fraud detection tool. These are software
programs that monitor your website traffic for irregular patterns, and then flag
potentially fraudulent clicks.

Some of the most popular click fraud detection tools include the following:

- AdWatcher (www.adwatcher.com)
- Click True (www.clicktrue.net)
- ClickLab (www.clicklab.com)
- WhosClickingWho? (www.whosclickingwho.com)

Viewing Invalid Clicks

Google tries to automatically identify and filter out any click fraud—what it calls *invalid clicks*—from your account.

 **LET ME TRY IT**

Generating and Invalid Clicks Report

You can see what Google has identified by running an invalid clicks report. Here's how to do it:

1. From the main AdWords page, select the Reporting tab and then select Reports.

2. On the Report Center page, click Create a New Report.

3. On the Create Report page, shown in Figure 21.1, go to the Report Type section and select Account Performance.

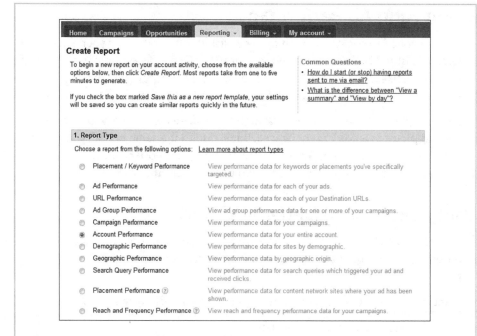

Figure 21.1 *Creating an invalid clicks report.*

4. In the Date Range section, select the desired reporting dates.

5. In the Advanced Settings section, click Add or Remove Columns.

6. When the page expands, as shown in Figure 21.2, go to the Performance Statistics section and check the Invalid Clicks and Invalid Clicks Rate options.

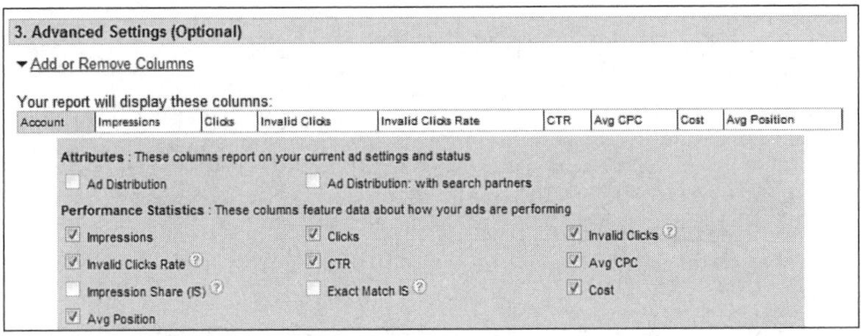

3. Advanced Settings (Optional)

▼ Add or Remove Columns

Your report will display these columns:

Account	Impressions	Clicks	Invalid Clicks	Invalid Clicks Rate	CTR	Avg CPC	Cost	Avg Position

Attributes : These columns report on your current ad settings and status

☐ Ad Distribution   ☐ Ad Distribution: with search partners

Performance Statistics : These columns feature data about how your ads are performing

☑ Impressions   ☑ Clicks   ☑ Invalid Clicks ⑦

☑ Invalid Clicks Rate ⑦   ☑ CTR   ☑ Avg CPC

☐ Impression Share (IS) ⑦   ☐ Exact Match IS ⑦   ☑ Cost

☑ Avg Position

Figure 21.2   *Displaying Invalid Clicks and the Invalid Clicks Rate.*

7. In the Templates, Scheduling, and Email section, enter a name for this report into the Name Your Report field.

8. Click the Create Report button.

The resulting report will show how many clicks Google has identified as fraudulent, and what percentage of your total clicks these fraudulent clicks represent.

LET ME TRY IT

Reporting Click Fraud

It's always possible that Google won't catch all the fraudulent clicks on your ads. If you identify a case of what you believe to be click fraud that Google hasn't identified, you need to report it to AdWords and ask for a refund. Google's fraud team then attempts to identify the source of the fraud, and (you hope) credits your account for the fraudulent clicks.

How do you report suspected click fraud? Here's what you need to do:

1. Document the suspicious activity. Include the keyword that was targeted, IP address of the clicker, date and time of the click, referring page (if known), and any other pertinent information (such as if the click is from a foreign IP). Do this for each suspicious click you identify.

2. Go to adwords.google.com/support/aw/bin/request.py?clickquality=1, shown in Figure 21.3, and enter the requested information—your name, email address, AdWords account number, and so forth.

Top questions: Click quality

Please provide the information requested below. We ask that you are as specific as possible to facilitate the escalation.

* Required fields

*Name:

*Contact email address:

*Customer ID Number:
(Found in the upper right-hand corner of any page in your AdWords account)

*Date range of suspicious activity: To
(Please note that we can only investigate a period of up to 60 days)   Please enter in this format: mm/dd/yyyy

*Campaign(s), ad group(s), and keyword(s) affected:
(e.g. Campaign #1, Ad Group Flowers, Keyword "tulips")

*Description of issue:

Suspicious IP addresses:
(Enter one IP per line in this format: 123.145.167.89. Blocks of addresses using the wildcard as the last 3 digits also allowed: 123.4.5.*.)

Suspicious search or content sites:
(Enter one site per line in this format: www.example.com)

Submit Request

Figure 21.3   *Reporting click fraud to Google.*

3. Go to the Description of Issue box and enter a description of the trends you've spotted. You should also ask for a refund or credit, based on the number of fraudulent clicks you've identified.

4. Enter IP addresses you suspect of fraudulent behavior into the Suspicious IP Addresses box.

5. Enter any websites you suspect of fraudulent behavior into the Suspicious Search or Content Sites box.

6. Click the Submit Request button.

The data you need to document your claim can be obtained from most third-party web analytics tools or from your server logs.

The good news is that Google cares a lot about click fraud, and has staff dedicated to investigating click fraud complaints and improving the overall quality of traffic. Chances are, if your claim is valid, you'll be made whole. Just remember, though, the burden of proof is entirely on you.

 SHOW ME   Media 21.3—A video about how to submit a click fraud report
Access this video file through your registered Web Edition at
my.safaribooksonline.com/9780131388666/media.

22

Ten Tips for Improving Your AdWords Performance

AdWords is a great way to drive traffic to your website and, if you have merchandise for sale, to convert that traffic into profitable transactions. But not every AdWords ad is equally effective; not every AdWords advertiser finds the program worthwhile.

There's no one key to improving your AdWords performance. You have to do lots of little things to maximize your click-through rate and achieve the highest possible return on investment.

To that end, in this final chapter I offer 10 things you can do to improve the performance of your AdWords ads. Following these tips won't guarantee AdWords success, but it's a good start toward achieving a return on your AdWords spending.

 SHOW ME   Media 22.1—A video about the top 10 AdWords tips
Access this video file through your registered Web Edition at
my.safaribooksonline.com/9780131388666/media.

Tip #1: Write a Compelling Headline

Let's start at the top of the ad, that 25-character headline that everybody sees first. As I've said before, first impressions matter, which makes the headline the most important part of your ad. This is particularly so for those placements in which only the headline is visible.

For this reason, you have to write a compelling headline for your ad. It should attract the attention of potential customers and compel them to click on the ad. It's the equivalent of a carnival barker—"Click here, click here!"

Naturally, the headline must inform customers of what you're selling or trying to accomplish; in this aspect, it needs to be informative. But the headline should also trigger a specific customer behavior, in most instances a click through to your chosen landing page.

A good headline includes words that grab the user's attention. I'm talking about words like *free* and *sale, new* and *more, discover* and *bargain*. These words cause users to read the rest of the ad or click on the headline to learn more. They're powerful.

Bottom line, it's worth spending a lot of time on the headline to get it right. In fact, the headline is so important that you might want to hire a professional copywriter to do the job. Yes, it's a short headline, but when every word (and every character!) counts, a pro can more than pay for himself.

Tip #2: Write Compelling Copy—With a Strong Call to Action

It's not just your headline that should be compelling. The two lines of descriptive or body text should also persuade potential customers to click through to your landing page.

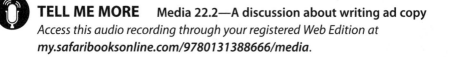 **TELL ME MORE**   **Media 22.2—A discussion about writing ad copy**
Access this audio recording through your registered Web Edition at
my.safaribooksonline.com/9780131388666/media.

Persuasive Words

To this end, you should use words that appeal to the customer's emotions. People want to be excited, comforted, or entertained; your copy should fulfill these emotional needs.

The best ads include specifics—percentages, dollar amounts, product names, and the like. For example, you can show users how to "Save 10%," "Increase profits by 25%," or buy something for "$19.99." There's no sense in being fluffy if you're offering a good specific bargain.

In addition, your copy needs to solve a problem or answer a question the customer might have. What does the customer need to do that your product does? That's the solution to push in the body of your ad.

Persuasive ad copy tells consumers how to save money, how to get something done, how to learn something important, how to do something better. You do this by using certain "power words" that invoke emotion and enthusiasm in potential buyers:

- Free
- Cheap
- Save
- Sale
- Special [offer]
- Bargain
- Bonus
- Limited time [savings or offer]
- Discover
- Learn
- Tips
- Tricks
- Enhance

Because you only have two short lines of copy to work with, you don't have space to talk about your product's features. Instead, you must focus on the benefits—that is, how the customer will benefit from buying what you're selling. If you're selling a weight-reduction aid, don't talk about its unique chemical compound; tell people that they'll "lose weight fast." Tell readers what's in it for them.

Because space is at a premium, it's okay to use space-saving abbreviations, such as the ampersand (&) for the word *and*. You can also use widely understood abbreviations and acronyms where appropriate.

You also need to set your product apart from the competition. To that end, play up your unique selling proposition—the thing that sets you apart from competing products. What makes your product better or different from everything else out there? That should be clear in your copy.

Action Words

Equally important, your copy should include a strong call to action. You have to ask customers to do something before they'll do anything at all.

What's a good call to action? Here are some common ones:

- Order now
- Buy now
- Download your free trial
- Sign up
- Get a quote
- Learn more
- Read our brochure
- Request more information
- Browse our site
- Join us today
- Start now

Remember, you want customers to do something specific—and you have to tell them what that is. Without a call to action, your ad is just a bunch of words on the page.

> The phrase "click here" is *not* a good call to action. First, it's implied in all PPC ads; the title is a hyperlink, after all. Second, Google doesn't like it, and might reduce your Quality Score if you include it. Third, clicking isn't really what you want users to do—you want them to get more information, buy now, or something similar. Focus on that.

Tip #3: Include Targeted Keywords

With text-based advertising, words are important. That goes for the keywords you use to trigger the display of your PPC ads.

To that end, you need to include your primary keywords in both your ad's headline and body copy. That's because people look for the keywords they've queried when they're viewing search results. If someone searches for *toboggan*, she's going to scan the search results page for the word *toboggan*. She's more likely to click on an ad that contains that word than one that doesn't; there's the implication that an ad that contains *toboggan* in its headline or copy is relevant to her search.

Google will boldface searched keywords on a search results page, further drawing attention to any ad that includes those keywords.

For this reason, ads that contain the same keywords that trigger the ad tend to perform better than ones that don't. Research your keywords carefully, and then include those keywords in your ads.

Tip #4: Bid on Misspelled Keywords

Here's a great tip for grabbing more traffic at a lower cost that helps you benefit from some common mistakes that people make.

You see, not everybody is a perfect speller. Lots of people misspell words when they're searching on Google; either they hit the wrong keys, or just don't know how to spell a particular word.

You can capitalize on these mistakes by bidding for the most common misspelled or mistyped keywords related to the topic at hand. If you're selling Harry Potter collectibles, for example, you could spend big bucks bidding on *harry potter*, or place much lower bids on the keywords *hary potter*, *hairy potter*, *harry poter*, and so forth. You'll pick up more traffic than you might imagine, at a fraction of the cost of the actual keywords.

Similarly, you can bid on "run-together" words, where people forget to put a space between two words in a phrase. For example, instead of bidding on the keyword *discount books*, bid on *discountbooks*—one mistyped word. Again, it's surprising how many people make mistakes like this when searching—and then see search results based on the incorrect query they entered.

Tip #5: Use Keyword Matching

Speaking of keywords, it's easy to get your ad displayed on a lot of different pages—too easy. If you used inexact keywords, such as those resulting from Google's default broad matching, you'll end up on search results pages not precisely related to your ad. This non-focused ad display typically has a lower clickthrough rate, which means it's not a good return on your advertising investment.

Avoid this type of non-focused display by taking advantage of AdWords' keyword matching options. Instead of using the default inexact match, use exact matching instead. You'll generate fewer impressions—meaning your ad won't be displayed as often—but potentially more and more targeted clicks, because you'll be reaching more appropriate prospects.

Learn more about keyword matching in Chapter 16, "Choosing the Right Keywords."

You employ exact matching by surrounding your keyword or key phrase with brackets, like this: **[*keyword phrase*]**. For example, if you're selling soccer balls, use the exact phrase **[soccer balls]**. This way, your ad won't get displayed when someone is searching just for *soccer*, or just for *balls*.

You can further fine-tune your ad display by using negative keywords. These ensure that your ad won't be displayed when someone includes a particular word in a search. Just put a negative sign (-) in front of any keyword you don't want associated with your ad, like this: **-keyword.** The result is that you avoid advertising to a lot of non-customers.

Tip #6: Bid High—Then Go Lower

Your bidding strategy affects both how much you spend on a given campaign and the campaign's return on investment. As you learned previously in this book, there are many different bidding strategies you can employ. The one that works best for the most advertisers, however, is one where you start bidding high, then reduce your bids over the course of the campaign.

Learn more about bidding strategies in Chapter 15, "Bidding the Right Price."

Key to this bidding strategy is establishing the first or second ad position right out of the gates, thus generating the maximum number of click-throughs—and improving your Quality Score. Once your Quality Score is high enough, you can maintain this ad position with a lower per-click bid.

This strategy works because Google factors CTR into the Quality Score. Obviously, a high ad position results in more clicks, thus increasing your Quality Score. It's kind of circular logic, but it's pretty much the only way to buy better performance.

Of course, this strategy costs a little more, at least initially. But after you've established a high Quality Score, you can drop back off the bidding a bit and run a more cost-effective campaign.

How long does it take for this strategy to work? For most advertisers, you can notice results in just a few days, or a week at the outside. Keep checking your reports to see when the minimum bid for the keyword in question has been lowered.

For example, when you create your campaign for a given keyword, you see that the current minimum bid is $1.50 for the top position. You bid over that amount— $1.60, let's say. After a few days, you see that the minimum bid has dropped to $1.00, given your Quality Score. You can now safely lower your bid to $1.10 or so. (In the meantime, your competitor—with a lower Quality Score—still has to bid that original $1.50 just to end up in second place.) Keep tracking these numbers over time and you might be able to take advantage of further bid reductions.

This strategy works more often than it doesn't, although it does require constant monitoring of results. That bit of work is worth it, though, both in terms of ad position and cost.

Tip #7: Point Users to a Customized Landing Page

I can't stress this enough. You cannot—you *must* not—drive potential customers to your website's home page. Customers don't want to see your home page; they want to see a page that follows directly from the ad they just clicked, that provides more information about the item they're interested in, and that lets them purchase that item if they so desire. Unless your home page also happens to be a product ordering page, you need to direct them to a different part of your site—a landing page custom designed for a particular ad.

You see, users are finicky. If they don't like what they see, they won't stick around long. Nor will they click any more than they have to—if at all—to find something that isn't obvious. This is why the page you link to from your PPC ad has to deliver on what customers expect. You have to put the information they want and need right in front of their faces, and make it easy for them to do what you want them to do (like place an order, for example).

If conversion matters more to you than raw clicks (as it should), you must create a landing page that encourages that conversion. The landing page should be attractive, easy to navigate, and informative. It should also carry forward the themes presented in your ad, and include all the same keywords and phrases. It should also follow through on any offers you make in the ad; there should be zero cognitive dissonance between your ad and the associated landing page.

Design the right landing page and you'll end up with a high conversion rate. Send users to a less-targeted page and you'll get a lot of traffic—but few sales.

ⓖ *Learn more about landing pages in Chapter 17, "Maximizing Conversion with a Custom Landing Page."*

Tip #8: Create Multiple Campaigns

The more organized your PPC advertising is, the more effective it will be. To that end, you need to create multiple specific campaigns rather than a single blanket one.

I find it best to create separate campaigns for each product offered. For example, if you offer three editions of a given software product, create three different campaigns, one for each edition. That might seem like campaign overkill, but it really helps to keep things focused.

In this example, you might also want to create a fourth campaign for the overall product line (all editions).

This approach lets you tailor the text and keywords for each ad to fit the specific product. It also lets you better track the results for each product you're advertising.

Tip #9: Optimize Your Campaign Settings

When you're first starting out with AdWords, it's tempting to go with Google's default settings for your new campaign. These default settings, however, might not be the most effective for you.

For example, you probably want to narrow the regions and languages in which your ads are displayed. If you're selling in the U.S., for example, you probably only want to advertise to English-speaking customers. It's also a good idea to refine the region where your ad appears; the default "U.S. and Canada" might be too broad. (Heck, the whole U.S. might be too broad if you have a local product or service.)

It's also a good idea to restrict your first ads to appear only on Google search results pages—the Google search option. It's a higher-cost display, but one that's worth the money, as it gets the best results. Opt not to display on the search network and content network, at least initially, as these networks have much lower click-through rates and can lead to disappointing overall results.

You can add the search network and content network back into your mix after you get your campaign established. They're good supplements to the main Google search, but not good freestanding choices.

Tip #10: Test, Test, Test

The final tip for improving your AdWords performance is that you probably won't get it right the first time. Or the second. Or the third. To be truly effective when advertising with AdWords, you're going to have to test the ads you run and the keywords you choose—a lot.

The most effective advertisers are in a constant test mode. They're always running side-by-side tests with different ad copy for the same keywords, or different keywords for the same ad, or even different landing pages for the same keywords and ads. There are lots of variables involved in PPC advertising, and you need to test them all. There's always a more effective combination available.

This means, of course, that you need to be comfortable with—and have the time for—managing multiple ads, ad groups, and campaigns. You also have to be comfortable using Google's tracking tools, so you can measure the performance of all the different variables.

All this testing is in the service of optimization. Even if you're already getting what you think are great results, your campaign can be further optimized. Maybe that optimization will result in paying less for your keywords; maybe the optimization will increase your click-through or conversion rates. The key is to keep tweaking things to make incremental improvements—and trust me, there's always something that can be improved.

Bonus Tip: What *Not* to Do

We'll end this chapter and this book with a bonus tip—what *not* to do in your AdWords campaign. Actually, there are a few things you should avoid doing. We'll discuss them all here.

Don't Waste Words

When you're writing ad headlines and copy, space is at a premium. Because of these space limitations, you can't afford to waste words.

To that end, you should avoid words that really don't matter. That means not using common words like *a*, *an*, *the*, *to*, and so forth. Remove every word that doesn't absolutely, positively have to be in the ad. (And, while you're at it, make sure you don't use two words that mean the same thing, such as "absolutely positively.")

Avoid Duplicate Keywords

It's tempting to include the same keywords in all the ad groups within a given campaign. Avoid the temptation. Duplicate keywords compete against each other; only the better-performing ad will get triggered by a given keyword.

For this reason, use a different set of keywords for each ad group within a campaign. Or, just follow the advice given in Tip #8: Create multiple campaigns, each of which can share keywords.

Don't Overbid on Content Network Keywords

One of the most common mistakes advertisers make is running their ads on both Google search and on Google's content network—that collection of websites that subscribe to Google's AdSense service. These AdSense pages are often less targeted than Google's search results pages, and have far less traffic, which means that you'll get a much lower click-through rate and fewer overall clicks when you advertise on the content network.

The mistake comes from overpaying for content network ads—which you'll do if you set the same bid level for the content network as you do for Google search. Instead, you should disable automatic bidding and bid lower for placement in the content network. You'll save some serious bucks without affecting your results.

Don't Be Annoying

The landing page you create for your ad should be direct and to the point. It should not include any little tricks that might annoy potential customers or infringe on their privacy. I'm talking scripts that launch pop-up windows, change browser settings, capture unnecessary customer data, and the like. Create a clean and discrete landing page—or risk Google lowering your Quality Score and shutting you out.

And That's That...

That last bit of advice wraps up this chapter, this section, and this book. I hope you've discovered how you can make money with both AdSense and AdWords—by running AdSense ads on your site and advertising your site and products with AdWords. The two programs are relatively easy to use, at least at a basic level, and can open up a whole new financial dimension to your online endeavors.

So go forth and have fun—and make money!

index